THE COLL...
RONALD HARWOOD

Ronald Harwood was born in Cape Town, South Africa, in 1934. He was Visitor in Theatre at Balliol College, Oxford, in 1986 and president of English PEN 1989–93, and was elected president of International PEN in 1993.

by the same author

Fiction
ALL THE SAME SHADOWS
THE GUILT MERCHANTS
THE GIRL IN MELANIE KLEIN
ARTICLES OF FAITH
THE GENOA FERRY
CESAR AND AUGUSTA
ONE. INTERIOR. DAY. – ADVENTURES IN THE FILM TRADE
HOME

Biography
SIR DONALD WOLFIT, CBE:
HIS LIFE AND WORK IN THE UNFASHIONABLE THEATRE

Plays
COUNTRY MATTERS
THE ORDEAL OF GILBERT PINFOLD
AFTER THE LIONS
TRAMWAY ROAD
THE DELIBERATE DEATH OF A POLISH PRIEST
INTERPRETERS
IVANOV
REFLECTED GLORY
POISON PEN

Television
ALL THE WORLD'S A STAGE
MANDELA
BREAKTHROUGH AT REYKJAVIK
COUNTDOWN TO WAR

Films
ONE DAY IN THE LIFE OF IVAN DENISOVICH
OPERATION DAYBREAK
THE DRESSER

Edited by
A NIGHT AT THE THEATRE
THE AGES OF GIELGUD
DEAR ALEC

The Collected Plays of
RONALD HARWOOD

Ronald Harwood

faber and faber
LONDON · BOSTON

This collection first published in 1993
by Faber and Faber Limited
3 Queen Square, London WC1N 3AU

Photoset by Parker Typesetting Service, Leicester
Printed in England by Clays Ltd, St Ives plc

Ronald Harwood is hereby identified as author of
this work in accordance with Section 77 of the
Copyright, Designs and Patents Act 1988.

All professional and amateur rights in these plays
are strictly reserved and applications for
permission to perform them must be made in advance
to Judy Daish Associates Ltd, 83 Eastbourne Mews,
London W2 6LQ. Tel: 071–262 1101.

A CIP record for this book is available from the
British Library.

ISBN 0–571–17001–3

2 4 6 8 10 9 7 5 3 1

CONTENTS

A FAMILY

for my mother

THE CHARACTERS

IVAN KILNER, *aged seventy-nine*
EMMA KILNER, *his wife, aged seventy-four*
FREDDIE KILNER, *his son, aged fifty-six*
MARGARET BARRETT, *his daughter, aged forty-eight*
MARC BARRETT, *his son-in-law, aged forty-six*
MILICENT PRICE, *his daughter, aged forty-three*
TOM PRICE, *his son-in-law, aged forty-five*
PAULA BARRETT, *his grand-daughter, aged twenty*

A Family was first presented at the Royal Exchange Theatre, Manchester on 11 May 1978 and subsequently, on 6 July 1978, at the Theatre Royal, Haymarket, London.

The Play was presented by Manchester Royal Exchange Theatre Company in association with Triumph Theatre Productions Ltd., with the following cast:

FREDDIE KILNER	Paul Scofield
PAULA BARRETT	Celia Gregory
MARGARET BARRETT	Eleanor Bron
EMMA KILNER	Irene Handl
TOM PRICE	Trevor Peacock
MILICENT PRICE	Sally Bazely
MARC BARRETT	Garry Waldhorn
IVAN KILNER	Harry Andrews

Director	Casper Wrede
Designer	Peter Bennion

ACT ONE

There is no formal set: lighting and small pieces of furniture are used to give an indication of place. Sounds of war. FREDDIE *walks into light, listening to these sounds. He hears his own voice:*

FREDDIE'S VOICE: What a day! What a place! What a crowd!
> (*Church bells, singing, cheering very loud.* FREDDIE *covers his ears. Silence. Light on his desk.*)

FREDDIE: What a day, what a place, what a crowd.
> (*A telephone rings, another, and another, until seven telephones are ringing, last of all* FREDDIE'S. *He reaches out and the moment he lifts the receiver, lights reveal* IVAN, EMMA, MARGARET, MARC, TOM *and* MILICENT *all forming a circle with* FREDDIE, *and all on the telephone.* PAULA, *who lies in bed, also forms part of the circle but she takes no part: she lies expressionless and motionless.* FREDDIE *listens but he, too, takes no part.*)

ALL: (*Except* FREDDIE *and* PAULA; *not simultaneously*) Good morning, hello, hello, hello, 'morning, how's tricks?

EMMA: Hello, I rang to remind you all tomorrow we're at Margaret's.

IVAN: And I've got a surprise for everyone. So be there on time.

MARGARET: Is it Sunday tomorrow?

TOM: All day. (*Laughs.*)

MARC: Are you sure it's our turn tomorrow?

EMMA: Of course I'm sure. Last Sunday we were at Tom and Milicent's –

TOM *and* MILICENT: Right, correct –

EMMA: This Sunday, Marc, it's you and Margaret.

MARGARET: I thought it was your turn, Mummy.

EMMA: Maggie, what's the matter with you? The Sunday before was me. Last Sunday it was Milicent. This Sunday it's you.

5

MILICENT: I only hope the weather lasts. What a spring! I just
　　want to lie in the sun and sleep –
MARGARET: That's all you ever do –
MILICENT: You're a fine one to talk. Perhaps you'll do us the
　　honour of changing out of your dressing-gown for once –
EMMA: Children, children –
IVAN: Did you hear what I said? I've got a surprise for all of you. I
　　want you all there. Especially early. All of you, mind. That's
　　an order.
ALL: Yes, Dad.
MARGARET: Sunday tomorrow, and I've got nothing in the house.
EMMA: Then you'll go to the shops today.
TOM: We'll bring something.
MILICENT: We always do.
EMMA: Milly, how's Danny?
MILICENT: Fine. He got an A plus in Physics.
EMMA: And Audrey?
MILICENT: She's having a lovely time. We had a letter from
　　Toronto last week. She likes Spenser's parents but she'll be
　　glad to get home.
IVAN: Oh? So they've got a postal service in Canada. Fancy. Tell
　　Audrey her grandparents would also appreciate a postcard.
TOM: She'll be back next week, Dad –
EMMA: And Maggie, how's Paula? She seemed so quiet last
　　Sunday.
MILICENT: And the one before.
MARGARET: Fine, fine, Paula's fine. Mummy, why can't Freddie
　　have us for once?
EMMA: Don't talk nonsense, Maggie. How can Freddie cope with
　　all of us on his own?
MARGARET: *I* have to.
EMMA: You've got a husband and a daughter.
MARGARET: You ought to invite us, Freddie. Once. Just once.
　　Even if you only offered and we refused. It's wrong that
　　Milly, Mummy and I have to do everything week after week.
　　All you do is come, eat, sleep and go. I don't expect a
　　bachelor to cook for the whole family but you've never even
　　once offered to take us all out. Have you ever once invited us

6

all to a restaurant? I don't mind for me, but it's Mummy I
care about –

EMMA: Maggie, please –

MAGGIE: I'm sorry, I have to speak my mind –

IVAN: Why?

MARGARET: Dad, please don't interfere. I'm talking to Freddie.
Freddie! Freddie!

FREDDIE'S VOICE: (*Recorded*) This is a telephone answering
machine. Dr Kilner's not available at present. In case of an
emergency please telephone 632 7141. Otherwise kindly
leave a message. Please speak now.
(*Everyone speaks at once.*)

EMMA: Children, children, please! Tomorrow's Sunday. We'll
meet at Margaret's. It'll be lovely. It's always lovely.
(*They are about to replace their receivers.*)

IVAN: And don't forget my surprise. Be there on time.

ALL: Yes, Dad.
(*They are about to replace their receivers.*)

EMMA: And Margaret, you're sure Paula's all right?

MARGARET: Sure.
(*Light remains only on* FREDDIE. *A traditional Italian love song
sounds. He begins to type.* MARGARET *enters. She wears a
dressing-gown and has a cup of coffee. She turns her face to the
light and soaks in the morning sun. After a moment, she turns and
goes to* PAULA's *bed.*)

MARGARET: Are you awake? (*No response.*) Did you sleep? (*No
response.*) How do you feel?

PAULA: The same.

MARGARET: Do you want any breakfast?

PAULA: No.

MARGARET: You must eat.

PAULA: I don't want anything.

MARGARET: If only you'd tell me what you feel. (*No response.*)
Paula, you can't go on lying day after day in bed.

PAULA: Ask Uncle Freddie to see me.

MARGARET: Isn't it better if I call in a stranger? I'll get Dr
Wadham.

PAULA: I want to see Uncle Freddie.

7

MARGARET: He's so off-hand, Paula. Dr Wadham's a good man.
(PAULA *begins to cry*.)
Paula, you've got to pull yourself together. It's Sunday today. It's our turn for everyone. Please, please, if you care anything for me, pull yourself together, have a bath, get dressed, put some lipstick on, come into the garden, it's a lovely day, be nice, smile, give Gran a kiss, please, be nice to Grandad, please. Otherwise they'll ask questions, everyone will want to see you, there'll be a fuss, they'll want to know what's wrong with a lovely girl like you who's got everything in the world, and what'll I tell them? What? I don't think I can stand it, Paula. Because you know who'll be blamed, don't you? Me, of course. Gran'll say I neglected you, Grandad'll say I'm too easy-going and Aunty Milicent will smirk her superior smirk. So, please, darling, for my sake get up and put on a good face.
(PAULA *cries*.)
Why do you punish me? Don't I suffer enough?
(*Pause*.)
PAULA: I just want to die.
(PAULA *weeps pitifully*. MARGARET *backs away*. MARGARET *rushes to the telephone, dials*.)
MARGARET: Mummy?
(*Light on* EMMA *on the telephone*.)
EMMA: What's the matter? Is everything all right?
MARGARET: Yes, yes –
EMMA: You sound upset –
MARGARET: It's nothing, it's not serious, it's just Paula –
EMMA: Oh my God, I knew it –
(*Light on* IVAN.)
IVAN: What?
EMMA: It's Paula –
(IVAN *picks up his receiver*.)
IVAN: What's the matter with her this time?
EMMA: Dad's on the extension –
MARGARET: I'm not sure, but she's not well –
EMMA: Has Freddie seen her?
MARGARET: It's not that serious –

8

EMMA: Since when are you a doctor?

MARGARET: No, but you know what I mean, Mummy. Freddie's always so indifferent. He says we fuss too much. All he ever does is stand at the end of the bed and say, 'And what's the matter with you?'

EMMA: Better to fuss too much than not at all. And it's only his manner, Maggie. You remember when I had the big op when they took out everything, he was at my bedside day and night. All doctors should be so indifferent.

IVAN: A young girl like Paula has no business to be ill. It's unnatural. Megs, you're too easy-going with her. Tell her from me she's not to be ill. I don't want her spoiling my surprise.

EMMA: But what's the matter with her?

MARGARET: That's just it, I don't know.

EMMA: Has she got a temp?

MARGARET: No.

EMMA: It can't be serious if she hasn't got a temp. I'll come at once. But Margaret, phone Freddie.

MARGARET: It's not necessary –

EMMA: Margaret, phone Freddie, if you don't, I will!

MARGARET: All right, I'll do it!

(MARGARET *is about to dial again when there is the sound of feet on gravel.* MARC *appears. He carries a jacket, looks dishevelled, walks wearily. She looks at him. He does not look at her, but continues on, head bowed.*)

How much did you lose?

(*He continues on his way.*)

Don't you care about anything? Have you forgotten what day of the week it is? It's Sunday morning, Marc. Do you know the time? Eight o'clock. 8 a.m. Don't you care about anything?

(*He stops.*)

Aren't you going to ask how your daughter is? Aren't you even going in to see her?

MARC: I thought we weren't supposed to be speaking.

(*He goes. Pause.* MARGARET *dials.*)

FREDDIE'S VOICE: (*Recorded*) 'This is a telephone answering

9

machine. Dr Kilner's not available at present. In case of an
emergency please telephone 632 7141. Otherwise kindly
leave a message. Please speak now.

MARGARET: Freddie, this is Margaret. It's eight o'clock, Sunday
morning. It's about Paula. She's not well. I don't think it's
serious but she won't talk to me. Or Marc. Perhaps she'll tell
you what's troubling her. She hasn't eaten a thing for four
days. She says she's not sleeping. Can you come a little
earlier today, Freddie? Have a look at her. Please. You know
what I think, Freddie? You remember when she was
thirteen, fourteen, she went through a stage, she was forever
saying she'd fallen down and hurt herself. She had her arm in
a sling for a month, she walked with a limp, you remember?
But you couldn't find anything wrong with her. And that
morning she said she couldn't move her legs. We thought she
had polio. God, I go cold at the thought. But in a day or two
she forgot all about it. You said she just wanted attention. I
think it's the same now. I think she wants attention. Why,
Freddie? Why? A lovely girl like Paula, clever, pretty,
everything she wants in the world she gets. Why should she
crave attention? Mind you, I'm not saying everything at
home is wonderful at the moment. (*Pause; begins to cry.*) I do
my best to keep up appearances but – (*Pause.*) I've no one to
talk to, forgive me, Freddie, going on like this. I know I talk
too much, I know I get on everyone's nerves, but Freddie,
I'm so unhappy, we're in such debt, Marc keeps me short,
yet he talks about opening another pharmacy and we haven't
got two pennies to rub together, and every third Sunday I
have to cater for almost a dozen people and still Marc goes on
finding the money to play poker night after night, where
does he get the money from, Freddie? Have a word with
him, please. He'll listen to you. He likes you. And we only
stay together because of Paula, otherwise I'd have divorced
him years ago but who can I turn to? It's not as if Paula –
(*Sound of feet on gravel.* MARGARET *quickly replaces the
receiver, wipes her eyes.* EMMA *enters.*)

EMMA: I came as quickly as I could. I ran. Me, at my age, with
my knees, I ran. I've got permutations.

MARGARET: Palpitations. Have you? Sit down. Rest.

EMMA: I'm all right. You've been crying.

MARGARET: It's nothing.

EMMA: Where's Marc?

MARGARET: Still asleep.

EMMA: What time did he come in?

MARGARET: Oh, early, midnight –

EMMA: Yes, midnight Tokyo time. Did he lose much?

MARGARET: No, he's not playing like he used to.

EMMA: No, heaven forbid –

MARGARET: He's not. Come and see Paula.

(MARGARET *leads* EMMA *to* PAULA. EMMA *peers at her.*)

EMMA: Mummy tells me you're not well, darling. (*Feels* PAULA's
forehead.) A fine strong girl like you. From a lovely home.
Say something to Gran, darling.

PAULA: I don't want to see anybody.

MARGARET: Paula –

EMMA: It's all right, Margaret, I'm not insulted. No temp.
(*To* PAULA.) I'm not anybody, I'm Granny, darling.

PAULA: Please go away. (*Weeps.*)

(EMMA *and* MARGARET *exchange a look, then withdraw.*)

MARGARET: She's been like that for four days. Five. Just lies
there. Hardly speaks. Hardly moves. Cries at the least
excuse. Doesn't sleep. Won't eat. Says the most awful
things.

(*Long pause.*)

EMMA: How long is it since she's been to the lavatory?

MARGARET: What?

EMMA: She could be constipated.

MARGARET: Oh, Mummy, it's more serious than that.

EMMA: Constipation can be serious.

MARGARET: It's not constipation. You only have to look at her –

EMMA: You ask Marc. He's a chemist. I bet he sells more laxative
than anything else.

MARGARET: She says she's depressed.

EMMA: Don't talk such nonsense. How can a young girl be
depressed. Did you telephone Freddie?

MARGARET: I left a message.

EMMA: On that robert?

MARGARET: Robot. It's an answering machine, Mum.

EMMA: I hate it. (*Pause.*) Is she due for her period?

MARGARET: I don't know.

EMMA: You should mark when she's due with an X in your diary. Freddie'll take one look at her, that'll fix her.

MARGARET: Freddie's not a miracle worker.

EMMA: He's a fine doctor. What he's forgotten about doctoring –

MARGARET: No, no, he's forgotten nothing, he knows everything, he's the greatest doctor who ever lived, given time he'll find the cure for cancer.
(*Pause.*)

EMMA: And do you think you were such an easy child? (*Pause.*) When Daddy and Freddie came back from the war, when you should've been the happiest little girl in the world, how did you behave? You treated me like dirt, as though I was a criminal, I've never forgotten –

MARGARET: Obviously not –

EMMA: Don't be so clever with me, Margaret, please. You deliberately burned a hole in Freddie's demob suit. I haven't forgotten that either.

MARGARET: I asked you here to look at Paula not to rake up the past. (*Pause.*) Sometimes I wonder if he's quite all there.

EMMA: Who? Freddie? Margaret, that's a terrible thing to say about your brother –

MARGARET: He doesn't seem to hear half of what anyone says to him. He walks around in a dream. Always with a faraway look in his eyes. Always humming. Always saying the same things over and over again. I have no contact with him. I know you all say I drive you mad because I talk too much, but Freddie on the other hand –

EMMA: With you it's nerves –

MARGARET: And with Freddie?

EMMA: Freddie fought a war. Who knows what happens to young men who fight wars? Who knows what they see, what they suffer? And to be a prisoner for two years, and to live like a wild animal for another two years on the run, and he was only a child, still wet behind the ears.

(*The love song comes again.* FREDDIE *begins to type furiously.*)

MARGARET: But what does he do with himself now? No wife, no children, no responsibilities, what does he do? He always seems like a child to me. Something infantile about him, un-grown-up, I feel like I'm a hundred years older than he is –

EMMA: You drive me mad, you talk, talk such nonsense –

MARGARET: But what does he do with himself? Has he got a girlfriend hidden away somewhere?

EMMA: Hidden away, what are you talking about, stop rattling, why should he hide a girlfriend?

MARGARET: You're right, when he came back from the war the life had gone out of him, as though he'd always be the age he was then, frozen, petrified –

EMMA: No one talks nonsense like you –

(FREDDIE *scrumples up the paper, throws it away, closes his ears to the love song.*)

MARGARET: And ever since then he's got madder and madder. I know you adore him, I know he's your favourite, but people laugh at him behind his back, I've seen it –

EMMA: You're determined to hurt me –

MARGARET: Ask him a question, he hums. He'll sit with us three, four hours of a Sunday and all he says is, 'What a day, what a place, what a crowd', until I could scream.

WOMAN'S VOICE: Federico-o-o . . . Federico-o-o . . .

MARGARET: Of course, Paula's his only friend in the family –

EMMA: Nonsense –

MARGARET: Stop saying nonsense, he talks to her –

EMMA: He talks to me, too. And Milly. He's closer to Milly than Paula –

MARGARET: They're close, that's true, like magnets, older brother, younger sister, more like twins, and me in the middle. Terrible to be the middle child.

(FREDDIE *paces.*)

EMMA: Better than being an only child.

MARGARET: Paula doesn't feel excluded.

(FREDDIE *goes to the answer machine, operates the controls.*)

MARGARET'S VOICE: (*Recorded*) 'Freddie, this is Margaret. It's

13

eight o'clock Sunday morning. It's about Paula. She's not
well. I don't think –
(*He switches off the machine, begins to put on his jacket,
humming tunelessly the Italian love song when:*)
WOMAN'S VOICE: *Dove vai*, Federico . . . *dove vai?*
(*He freezes, one arm in the sleeve of the jacket. Sound of feet on
gravel.* TOM *and* MILICENT *enter.* TOM *carries parcels.*
FREDDIE *goes.*)
TOM: Mum, Margaret, how's tricks?
(*Greetings and kisses are exchanged.*)
EMMA: And where's Danny?
MILICENT: At home. He's working.
EMMA: Work, work, work, I've never known a boy work so hard.
And with a brain like that I don't understand it. Paula, I can
understand, she has to work, she's a girl, but Danny? What's
he need to work for? He's got a photogenic memory.
(*The others are secretly amused by her malapropism.*)
TOM: Dad not here?
EMMA: Any moment. I came early.
TOM: What's this surprise of his?
EMMA: Search me. You know how secretive he is. He never got
over his time in Intelligence during the war.
MARGARET: I've got to hand it to you, Mil, that's a very smart
outfit.
MILICENT: Thank you, I picked it up very cheaply.
TOM: Correction. Me she picked up very cheaply, the outfit I paid
plenty for. (*Laughs.*)
MILICENT: It's very versatile. I can take off the top and sunbathe
in it.
MARGARET: And your nails are always so nice.
TOM: Didn't I tell you you looked a picture?
MARGARET: How do you manage it?
MILICENT: We bought a new washing-up machine.
TOM: (*Wriggling his fingers*) The old one's got rheumatism.
(*Laughs.*) But now see what I've brought you. You said you
hadn't got anything in the house. All right, hey presto, pâté,
meat loaf, hamburgers, enough to feed the Russian army.
And not bought, mind. Home-made. And by whom? By me.

14

EMMA: You made them, Tom?

TOM: I certainly did. Besides a new washing-up machine I also bought a new mincer. Correction. It doesn't mince, it chops. So, what I'm going to do in future is, on Saturdays, I'm going to make delectables for the week –

MILICENT: (*Smiling*) Ah, that's what you're going to do on Saturdays, is it?

TOM: Yes, I am. Make tit-bits, tasties, put them in the deep-freeze, forget about them, when I need them I'll thaw them. That way Milly doesn't have to lift a finger –

MARGARET: Except to paint her nails.

TOM: I like cooking. I also made a chocolate cake.

(MILICENT *lies on a deckchair and suns herself.*)

EMMA: Oh, chocolate cake.

MILICENT: Tom, don't go on, it's boring –

TOM: Doesn't she look a picture? I don't know what I see in her.

MILICENT: I've been wondering that, too, recently.

(*He laughs.*)

TOM: Where's Paula?

MARGARET: Sleeping.

TOM: I'll wake her.

MARGARET: No, no, let her sleep.

TOM: I've got something for her. As I was leaving the factory on Friday, they caught my eye and I said to myself Paula will be a sensation in these. They're our up-market line – the latest thing – (*He opens a package, produces two hideous dresses, holds them up. Silence.*) Export rejects.

EMMA: We can see.

TOM: It's in the stitching, you can't notice. (*Pause.*) Well? Don't you like them?

MILICENT: They're vile, Tom.

TOM: On you they'd be vile, agreed, but on Paula, they'd be fine. She's got a style of her own.

MILICENT: She'll need it.

TOM: I'm amazed. I liked them. I even sent Audrey two of each in different colours in Toronto.

EMMA: Audrey? She'll look like a barrage-balloon in those.

MILICENT: She's lost weight.

15

EMMA: If I know Audrey she'll find it again. She's like Aunty
　　Hilda –

MILICENT: She's nothing like Aunty Hilda.

EMMA: Aunty Hilda paid a fortune to a health farm for a week. A
　　very strict regiment, she said –

TOM: (*Winking at* MILICENT) Must've been the Irish Guards –

EMMA: Lemon juice for breakfast and lunch, then over to the café
　　opposite for cream teas in the afternoon. Now she says these
　　crash diets don't work.
　　(*Pause.*)

TOM: (*Holding up one of the dresses*) Not the pink?

EMMA: Especially not the pink.
　　(FREDDIE *enters.*)

FREDDIE: What a day, what a place, what a crowd.

EMMA: Freddie, darling.

MILICENT: I didn't hear you come down the drive.

FREDDIE: That's because I came round the side.

MILICENT: (*Laughing quietly*) Typical.
　　(*He kisses the women.*)

EMMA: Freddie, isn't your hair too long?

FREDDIE: Mummy, I'm a big boy, I'm over fifty, you know –

EMMA: You could be over a hundred, your hair's still too long.

TOM: Read any good prescriptions lately? (*Laughs.*)

FREDDIE: Hello, Tom, how are you?

TOM: Sitting up and taking nourishment, thank you. (*Quietly.*)
　　Fred, when you've got a moment, I'd like a word with you
　　(*Gestures vaguely.*)

FREDDIE: Is Marc about?

MARGARET: He'll be down in a moment –

FREDDIE: I'll go and look at Paula –

MARGARET: Let me see if she's awake. And Freddie, I'm sorry I
　　left such a long message, going on and on –

FREDDIE: What long message?
　　(*She turns and goes. He hums.*)

MILICENT: What's wrong with Paula?

EMMA: Nothing serious. A mood. But Freddie, here a moment.
　　I'm worried about Dad. He overdoes it. He says every time
　　he moves his neck he gets a pain in his chest.

FREDDIE: Tell him not to move his neck.
  (*The love song sounds.*)
MILICENT: Freddie, you all right?
FREDDIE: Yes, yes.
  (MARGARET *re-enters.*)
MARGARET: She's asleep.
FREDDIE: Then wake her up.
MARGARET: No, no, she needs the rest. She hasn't slept for, I don't
  know, she doesn't eat. Let her sleep. You can go in later.
  (*He hums to the love song.*)
MILICENT: It's not serious, is it, Meg?
MARGARET: No, a little depressed, you know kids.
TOM: Perhaps she's got trouble with her boyfriend, Chesney.
  Chesney! If I had a boyfriend like that I'd also be depressed.
MARGARET: No, I don't think it's him. He telephones every week.
  It's a pity he's so far away.
EMMA: I'm with Tom. I don't like the boy.
MARGARET: Chesney's all right.
EMMA: He doesn't stand up when I come into the room.
MARGARET: Young people don't stand up any more, Mummy.
EMMA: Don't tell me, a little more standing up, a little less sitting
  in we'd have a better world. Freddie, do you think it could be
  boyfriend trouble? She talks to you.'
  (FREDDIE *stares into space.*)
  Did she say anything about Chesney? Do you think it could be
  a lover's twist, Freddie?
MARGARET: Tryst, not twist.
EMMA: Freddie, what do you think?
FREDDIE: (*Lost in memory*) We could be married, Ardella. One day
  I'll take you home. Ardella, Ardella, don't cry. We have our
  whole lives before us. You know what I see when I think of us
  together? Green fields and bright spring flowers. And we're
  walking hand in hand, and there's a soft and gentle rain. And
  the green field is endless. Marry me, Ardella. Will you? Will
  you?
EMMA: What do you think, Freddie?
FREDDIE: Mummy, you're always worried. If you're not worried,
  you're worried about not being worried.

17

EMMA: You don't listen to a word I say.

MARGARET: Freddie, what do you think, would you rather I called Dr Wadham?

EMMA: Gerald Wadham?

MARGARET: How many Dr Wadhams do you know?

EMMA: Don't be so clever, please, Margaret –

MARGARET: Of course Gerald Wadham. He's our doctor. We only use Freddie when it's something serious. On second thoughts I think it's better Freddie doesn't see Paula. I don't want a fuss. I'm sorry I told any of you now. I always act without thinking.

MILICENT: (*To* TOM) She drives me mad.

EMMA: Gerald Wadham. His father was an actor.

MARGARET: So?

EMMA: My mother used to take in actors when I was a little girl. Charged them sixpence for a bath. We didn't get rich. Before Gerald Wadham examines a grandchild of mine, I'd tell him to wash his hands. And I'd stand over him to make sure he did it. Gerald Wadham. He's got as much nose for doctoring as a chiropodist.

(MARC *enters.*)

MARC: Sorry, I overslept. (*Kisses the women.*) Mil, you look lovely. (*To* MARGARET.) Sorry, darling, anything need doing?

MARGARET: Everything's under control, thank you, dear.

FREDDIE: Marc –

(*He draws* MARC *aside.*)

MARC: Look, if it's about the money. I'll pay it back next month, I promise, I've got something rather big on, plans –

FREDDIE: It's not the money. No. More important. Would you do me a favour? Could you possible nip down to your chemist shop and bring me a bottle of these –

(*Hands* MARC *a prescription.*)

MARC: Who's it for?

FREDDIE: Me.

MARC: Again?

FREDDIE: What'd you mean again?

MARC: Last year, I remember –

FREDDIE: For once a year you can't say 'again', Marc. Call it
    spring fever, summer madness, just bring the stuff.
MARC: You're sure you shouldn't see someone? I know you
    doctors, you're the worst patients in the world. Why don't
    you call Charlie Rosen? He's a top man.
FREDDIE: I've known Charlie Rosen all my life. We were taken
    prisoner together. After the war, we qualified together. All
    Charlie Rosen knows is why rats get hungry when you ring
    bells. Just bring me a bottle of the stuff, Marc.
MARC: You're the doctor, but Freddie, take care of yourself.
    You're the best, I mean this, the only decent one –
FREDDIE: Marc, if you're going to go on like this, bring two
    bottles.
TOM: Look, Dad's just turned the corner. What a man!
MARC: Shit.
TOM: Marc, language, please.
MARC: I'll go down to the shop –
FREDDIE: I think I'll come with you –
MARC: I can manage –
FREDDIE: No, I'd like to –
TOM: But Dad's just coming, he wanted us all here early –
FREDDIE: We'll slip round the side. Tell him we won't be long.
    (*They go quickly as jogging feet sound on gravel.* IVAN *enters. He
    wears a tracksuit.*)
IVAN: Twelve minutes, forty-two seconds. And I didn't sprint,
    just kept up a good steady pace. From door to door. Even
    had time to exchange words with Uncle Simon who was on
    his way to buy his papers in his dressing-gown and
    unshaven. 'When is your seventieth birthday?' he asked me.
    'Nine years ago,' I said. 'Be sure to invite me to the party,' he
    said. His mind's gone. Second childhood. How he made
    such a fortune I'll never know. And he's five years younger
    than me, sans teeth, sans hair, sans everything but money in
    the bank. Of course, he's careful with money, not to say
    mean. He wouldn't give you ice in winter. And I've never
    really forgotten him for the speech he made at Margaret's
    wedding, saying I ran a second-hand bookshop. I had to
    stand up and correct him. An antiquarian book-seller, I said,

that's entirely different. Well! Good morning!
(*Everyone greets him and he greets everyone, kissing both the women and the men. When he comes to* MARGARET:)

IVAN: Darling.

MARGARET: Dad.

IVAN: How's Paula? I hope she's recovered. I don't approve of her being ill. (*Slips her a cheque.*) Here's a little something for you. I know Marc keeps you short.

MARGARET: (*Kisses his cheek*) Oh, Dad.

TOM: Well, Dad, don't keep us in suspense. What's the surprise?

IVAN: Tom, you couldn't have asked me a nicer question. This is the moment I've been looking forward to all week. I've had such a wonderful idea, something we can all enjoy, be proud of, revel in. A real family occasion. Everyone gather round because we have to celebrate. I'm going to ask you all to cast your minds back – (*Breaks off; looks around.*) Nobody's here.

MILICENT: (*Smiling*) *We're* here, Dad.

IVAN: Where the hell's Freddie? He has to hear what I've got to say, it concerns him deeply, profoundly, it concerns him, where is he?

EMMA: Don't get excited first thing in the morning –

IVAN: And Marc, it's his house, where's Marc? I wanted everyone here when I arrived.

TOM: They slipped down to get some medicine –

IVAN: Medicine. (*Grunts with annoyance.*) Damnation, I said to you all on the phone to be sure to come especially early and now it's unusually late. My pleasure is entirely spoiled. I was looking forward all week to telling the whole family. And where's Danny?

EMMA: What are you doing, Ivan, taking a roll call?

MILICENT: Danny's got homework.

IVAN: I should have thought the one day of the week we all come together, Danny could have given his lessons a rest.

TOM: He's conscientious, Dad.

IVAN: So was Attila the Hun. Conscientiousness doesn't impress me. Liveliness impresses me –

EMMA: Don't tell us –

IVAN: Lively mind, lively body, lively spirit, lively people coming together at a reasonable time –

EMMA: You've waited so long to tell us your surprise, another ten minutes won't hurt. It's not such a terrible thing. So sit down, relax, stop laying down the law –

IVAN: I'm not laying down the law, I'm stating a fact. People are late when I ask them to be early. That's a fact, not a law. And Paula's so ill she can't listen to what I have to say. I shall insist she's here when I tell you all –

MARGARET: Dad, she's not well, she doesn't want to see anybody.

IVAN: I'm not anybody, I'm her grandfather.

EMMA: Exactly what I said, but she told me she didn't want to see me either.

IVAN: Oh, so you've seen her, have you? Why can't I see her?

EMMA: Oh, you're such a difficult man. If you don't calm down, you'll fall down. For good. I think those pills Freddie gives you are get-you-goings not take-it-easies.

IVAN: I don't take those pills. I threw them away. I don't feel my age.

EMMA: Who said anything about age? A man of your temperament is a volunteer for a coroner.

IVAN: Coronary!

TOM: Same thing. (*Laughs.*)

IVAN: Let me tell you I feel no different from the time I was forty-five. I could still make a parachute jump even now.

EMMA: Yes, from a billiard table.

IVAN: I could, I'm telling you, I could! 'Tuck your legs in, Captain Kilner, sir!' Certainly I could.

EMMA: Ivan, pardon my French, but for a clever man you're a bloody fool.

(*General laughter which annoys* IVAN.)

IVAN: I'm going to see Paula.

MARGARET: Daddy, please leave her alone.

EMMA: Ivan, you're a baby –

IVAN: She's my grandchild, I demand to see her!

EMMA: Stop behaving like a bull in the china department –

MARGARET: You'll upset her –

IVAN: Me? Upset her?

MARGARET: Daddy, be gentle with her –

IVAN: Sweetheart, of course I'll be gentle with her. What do you take me for? Of course I'll be gentle.

(IVAN *goes to* PAULA, *followed by everyone else. They crowd round the bed and peer at her.*)

So what's all this nonsense about being ill?

MARGARET: It's all right, darling, Grandad just wanted to see you.

IVAN: I don't approve of illness, you know that.

EMMA: Ivan, have a little sympathy. You make it sound as if it's deliberate.

IVAN: All illness is deliberate. You open yourself to microbes, mental and physical. You let them into your system. Good health is a mixture of iron will and massive indifference. I've never had a day's illness in my life –

(*Everyone finds wood to touch.*)

– and I never allowed my children to be ill either.

EMMA: He's mad –

IVAN: I cannot remember ever having a common cold. My will would never allow it. And I am indifferent to the prevailing microbes. I have no sympathy for the sick. In fact, I hold them in utter contempt. If you wanted to be well, Paula, you could be well. It's mind over matter.

MARGARET: Daddy, enough, please come out of here –

IVAN: Margaret, don't teach your father about children. All this lying in bed, not eating, feeling sorry for yourself, it's a modern complaint, in my day we had no time for such things.

MARGARET: Dad, can't you see she's upset?

IVAN: What I'm saying is for her own good. You want to grow like Aunty Lola, Paula? She was the most complaining woman I ever knew –

EMMA: Ivan, Lola was a chronic invalid –

IVAN: Exactly, she didn't want a life, she wanted an illness. It's elementary psychology –

EMMA: Yes, piss-psychology –

IVAN: Don't be coarse, Emma, it doesn't become you. We fall

into these habits of illness, these patterns of thoughts because they're comforting. But it's not impossible to break them, Paula. You mustn't make illness a life sentence. With perseverance, will, inner strength, these patterns can be changed. There is nothing in the world that cannot be changed.

EMMA: Meet Professor Young.

IVAN: Jung, Jung, Young, Jung! So, Paula, I've always thought of you as a lively girl and so I don't like to see you not a hundred per cent. And you know something else? An illness like yours, not one thing or the other, neither fish nor fowl, just a general illness, is a way of drawing attention to yourself. Paula, I want to assure you that we all love you. You come from a lovely home. You've got us all to rely on. A fine mother and father. If you're in any sort of trouble you have only to tell us and you'll have a battalion to support you. A battalion? An army. So, now I'll tell you what I want to do. Get up, get dressed, come out, join us, and listen to the surprise I've got for all of you. What do you say, Paula? (*A long pause.*)

PAULA: Fuck off. Just fuck off.
(*She buries her head beneath the bedclothes. Shocked silence. Eventually* IVAN *retreats.* MARGARET *and* EMMA *either side of him,* TOM *and* MILICENT *following.*)

MARAGET: She didn't mean it, Dad.

EMMA: What did she say? I didn't hear what she said –
(MARGARET *bursts into tears.* EMMA *goes to her.* IVAN *stands immobile. Unnoticed,* FREDDIE *and* MARC *re-enter.*)

FREDDIE: What a day! What a place! What a crowd!
(*Silence. He hums.*)

IVAN: I've never known a day go so sour.

FREDDIE: Isn't anyone going to tell us what happened? (*Silence.*) Let me guess. Somebody insulted somebody. I know this family.

IVAN: (*Quiet, shocked*) We have an illness in our midst.
(FREDDIE *hums.*)
How can a child speak to her grandfather like that? How can a child who comes from a background like this utter such

23

filth to her own grandfather. To use the language of the gutter (*He lapses into silence.*)

EMMA: Freddie, go and see Paula at once. I think it's more serious than any of us imagine.

IVAN: Every time I think about it I feel dizzy.

FREDDIE: Then don't think about it.

EMMA: Ivan, sit down. Breathe. Be calm. Freddie, will you do as I say and go and see the child? Margaret, I'm sorry to say this but you neglect her.

TOM: (*Really shocked*) I've never heard such language.

MILICENT: Yes you have, Tom, don't be such a prude.

EMMA: Nobody will tell me what she said.

FREDDIE: Nor me.

TOM: Swearing like that –

MILICENT: Oh, Tom, everybody swears nowadays.

TOM: At their grandfathers?

EMMA: And Marc, you take no responsibility, you act as if she's not your child, as if you have no concern –

MARC: What should I do? I don't know what to do. I don't even know what happened.

EMMA: You let everything fall on Margaret's shoulders –

MARGARET: I'm all right –

EMMA: Freddie, go and look at Paula. She needs attention.
(FREDDIE *goes to* PAULA *and stands at the foot of her bed.*)

FREDDIE: What's the matter with you?
(PAULA *remains hidden under the bedclothes but is weeping.* FREDDIE *hums.*)
What did you say to your grandfather?

PAULA: (*Emerging slowly*) I couldn't help it.
(*He goes to her, takes her pulse. She suddenly holds him tightly.*)
I need your help, I need your help.
(*He disentangles himself.*)

FREDDIE: If you let go of me, you'll get my help.
(*She lies back. He takes a thermometer from her bedside, jams it in her mouth. Pause, he hums.*)
Your mother says you're not eating.
(*She nods.*)
How long's this been going on?

24

(*She holds up five fingers.*)
Nothing, really nothing for five days? That's not clever. Last
Sunday you were all right. Weren't you?
(*Shakes her head.*)
Why didn't you speak to me then? Why did you leave it a
whole week?
(*Pause. He removes the thermometer.*)
PAULA: I can't stop crying.
FREDDIE: Is it your boyfriend?
(*Shakes her head.*)
What, then?
(*Pause.*)
PAULA: When I think of being dead, I cry.
FREDDIE: Then don't think of being dead.
PAULA: I can't help it.
FREDDIE: That's not like you. You've always been sensitive, I
don't deny, but I'v never known you morbid. As a matter of fact,
that's why we get on so well together, you laugh at my jokes.
PAULA: Don't try to cheer me up. I get that all day long.
FREDDIE: I'm not trying to cheer you up. I'm trying to cheer
myself up. And I speak the truth. We get on well. I like to hear
your news. I like to hear what's going on in your life.
PAULA: I'm a messenger, that's what's going on in my life.
FREDDIE: An interesting occupation, but I thought you were a
librarian.
PAULA: I carry messages.
FREDDIE: For whom?
PAULA: For my mother. For my father.
FREDDIE: They send you on messages?
PAULA: They don't speak.
FREDDIE: Marc and Maggie aren't speaking? They seemed
friendly enough a moment ago –
PAULA: You should know by now that as a family we excel at
keeping up appearances.
FREDDIE: They don't speak at all?
PAULA: Ask your father if he needs a clean shirt. Do you need a
clean shirt? Of course, I need a clean shirt. Yes, he needs a
clean shirt.

FREDDIE: How long's this been going on?

PAULA: Three weeks. Four. Don't tell them I told you.

FREDDIE: Why not?

PAULA: You know why not.

FREDDIE: If I knew, I wouldn't ask. Why mustn't I tell them what makes you unhappy?

PAULA: Because of Grandad and Grandma, Aunty Milly and Uncle Tom, because of Danny and Audrey and Spenser and Uncle Simon and Aunty Hilda and Uncle Ollie and Aunty Rita and Gerald and Leon and Kevin and Lionel and Gloria and Marjorie and Rollo and Lynnette and Sharon –

FREDDIE: All right, all right, there's a lot of us, you've made your point.

PAULA: No one must know that anyone else is unhappy.

FREDDIE: All right.

(*Pause. He hums. She begins to cry.*)

PAULA: I feel I'm being crushed.

(*Pause.*)

FREDDIE: You'll marry soon, have children of your own, it won't seem so bad.

PAULA: And spread the disease.

FREDDIE: The disease?

PAULA: I just want to die.

FREDDIE: Is that what you said to Grandad?

(*Shakes her head.*)

Worse?

PAULA: I told him to fuck off.

FREDDIE: (*Smiling*) That's a terrible thing to say.

PAULA: He stood over me, lecturing –

FREDDIE: He likes to lecture.

PAULA: All they think of is themselves.

(*Pause.*)

FREDDIE: I'm sorry your parents are going through a bad patch. I'm sorry everything's getting you down. But why suddenly so despairing?

PAULA: It's not sudden. It's been all my life.

FREDDIE: Paula, Paula, don't quote from the books on your shelves. You? Unhappy all your life? Why lie to me such an obvious lie? Have a little respect for my intelligence. I know doctors don't have to be clever, but we have got good memories, and I remember you happy. Sunny. Full of life. (*Pause.*) We all get depressed from time to time. With me, it's seasonal. Late spring. Early summer. Certain dates. An anniversary. There's one next month. The 8th of June. I know I'll have a black day. I always do. Even as I'm talking to you, there's this – this accompaniment, like having the radio on but not really listening. (*Pause.*) I've taken a pill. Two. I – I – (*Hums.*) I can't tell you how long I've been plagued like this. Years. And recently, I've been thinking I should write it down, for my own sake, you understand, what happened to me, to try and exorcize the memory. (WOMAN'S VOICE 'Federico . . . Federico . . . ') You've read my short stories. You're the only one who has. There's a long and honourable tradition of medical men turned writer. But, Anton Chekhov I am not. Still, I believe, I could help myself by having to face the source of my pain. Correction, as Uncle Tom would say. An ache. No, another over-statement. A pinprick. No. An absence of feeling.

(*Light changes. Warm, reassuring.*)

Why are you crying, Ardella? You mustn't cry. We won't be parted. I won't allow it to happen. I swear it, Ardella. On the lives of our dead comrades. Never. *Mai*. Never.

(*Light returns.*)

A longing. A sense of loss. I'm telling you this, Paula, not so you should have sympathy for me, but to let you know I understand a little of these things. We all have good and bad days. Only idiots and corpses are placid. Don't make too much of your sadness, whatever. Don't overdo it. Don't indulge yourself. You begin to believe in your own despair and that's truly dreadful. (*He listens.*) We're friends, Paula. And all that's required of friends is that they speak to each other. (*He hums.*) See the funny side. As you've always done. Hitherto.

(*Sound of aeroplanes overhead.*)

These bloody pills do no good at all.

(*Sound begins to fade.*)

Aunty Hilda came to see me the other day. She said she was off to a health farm and wanted a check-up. I said 'No cream teas in the afternoon now' and she said, 'Freddie please, I didn't come here to talk politics'. As Gran would say, she's not a well woman. (*He hums a little. Silence.*)

PAULA: You're no different, Uncle Freddie. I'm crying and what do I hear? The reason for *your* tears. Mummy's the same. Only Dad keeps silent. There's no hope, Uncle Freddie. I feel punished. And for what? I can't keep thoughts of death out of my mind.

IVAN: (*Calling*) Freddie!! Freddie!!

PAULA: When they argue I want to hide. I've no control over myself . . . I go cold inside. I dropped a glass the other night. I yelled for twenty minutes at the sight of broken glass.

IVAN: (*Calling*) Freddie, we're waiting for you

PAULA: I feel lost. I've nothing to hold on to. I just sit and stare and think and cry.

(*Pause.*)

FREDDIE: Is that a quotation?

(PAULA *looks shocked.*)

You see it doesn't ring true.

(*She buries her face in the pillow.*)

Exaggeration is a family failing, that I understand. But sitting – staring – thinking – crying from you? (*He laughs.*) I've never known anyone lie as compulsively as you do. It amuses me. You'll be all right in a day or two.

(*He leaves her and joins the others. They all look at him expectantly except* IVAN, *who is pacing impatiently.*)

MARGARET: Well?

FREDDIE: Something's not quite right.

MARC: Serious?

MARGARET: Did she tell you about when she broke the glass?

FREDDIE: I may want a second opinion.

MARGARET: Oh God.

FREDDIE: No. Just an ordinary doctor will do. All I want is a second opinion to confirm my opinion that there's nothing wrong with her.

IVAN: You want a second opinion? I'll give you a second opinion:

ignore her. Take no notice. Behave as if she didn't exist. You'll see, in a day or two she'll get bored with being ignored, she'll get up and start showing off in some other way. Do not allow her to interfere with our Sunday. That's what she wants. I will not give her the satisfaction of seeing me upset. So, instead, I'm going to tell you my surprise and Paula can partake or not. But if it's up to me –

EMMA: She's our grandchild, Ivan –

IVAN: (*Exploding*) Don't tell me about my responsibilities. I think I have performed my obligations as well as any man.

EMMA: She needs our love.

IVAN: Emmy, for God's sake, you talk like a woman's magazine rubbish basket. Love, love, you think love is standing about with a treacle smile and tears in your eyes. You think love is indulging the worst side of the object to be loved. I'll tell you what you think: you think love is three telephone calls a day to all and sundry telling them how much you love them. But I say unto you, love is a muscle, love is a hammer, love is a parachute jump from 12,000 feet at the age of forty-five. Love is an *effort*. You think it's easy for me to be hard on that child? You think I'm so stupid I don't know she must feel pain to act in the way she does? Of course I know these things. But I am telling you this is a *community* of love. We're all part of it, no matter what. Even Audrey, married now, to that husband of hers whom I hardly know and whose name I can never remember but who always reminds me of the fairy queen –

MILICENT: Spenser.

IVAN: Spenser. Even Audrey and Spenser are part of that community still. You allow one member to believe that the individual is more important than the community and you bring down the Temple. It's up to Paula to return to the circle but that means there must be a circle for her to return to, which means the circle must remain unbroken. We must not allow ourselves to be provoked. Our values, habits, behaviours must remain constant and recognizable. When she sees we are undisturbed, she will come running to join the dance. Just hold fast, put her from your minds and wait.

(*Pause.*)

EMMA: I don't phone anybody three times a day.

(IVAN *growls with irritation* .)

MARGARET: (*To* FREDDIE) He's never liked Paula. They're so similar.

(FREDDIE *hums.*)

IVAN: And, my friends, I'm going to tell you something else –

MILICENT: Dad, please, we're not a public meeting –

IVAN: – it's perfectly appropriate that we've had this little how-do-you-do.

TOM: How d'you mean appropriate, Dad?

IVAN: It gives more piquancy to my surprise.

EMMA: What's that mean?

IVAN: It means that Paula should be made aware of the privilege she has in life to belong. Here. With us. Because we have cause to rejoice in who we are, what we are, why we are.

EMMA: Is this the surprise?

IVAN: We are going to have a party.

MILICENT: Oh, Dad, not another party –

MARGARET: We're always having parties –

EMMA: I agree with the girls, you can have too much of a good thing –

IVAN: Not just another party, a celebration.

EMMA: Of what? We've had our golden wedding.

IVAN: Will you shut up, Emma, and just listen?

TOM: What are we going to celebrate, Dad?

IVAN: An event that took place thirty-three years ago.

(FREDDIE *hums.*)

EMMA: Thirty-three years? What kind of an anniversary is that?

IVAN: June the 8th, that's what kind of anniversary.

MARGARET: June the 8th?

EMMA: Ivan, you're mad, who celebrates thirty-three years from anything? Honestly, Ivan, you're the most concentric man I know.

MARGARET: Eccentric.

TOM: What's so special about June the 8th?

IVAN: On June the 8th, thirty-three years ago, Freddie was liberated.

30

(*General understanding: the love song sounds.*)
An event I consider the most important in my life or anyone else's for that matter –

EMMA: Anyone's else's, he's crazy –

IVAN: I'm an old man. The events of the past begin to be more vivid and more important to me than what happened yesterday or this morning. I want to mark June the 8th. I have a desire so strong to make everyone aware of what happened. And time is not on my side. Next year I may not be here. Or worse, I may be incontinent. We will give a party and I will tell the story of what happened. I want the young ones, Paula and Danny especially, to hear. It's important the young know the exploits of the old.

FREDDIE: I won't be there.

IVAN: Now let's make lists. What shall we say? Forty, fifty people? For my own part, I'd prefer not to ask Uncle Simon because I can't bear to hear him eat –

EMMA: You've got to ask Simon, how can you leave out Simon?

FREDDIE: I won't be there.

IVAN: And Aunty Hilda should be invited at the last possible minute in case, luck being with us, she has another engagement.

FREDDIE: I won't be there. There will be no party, no celebration, no anniversary. There's nothing to celebrate.

IVAN: Freddie, Freddie –

FREDDIE: I don't want it, I want no part of it, I don't want to hear another word about it –

EMMA: Freddie, don't speak to your father like that –

IVAN: Freddie, darling, why are you so upset? You remember that day, the crowds, the cheering, they rang the bells in a dozen churches.

FREDDIE: I'm not listening to you, Dad, I don't want to hear. In front of witnesses I tell you I won't be there. And if you hold such a party I won't speak to a single one of you ever again. There's nothing to celebrate.

IVAN: Freddie, darling, calm down, I didn't mean to upset you. I only want joy for all of us. I'm an old man, Freddie, give me the pleasure. It may be my last opportunity. Who

31

knows where we'll all be next year?

TOM: You'll be here, Dad, it's us I'm worried about – (*Laughs.*)

FREDDIE: Next year, ten years, never, never, *mai*. Never, never, never!

(*He moves away from the rest, sits apart, hums.*)

WOMAN'S VOICE: (*Anxiously*) *Dove vai*, Federico . . . *dove vai*?

(IVAN *goes to* FREDDIE.)

IVAN: I'm asking you, Freddie, as a favour to me. Indulge me. Be there. Don't deny you think often of that day. Recently, I've been unable to think of anything else. I don't believe in premonitions, but before I die, I want all of them to know.

FREDDIE: They know.

IVAN: They don't. And even if they ever did, they've forgotten. The girls were young. Mum doesn't like to think of the past. When I say all of them, I suppose I mean I want the young to know. I can't tell you how often I've had the urge to draw the grandchildren round me, to tell what happened that day, because I see in those events a symbol.

(*Love song sounds.*)

We're unusual. Because in an unfeeling world, we feel. And when I ask myself why, the answer comes because of what we did that day. You and I. Freddie, I tell you, I wouldn't tell the others, but how long can I have left? I feel an *urgency* to mark the event.

FREDDIE: Mark it, do what you like, I won't be there.

IVAN: Have you ever thought that you may be helped if we celebrate? Oh, I know you think I'm an insensitive man, but I'm not so insensitive I can't perceive the sadness in your eyes, the silences, the preoccupation. Last year, on the anniversary of that day, when I telephoned, you said you were ill: you think I didn't know you were drunk?

FREDDIE: I'd taken pills –

IVAN: And the year before. And the year before that. You think I can't put two and two together? I'm your father. Since a little boy I've known without being told what you think, what you feel. Celebrate with me. A father. A son.

FREDDIE: A father, a son, not Siamese twins!

IVAN: Freddie, turn your sadness into joy. Do it. For your own sake.

32

FREDDIE: Ah, it's for my sake, is it?

IVAN: All right, for my sake. I want you to bless what I did that
day. (*Silence.*) Don't make me determined, Freddie. We'll
all regret it. They don't call me Ivan the Terrible for
nothing. (*Smiles.*)

FREDDIE: You're determined already.

IVAN: For an old man's sake. I need peace, too.

FREDDIE: Dad, you'll do what you want to do. Allow me the same
freedom.
(*Silence.*)

IVAN: Talk about a kick in the teeth. (*Long pause.*) What time's
lunch?

TOM: I'll go and start now. Shall I? It won't take long.

IVAN: I need to jog, to move, to think. I've never known a day
leave such a bitter taste.
(*He jogs off.*)

EMMA: Where are you going? What does he need to jog for?
Honestly, he always overdoes everything. (*Pause.*) Why
didn't I marry Norman Teller? He was such a quiet sort.

TOM: Come on all of you, help me make lunch, eh? We'll have
some fun. All of us together.
(*He goes.* MARGARET *follows.* EMMA *sees* MARC.)

EMMA: Marc, you can come and help too. It's your house.
(*She nods to* MILICENT. MILICENT *understands and goes to*
FREDDIE. MARC *hovers.*)

MILICENT: Brother mine.

FREDDIE: Sister mine.

MILICENT: You want to talk?

FREDDIE: Go and help them with lunch.

MILICENT: I prefer to sit with you. I won't ask questions.

FREDDIE: Thank you.
(MARC *approaches.*)

MARC: Freddie, did you tell her my news? (*No response.*)
Something cheerful for a change. You want to hear, Mil? (*No
response.*) I'm thinking of opening a second pharmacy.

MILICENT: Not now, Marc.
(*He turns sharply and goes.*)

FREDDIE: I think Mum's right. We're all concentric. A wayward child, a sour surprise, a second pharmacy. How come that a wet like Marc can do so well?

MILICENT: Damp always rises.

FREDDIE: We crushed him. He used to be livelier. I suppose he's had to develop an instinct for survival.

MILICENT: He was always wet.

FREDDIE: You were clever to turn him down. Clever to choose Tom. Poor Margaret.

MILICENT: It's a pity Paula doesn't take after her father. At least we'd have a quieter time.

FREDDIE: No, she's a Kilner all right.

MILICENT: I never know with you, is there something seriously wrong with Paula?

FREDDIE: No. She gets it into her head that to be ill is to be special. It's a sort of showing-off. But why? (*Pause.*) I've been a doctor too many years.
(*Pause.*)

MILICENT: You were stupid to rant and rave. You know our father as well as I do. There's nothing he likes better than opposition, nothing he enjoys more than an obstacle to be moved. Let him puff, let him blow, only don't *oppose* him. That's when he becomes persistent.

FREDDIE: Becomes persistent? When was he anything else? You think I don't know? One way or the other we'll all gather, the champagne corks will pop, and he'll tell the story of June the 8th. Persist? When has he not?
(*Silence.*)

IVAN'S VOICE: There! There! My son!
(*Silence.*)

MILICENT: Freddie, you look tired. Go and lie down. Sleep. I'll wake you for lunch.

FREDDIE: I shall sleep away the 8th of June. Will you wake me then?
(*She kisses his cheek.* MARGARET *goes in to* PAULA. PAULA *breaks a glass and threatens* MARGARET.)

MILICENT: Tom's dropped something, I bet.

PAULA: Come near me and I'll cut my wrist, I swear it, leave me alone, leave me alone, leave me alone, leave me alone! (*She*

34

throws down the broken glass, and runs out, screaming.) Leave me alone . . .

(MARGARET *swoons, sobs.* MILICENT *helps her.*)

EMMA: Freddie, go after Paula. Marc, try to find Dad. Tell him what's happened but tell him gently, don't let him get excited.

(MARC *runs off.*)

Freddie, go and find Paula. Bring her back.

IVAN'S VOICE: I've come to fetch you, my son.

(FREDDIE *laughs.*)

EMMA: Freddie!

(*Laughing, he goes.*)

(*Blackout.*)

ACT TWO

Light on FREDDIE *taking* PAULA's *pulse. She is hidden in the bedclothes.*

IVAN'S VOICE: There's nothing wrong with her. The MO says so. It's an old trick. They'll do anything to keep you. She's not dying. She only took eight aspirins.

(FREDDIE *covers his ears involuntarily.* PAULA's *bed is now centre.* FREDDIE *gives her an injection. Around the bed sit* EMMA, MARGARET, MILICENT *and* TOM. FREDDIE *leaves the bedside, sits and begins to eat a hamburger.*)

MARGARET: How far can an old man run? Marc should have found him by now. Of course, Marc is out of condition and he's sitting on a pavement somewhere nursing blisters. Or suffering from cramp. He suffers from cramp. (*Laughs too loudly.*) Once, years ago, when we were first married, at a most delicate, I mean *most* delicate moment, he suddenly sprang out of bed and began to stamp his foot on the floor. I said, 'Whatever gives you pleasure!' and he said 'I've got cramp, you bloody fool!' (*Laughs, cries softly.*)

MILICENT: (*To* FREDDIE) Physician.

(FREDDIE *rises, goes to* MARGARET, *gives her two pills from a bottle in his pocket which she swallows.*)

FREDDIE: Anyone else in need? Only three of us on sedatives? What's happening to us all? You disappoint me. We're unusually calm.

TOM: Listen, everybody, you know what I say? I say, look on the bright side.

MILICENT: Be quiet, Tom.

TOM: No, I won't be quiet, why should I be quiet? I have as much right to speak as anyone else. I say look on the bright side because there's no need to exaggerate. She ran away, she's

come back – correction – she was brought back. There *is* a
bright side: she's here, she's well. That's the bright side.
(*Pause*.)

MILICENT: God help a child of mine who did this to me.
(*Pause*.)

EMMA: (*To* FREDDIE) Freddie, eat a little less noisily, please. I
can't hear the band.

MARGARET: (*To* FREDDIE) How can you eat at a time like this?

FREDDIE: By opening and closing my mouth.

(MARGARET *goes to* PAULA, *sits on the bed, caresses her
forehead*.)

MARGARET: Sweetheart, little sweetheart, try some soup. (*No
response*.) An egg. Soft boiled. Crustless bread. (*No response*.
To FREDDIE.) What is she trying to do now? Starve herself to
death? (*Laughs too loudly*.)

FREDDIE: Leave her be. I've given her a sedative.

EMMA: Margaret, sit down. Paula, we're here. Don't be
frightened, angel. We all love you.
(*Pause*.)

TOM: Would someone please explain why we are sitting like this?
We seem to be waiting for something. For what? For what
are we waiting?

FREDDIE: The Eumenides, then we can have a proper reunion.

MILICENT: We're waiting for Dad.

TOM: Why? What do we expect Dad to do?

FREDDIE: Persist.

EMMA: I'll tell you what worries me: did anybody see her?

TOM: Who?

EMMA: Who, who! Paula, of course! The neighbours, did they see
her?

FREDDIE: How could they help it? In her nightdress? Screaming?
Not a sight easily ignored.

EMMA: We must try to keep it quiet. Somehow.

MILICENT: One thing's certain, we mustn't tell Aunty Hilda.

TOM: Right. There are three forms of communication.
Telephone, television and tell Hilda.

EMMA: Don't joke, please Tom. A child runs screaming down the
street in her nightdress. What will people think?

37

FREDDIE: They could think she's had a bad case of constipation.

EMMA: Freddie. (*Pause*.) Had she shaved under her arms?

MARGARET: Mummy, please, yes, she'd shaved, she'd used deodorant and talcum powder, tampons and suppositories –

EMMA: Margaret, control yourself!

FREDDIE: Take comfort she's got a good figure. Imagine if Audrey ran down the street in her nightdress.
(*Pause*.)

MILICENT: No child of mine would dare do such a thing.

TOM: Shouldn't we all go to our respective houses? Let Freddie deal with it as a doctor?

FREDDIE: It's all dealt with, Tom.

EMMA: And leave Margaret alone? At a time like this?
(EMMA *sits on the bed, dabs at* PAULA'*s forehead with a cloth*.)

MARGARET: Tom, don't talk of leaving, please.

TOM: All I'm suggesting –

MILICENT: Tom – (*Beckons him aside*.) Don't go on. Can't you see? There's comfort in our being here. Especially you and me. We're a support. We have to be calm. And we must wait for Dad. It would be terrible if he got back and found we'd all gone. We have to give comfort.
(MILICENT *goes to* MARGARET, *holds her hand;* MARGARET *puts her head on* MILICENT'*s shoulder and rests.* EMMA *nurses* PAULA. TOM *goes to* FREDDIE, *sits by him, smiles.*)

TOM: And you sit here and stuff your mouth as if nothing's happened.

FREDDIE: I'm still to be convinced something has.

TOM: You went after the girl, you saw her, you know what state she was in, you brought her back –
(FREDDIE *hums, eats.*)

FREDDIE: Talk to me, Tom. You wanted to talk to me.

TOM: Not now. This is neither the time nor the place. It'll keep.

FREDDIE: Talks to me. Tell me something ordinary and commonplace. Talk to me of haemorrhoids and hernias. Tell me you want your ears syringed. Tell me that you fart when you least expect to. (*Pause*.) Excuse me. The doctor has taken his own medicine and is unnaturally quiescent. As we all are. I hear nothing in my head. The battery has run down.

38

I am bereft of memory. There is no peace like the present. Make the most of it. You asked why we sit here waiting? We are to be buffeted. We all know it. It is inevitable and unstoppable. That's why we must all remain together. We must have something to hold on to when the storm breaks. Crack your cheeks, rage, blow. Can the house stand it? We've never had anything like this before. We need an act of healing; we'll get an act of war.

(*Pause.*)

TOM: It doesn't seem tight to talk of my troubles when a young girl is having a breakdown.

FREDDIE: There may never be a better opportunity.

TOM: Well. If you won't think badly of me, talking of myself, when our thoughts should be elsewhere. (*Pause.*) I have a confession to make.

FREDDIE: Good. (*Hums.*)

TOM: And this is confidential, Freddie.

FREDDIE: An unnecessary enjoinder: the secrecy of the surgery is absolute. Speak.

TOM: This is difficult for me. (*Pause.*) I'll come straight to the point. (*Pause.*) Look: I'm faithful to my wife.

FREDDIE: I can see the need for secrecy, you don't want to let that sort of thing get about.

TOM: No, no, I tell you that as a preamble, so you'll understand what's to come.

FREDDIE: Ah, there's more.

TOM: I've been faithful to Milicent since the day we were married. Twenty-one years, one woman, I want you to know that. And don't think it's a virtue, it's not. Fidelity comes easily to me; I prefer it; I enjoy it and I've always taken pride in it. (*Pause.*) I came from an orphanage, as you know. So being taken in by you all was a blessing and a privilege, like being admitted to an exclusive club. You don't go about deliberately breaking the rules if you want to go on being a member. And fidelity seemed to me a cardinal rule of this particular club. I've never told anyone this, Freddie. As a matter of fact, when the travellers come round to the factory, we sit and natter. I sometimes lie, pretend I've got something

39

on the side, because nowadays your virility's in question if you're not having if off twice a week with some blonde little scrubber in Accounts. (*Pause*.) Milicent and I have led a very orderly married life, regular, satisfactory, perhaps people think it boring and dull, I don't know. Every Saturday night. Once. Once only. In marriage that's enough. But there's the problem, started two months ago and no apparent sign of alleviation. I can't get it up.

(FREDDIE *hums*.)

The first time, you can joke; the second time you manage to smile; thereafter, your whole life is put in jeopardy. Last night, no change, except I dreamed I was an inch high and trying to climb a giant wax candle which kept on melting. What must Milicent think? She must, it's only natural, she must think I'm being taken care of elsewhere, and who would blame her? And how can I explain the reasons for the way I feel without hurting her? How can I tell her that every time I touch her I feel almost as though I'm committing incest, as though the flesh I'm touching is too much part of me, as though I'm doing something sinful. (*Shudders*.) Is there anything you can give me, Freddie? Is there a medicine?

FREDDIE: For incest?

TOM: Don't joke. I've even thought I should go and see a psychiatrist. Charlie Rosen, perhaps, what do you think? The other day I bought a little book. The author says impotence can come from an unnatural attachment to one's mother or one's sister: I didn't have either, so who are you to believe? Should I go and see Charlie Rosen? He's a top man.

FREDDIE: Have you thought, perhaps, of going to a whore?

TOM: Won't work. Tried it once. When I was eighteen. Afterwards I washed for a week. I spent seven days in and out of the bath.

(*Pause*.)

FREDDIE: You may have come to the wrong doctor.

TOM: Freddie, I need medical advice.

FREDDIE: (*Smiling*) I've needed it for thirty-three years. (*Hums*.)

IVAN: She did what? She did what? She did what? She did what?

(IVAN *enters.* MARC, *breathing heavily, is a little behind him.*)

MARC: That's all he's said since I told him. 'She did what? She did what?' That's all he says. (*Goes to* PAULA.) How are you, baby?

EMMA: Ivan, it's all right, only a few people saw, no one need know, Freddie's given her a sedative –

IVAN: Let me understand: she ran down the street in her nightdress –

EMMA: Screaming, but not many people around, thank God it's Sunday, and we'll keep it among ourselves –

IVAN: Why did she do it?

FREDDIE: Why do people run away, Dad?

MARC: She broke a glass, threatened to cut her wrists.

MARGARET: And funny, she doesn't like broken glass. (*Laughs too loudly.*)

IVAN: Why

EMMA: Who knows why? She's not herself. Sit, Ivan, sit. How far did you run? You're sweating. Sit, sweetheart, sit.

IVAN: I don't understand. Threatens her life. Runs away. Why? If she needs help, we're here. What does she need to run away for?

MARGARET: Would you like something to eat, Dad? You haven't had lunch. A drink, perhaps? Whisky, tea, coffee, a sandwich, brandy? What would you like?

FREDDIE: In time of crisis, offer food and drink.

IVAN: I have no appetite. Neither am I thirsty.

PAULA: Uncle Freddie.

(*All turn to her.* FREDDIE *goes to her; the others retire to their chairs,* EMMA *and* MILICENT *attending* IVAN.)

FREDDIE: Yes, Paula, I'm here.

PAULA: Will I have to go to hospital?

FREDDIE: What for? You're not hurt.

PAULA: No, I meant, I thought perhaps you'd say I was in need of a different sort of treatment.

FREDDIE: You mean another patient for Charlie Rosen? Anyone would think he was touting for business around here. No, I'm qualified to cope. I've given you something to calm you down and you seem calmer – (*The love song sounds; he*

41

hesitates a second.) – we'll talk tomorrow, when we can be alone, perhaps I'll prescribe something stronger, although I know medicine isn't the be all and the end all, it wears off, the respite from pain is brief, but who knows? We may make progress – (*Puts a hand to his head; love song a little louder*.) Or we may not.

PAULA: What will happen to me?

(IVAN *stands suddenly, comes forward*.)

IVAN: I'm going to speak my mind. I cannot keep silent. I have a duty. You must learn, Paula, to have more concern for those nearest and dearest to you. You must stop behaving like a childish, self-indulgent, selfish, unbalanced exhibitionist – (*The sounds of war*.)

MARC: Dad, don't speak like that to her, please.

IVAN: I have a duty to perform –

MARC: She's my daughter, it's my house, Dad –

IVAN: It's my mortgage. You're so keen to assert your rights, take from me the debt, please, my wife and I could travel a little more, we could see a bit of the world. It's your house, Marc, but I pay for it.

MARC: Shit.

TOM: Marc –

EMMA: Ivan, darling, don't get so worked up –

IVAN: I am worked up. This girl has to be told a thing or two. Does she know how privileged she is? She has to be told what people go through, what struggles, what pain, what feats of daring and danger just so that she could be born into comfort and contentment, love and devotion, safety and freedom, just so she could be born. Not so she could run away.

EMMA: He should have been a politician. Ivan, you want to explode?

MARGARET: (*Crying*) Dad, you'll make matters worse –

IVAN: That would take some doing, Margaret. But so be it. Let the heavens fall, let us all be struck down with pestilence but I would never forgive myself if I didn't say what I have to say. And to her directly, so she may hear and understand and get well.

(*Sporadic machine-gun fire*.)

42

EMMA: Freddie, as a doctor, forbid it. Order your father to be
quiet. Order him to go home and rest. Tell him the child
needs peace. Tell him he needs peace.
(*Light changes.*)

FREDDIE: I'll go to him, Ardella. I'll tell him what I've decided.
He'll listen. He'll understand. Why did you do it? What
good would you be to me dead?

EMMA: Freddie, please, you're the only one who can help –
(*Light returns.*)
Why don't you listen to your mother, Freddie?

FREDDIE: (*Laughing*) The animals go in two by two, hurrah,
hurrah!

IVAN: The rest of you leave if you wish, but I'm determined to be
heard. (*Advances on* PAULA's *bed.*) Had we been living in
another time, had I been my father or my father's father, I
would have cursed you and cast you out of this house. Do
you know what you've done? Do you know the reprehensible
nature of your act? You have caused pain to those who love
you, but worse: I am told you threatened to take your own
life, and that's more vile than saying you didn't ask to be
born.

FREDDIE: You're in fine form today, Dad –

IVAN: Freddie, this is a serious matter for concern. Where was I?
You disturb my thoughts.

FREDDIE: Dad, I think you should stop.

IVAN: I still have things to say –

MARGARET: No, there's no stopping him now. All our lives we've
been lectured. Other children were scolded, slapped or
locked in their rooms without food, we were treated to
sermons on the mount. But I say unto you – (*Laughs, cries.*)

IVAN: And have you turned out so badly?

MARGARET: Yes, my God, yes, we have –

IVAN: If you have nothing to say, Margaret, keep your mouth
tight shut. We're not criminals. We neither rob nor steal.
Where will you find kinder, more hospitable, more generous
people? Where? We live as best we can without damaging
our neighbours –

MARGARET: But what about ourselves?

43

IVAN: No one talks more rubbish than you. Where would you be
without us?

(FREDDIE *hums*. *Silence*. IVAN *turns on* PAULA.)

Don't misunderstand me, Paula, I have no intention of
punishing you. That's not my interest, not my bent. But you
must get it into your skull that you are not the only person to
walk on this planet, that the world wasn't created for your
pers al pleasure a second after you were born. You are not
solitary and self-contained. There are others in the world.

FREDDIE: A difficult philosophical concept –

IVAN: Your uncle scoffs, but he knows the truth of what I say
better than most. You, Paula, are privileged. And why?
Because you have enough to eat? No. Because you are warm?
Wrong. Because your mother buys you too many clothes or
because you can go on holiday once a year –

MARGARET: Twice last year –

IVAN: Margaret, please. No. None of these things. So I'll tell you
why. You were born with the privilege of possibility. (*He
looks round to measure the effect.*)

EMMA: When you do that, Ivan, you remind me of one of the
actors my mother used to take in when I was a girl.

MILICENT: I hope he bathed.

MARGARET: I often thought Paula should have been an actress.

IVAN: Listen to me, Paula, and learn something for a change –

MARC: Dad, she's upset, she's been given a sedative, how can you
be so insensitive?

IVAN: It's for her own good. Possibility, Paula. You were born
with the possibility to live fully, to inherit the riches of
thought, expression and freedom. You have the possibility of
culture, of books, which I know you love, of painting and
poetry, the theatre and music –

EMMA: She was never very musical –

MARGARET: She did Grade Five on the piano –

IVAN: Shut up, the pair of you! I am trying to help the child.
Possibility, Paula, to express the talents within you, to open
yourself to beauty and truth, to struggle with complex
thought, to worship nature, all these things were, at birth,
yours for the asking. And there was only one obligation upon

you: that you cared for and protected your inheritance, that, in time, they may be passed on enriched by your presence on this earth. Now, if you don't want that, if you cannot comprehend that simple beauty, go into a nunnery. I personally will purchase the veil for you. But do not spit in the face of those who have made these things possible. (*Pause.*)

EMMA: Good. I think he's finished, now we can get up, go home, leave the girl in peace, we'll come tomorrow, Margaret.

IVAN: Emma, I might strike you for the first time in fifty-six years of married life. I am not yet finished with her.

FREDDIE: He's not yet finished, I thought as much –

IVAN: Paula, are you taking in what I said? There is nothing personal in this between you and me. Paula. I don't mind for myself that you should speak to me as though I were a social misfit, though where you should learn such langauge, I don't know –

FREDDIE: From Chesney, I bet –

IVAN: Paula, your inheritance is there to be used not squandered, to be nourished not scorned.

FREDDIE: (*To* MILICENT, *smiling*) Ah, he's off.
(*The sounds of war, distant but continuous now.*)

IVAN: Family feeling. It's thought to be a sentimental concept nowadays, a concept much derided. But the change of attitude to a concept doesn't change the concept.

EMMA: Ivan, it's getting late, come, sweetheart, enough, we'll talk philosophy another day. Come on, darling –

IVAN: (*Exloding*) I am going to tell her what she has to learn, now. I know what I'm doing! The privileges she chooses not to exercise were earned by struggle, by duty, by sacrifice, by our history.

EMMA: Oh, history, no, Ivan, don't rake up the past, I hate the past –

IVAN: She hates the past, your grandmother. Well, well, I'm not so squeamish. You run away. You threaten to end your own life. Have you any idea what that would do to those who remained behind? Have you any notion of what separation means? Do you know what it means to lose a loved one?

45

EMMA: He's telling not asking.

IVAN: Look, look at your grandmother. You wouldn't think a telegram could turn a woman's hair white in a week. White.

EMMA: Give ancient history a rest, Ivan –

FREDDIE: Let the trumpet sound.

MILICENT: Dad, a young girl in a state of shock, she can't take anything in at the moment, what good does it do to lecture her now?

IVAN: Milicent, I never struck you as a child unless in anger. I am not the man to come back tomorrow in the cold light of day.

FREDDIE: Thank you, Mill, but too late. The dogs are unleashed. He'll never have another opportunity like this one. I know what's coming: family feeling is a parachute jump from 12,000 feet.

IVAN: Yes, all right, a parachute jump. Mock me, but I did it. No one will deny me that leap. Certainly not Paula.

FREDDIE: What Paula's done has nothing to do with your parachute jump. You're just looking for an excuse, any excuse, because you're determined to persist, determined to have your celebration. Celebration?

IVAN: Wrong. Had I not jumped none of us would be here. Our whole world would have been different. She would have had no possibility, no privilege. She would have inherited nothing but sorrow.

EMMA: Anyway, there were two telegrams not one.

IVAN: Two? There was only one, Emmy –

EMMA: Forgive me, two. I should know. When the first came, you were still running the Transport Depot, Captain Kilner. Afterwards you joined Intelligence. The second telegram turned me white.

IVAN: The second?

EMMA: First came missing believed a prisoner.

MARGARET: Mum's right. I remember because we used to pray at noon each day for Freddie's safety.

MILICENT: Yes, let him be repatriated, O Lord –

EMMA: Then came a prisoner's postcard, they called it, through the Red Cross –

FREDDIE: Dear Mum and Dad, the only English book they've got here in the camp is *Alice in Wonderland*.

EMMA: (*To* IVAN) *Then* you went to see Professor Ingles.

IVAN: Ingles, I'd forgotten all about Ingles. A faithful customer before the war. Always asking about early editions of the metaphysicals.

EMMA: Nonsense, he was questioning the boys who'd escaped from POW camps.

IVAN: Ingles, at my suggestion, transferred me to his staff. That's how I learned that Freddie had escaped, and instead of making his way to Switzerland, had joined the partisans.

EMMA: Then came the second telegram.

IVAN: What a memory you've got, Emmy –

EMMA: A good memory is a curse.

FREDDIE: Missing believed killed.

IVAN: Someone who'd escaped with you had seen you fall. A place called San Angelo. Snow covered. Someone had seen your blood.

EMMA: (*Touching her hair*) Yes, yes, white as snow.

IVAN: Are you listening, Paula? I'm telling you of family feeling.

FREDDIE: Missing believed killed.

IVAN: I refused to believe it. Refused. It is not so, I said. *He is not dead*. My son. My only son.

TOM: Why didn't you believe it, Dad? Why?

FREDDIE: Yes, Dad, why?

IVAN: Forgive me, Freddie, but you don't have children so you can't understand. I would not believe in your death. Had they shown me your corpse, I still would not have believed in your death.

FREDDIE: Mad –

IVAN: No doubt, but I remember reading of a man, also a father, after some war or other, waiting on the quayside for a ship carrying prisoners home. When the last man came down the gangplank and he saw that it wasn't his son, he took out a gun and shot himself. How can you explain? A father. A son.

EMMA: (*Crying*) Stop now, Ivan sweetheart, it's in the past, the young hate the past, who needs to be reminded?

FREDDIE: He does.

IVAN: You understand, Paula, the meaning of these events? Since

47

I would not, could not believe in Uncle Freddie's death, I
had to believe in his life.

EMMA: Bring him back, oh bring him back.

IVAN: Not knowing how, unaware of obstacles, careless of
danger, I determined to find him, to bring him home. Who
else would do such a thing? A clerk in a war office? A
commanding officer in the field? No, a father for a son.

EMMA: Oh, my little boy.

IVAN: I will bring him home. I. His father. Let the war rage. I
swore to find my son. Up to the long Italian leg, the battle
raged, and like a rash the allies advanced.

FREDDIE: San Angelo, they could have by-passed San Angelo –

IVAN: I studied the map. San Angelo. Far behind the enemy line.
There was only one way to reach that town and find my son.
I would have to drop with the paratroops. 'Tuck your legs in,
Captain Kilner, sir.' 'Give me a chance, I'm forty-five years
old!' 'Tuck your legs in, Captain Kilner, sir!' Like a puppet
cut loose from his master, I, Ivan Kilner, dealer in dust and
leather, dropped and floated, descended on the snow-
covered land, thinking that somewhere down there is my
son.

(*Light changes.*)

FREDDIE: We could be married, Ardella. One day I'll take you
home. Ardella, Ardella, don't cry. We have our whole lives
before us. You know what I see when I think of us together?
Green fields and bright spring flowers. And we're walking
hand in hand, and there's a soft and gentle rain. And the
green field is endless. Marry me, Ardella. Will you? Will
you?

(*Light returns.*)

IVAN: (*Speaking over the last of* FREDDIE's *speech*) Into the snow I
fell, ploughing a black furrow in white, dragged this way and
that, struggling to free myself of the harness, impatient to be
on my way, anxious to set out on my quest. In my pack a
parcel. A uniform made by a tailor in Verona to Freddie's
measurements. My belief in Freddie's survival was absolute.
I commandeered a car and a driver, headed north-east,
seeing at a distance the enemy harried by partisans. Every

yard of the way, I thought Freddie may have walked here,
Freddie may have travelled this road, Freddie may be hiding
and fighting in those hills. And, as though I were a
participant in a miracle, I came through unharmed. At last,
up the cobbled main street of San Angelo we drove, the only
Allied officer in the town, besieged and surrounded by
screaming partisans believing me to be a fleeing enemy in
disguise. In time, my identity proved to their satisfaction, I
was marched into the town hall and there the mayor fell upon
my neck, kissed me on both cheeks, saying 'The very man.
You, sir, must take the surrender of the enemy garrison.'
The German commandant would not surrender to what he
called the partisan rabble, so, I was the very man. They
needed me. And I them. I asked for the partisan leader. He
was brought to me. I asked him, 'Have you any escaped
Allied soldiers fighting with you?' 'Only two left,' he said,
'the rest have been killed.' Hold tight. All your courage now.
'Is one of them named Frederick Kilner?' He did not know
their names. 'There are two,' he said. From my pocket I took
Freddie's photograph. 'Is this either of them?' He studied
the photograph for a lifetime. His answer was a shrug, small,
infinitely expressive. 'It could be,' he said, 'and it could not
be.' I passed out and came to with the taste of brandy on my
tongue.
(*Crowd cheering. The ringing of bells.*)
Confused, bewildered, in agony, I received the enemy's
surrender from the man who might well have ordered the
death of my son, and then stepped out on to the town hall
balcony to the cheers of a seething multitude.
(*He turns to* FREDDIE *who is lost in memory. A partisan song is
sung by the crowd, and* FREDDIE *joins in.*)
FREDDIE: Look at the crowd, Ardella, have you ever seen so
    many people? Is this what liberation means? Hold my hand,
    Ardella. We mustn't be separated, not now. Don't resist, let
    them carry us. Hold tight. Hold tight.'
IVAN: There! There! My son! Freddie! Freddie! My son!
FREDDIE: Dad, what are you doing here?
IVAN: I've come to fetch you, my son.

(FREDDIE *stumbles forward. They embrace passionately. Bells, cheers at their loudest.* FREDDIE *turns, arms outstretched, joyful.*)

FREDDIE: What a day! What a place! What a crowd!
(*Love song sounds forlornly.*)

MARGARET: I prayed to God Dad wouldn't find him.

EMMA: He did it for me. He didn't want to watch me wither away and die.

MARGARET: I didn't want Freddie to come home.

EMMA: Margaret, you talk such nonsense.

MILICENT: I sat on Freddie's knee. It was the first time I was allowed to stay up after midnight.

TOM: I like to think my father, whoever he was, would have done the same for me. I don't know. Sometimes I think we're too close.

MARC: I wish I felt more for Paula. You like people to be in your debt every which way, money, favours, love. Always owing. Always behind. If only I could get some money together I'd be free.

MILICENT: I'm the only one who knows how to deal with Dad. Get out of the way and let him blow himself out.

MARGARET: I stole money from Dad's wallet. I burned a hole in Freddie's demob suit. No one's interested. You pour your heart out as he says 'What long message?'

EMMA: He brought me back my son.

IVAN: (*To* PAULA) A father, a son, but more, much more. One day when you have children of your own, when to see them ill is to wish yourself in their place, when to see them sorrowful is to beg to be given their suffering, then you will come to know and understand what deeds were done that day –

FREDDIE: But there's more, Dad, there's more. You've left out the most important part –

IVAN: (*Ignoring him*) We're not bound by chains but by hands willingly clasped –

FREDDIE: Let's hear the rest of the story, Dad –

IVAN: You've danced in a circle, haven't you, Paula, when one member falls and drags the others down? As long as I live I will not allow the circle to be broken. Not by anyone!

FREDDIE: But you didn't tell how, Dad. How do you keep the circle intact?

IVAN: Not by war or famine, not by distance of a million light years –

FREDDIE: Finish the story!

IVAN: (*Beginning to lose his breath*) – because in an unfeeling world – (*Chokes.*) – someone give me a hand.

(FREDDIE *rushes to him; so do the others, they get him a chair.* MILICENT *goes to get water.*)

EMMA: Sweetheart, sweetheart, are you all right?

(FREDDIE *examines him.*)

FREDDIE: He's all right.

MARGARET: Daddy, Daddy, Daddy.

FREDDIE: Give him air.

MILICENT: (*Returning with water*) Is it serious? What's the matter with him? How is he?

FREDDIE: He's seventy-nine, that's how is he.

IVAN: (*Trying to stand*) I'm much better now.

FREDDIE: Sit down.

EMMA: Better still, sweetheart, lie down.

IVAN: I don't want to lie down.

FREDDIE: Do as you're told.

IVAN: Of all the professions a son of mine could have chosen, that of a doctor is the most reprehensible. Only doctors need illness.

EMMA: Ivan, for once, obey. Just don't get going again, you'll blow your gusset.

MARGARET: Gasket.

EMMA: Such an obstinate man. When did you last go to the lavatory?

IVAN: A year ago. It was a Tuesday, I remember.

EMMA: Don't be so clever.

IVAN: Stop fussing, Emma, and don't worry. I'll tell you when I'm ready to be buried. Someone stay with Paula.

(IVAN *goes escorted by* EMMA, MARGARET *and* MILICENT.)

TOM: I have something to say. I think Dad deserves his celebration. We should have a party, just as he said, with

51

speeches and champagne and fireworks, if necessary. Let him see that we are full of admiration. Well, I am. Full. And he deserves it. Doesn't he deserve it? What he did, think about it, that's what I call amazing. Correction. Heroic. I'll pay for the party myself. We'd be failing him and ourselves if we didn't celebrate such an event. It's not just an anniversary, it's a victory. Come on, Marc, Fred, let's hear the cheers.

(MARC *moves away, sits.* FREDDIE *hums.*)

I don't know what's the matter with you people. Where's your gratitude?

(FREDDIE *goes to* PAULA, TOM *sits.* FREDDIE *stands at the foot of* PAULA'*s bed. From his pockets he takes two tin-foil packages which he unwraps and places on the bed: one is a hamburger, the other a piece of chocolate cake; both he has secreted at some previous moment.*)

FREDDIE: And Paula, how are you? (*No response.*) Do you feel calmer?

PAULA: Calmer, yes.

FREDDIE: Suspended animation, would that describe your state?

PAULA: If you like.

FREDDIE: Not if I like, Paula, if you like. I want to understand your state of mind.

PAULA: Calmer, I said.

FREDDIE: I wonder why you feel calmer?

PAULA: Because of the sedative, I suppose.

FREDDIE: The sedative.

PAULA: The stuff you injected.

FREDDIE: You must be mistaken, Paula. I injected nothing. (*Hums.*) Unethical, I don't deny it. Treacherous, I stand guilty. (*Hums.*) A girl threatens to cut her wrists, and in her nightgown runs screaming down the street, waving her arms like a dervish, to be caught by her uncle, a general practitioner in family scandals, who fights and struggles with this girl while she, in a state of high excitation, resists, screams abuse at the milkman on his Sunday rounds, at old and young alike, and, struggling still, is brought back to her bed where one shot, 5ccs of absolutely nothing at all instantly calms her. Amazing. You're a little bitch, Paula.

PAULA: I felt the prick of the needle.

FREDDIE: Don't persist, it's a family failing. The prick of a needle is not proof of an injection. You're a rotten little bitch, Paula.

(*Pause.* PAULA *grabs the food and begins to devour the hamburger and the chocolate cake.*)

PAULA: (*Mouth full, nervous laugh*) Will you tell them?

FREDDIE: Tell them what?

(*She eats.*)

Come, come. I want you to explain: what is it I should tell them?

(*She begins to cry.*)

To eat and to cry simultaneously is not seemly, Paula. I am impervious to your tears. You will find it difficult to engage my pity. Try another tactic: try the truth, try telling me why. Try telling me why you take to your bed for a week, pretend to be depressed and suicidal, tell us you haven't eaten or slept, insult your grandfather, and perform, in general, like a demented lemming. I may not look it but I'm all ears.

(*Pause.*)

PAULA: You wouldn't understand.

FREDDIE: Paula, Paula, you just put a knife between my ribs, acid in my eyes. You wouldn't understand. My God, what profundity. To mothers and fathers you say such things, not to kindly, intelligent, sympathetic uncles. You wouldn't understand. Paula, words of advice: don't give me any more shit.

PAULA: I say you wouldn't understand and I mean it. You love them.

FREDDIE: Why are you turning it on to me when it's you we're talking about? When you say I love them, like an accusation, does it mean that you don't?

PAULA: Of course I love them. And I hate them. And I want to stay here. And I want to run away.

FREDDIE: Perhaps you're right: for comprehension I get two out of ten.

PAULA: I reach the front door, suitcase packed, and I stop.

Physically and emotionally I'm unable to walk out. I'm on a rein. I can't explain the intricate organization of my responses any clearer than that. I am shackled.

FREDDIE: But that I understand. Families make good prisons.

PAULA: When I have children they won't feel like that.

FREDDIE: That's what I used to say. I was never able to prove it.

PAULA: You chose not to.

FREDDIE: Really? You seem to know more about it than I do.

PAULA: You stood on that Italian balcony exultant, arms outstretched, I can just imagine, embracing all those strangers, rejoicing that your father had risked life and limb, defied the entire war effort to find you. He asked me if I understood the meaning of his heroic action. Yes, I understood. What was it he said when he saw you? I have come to fetch you, my son.

FREDDIE: I wish you wouldn't talk so much about me, Paula. It's you I'm interested in.

PAULA: You should be more perceptive.

FREDDIE: A mind-reader I am not.

PAULA: You were to see that I was ill. You were to say this girl is having a breakdown. You were to put me out of their reach, because I don't possess the strength to escape on my own.

FREDDIE: Is that why you talked of treatment and hospital? You pretended to be ill in order to escape? To go to such lengths may in itself constitute a more than slight mental imbalance. (*Hums.*)

PAULA: I wanted you to diagnose mental, physical, emotional exhaustion, anything at all, but what did you say? You'll be all right in a day or two. I wanted you to order me out of this house. And what did you do? Accused me of lying, saw through me and still didn't wonder why I'd gone to such lengths. I wanted you to unlock the cell door and to throw away the key. Instead, what happens? It was you who ran after me and brought me back. I have come to fetch you, my son.

FREDDIE: You think I should have left you out in the street, in your nightdress, on a quiet Sunday, yelling obscenities at the milkman? I wonder from whom you've inherited this persistence.

54

PAULA: (*Breaking down*) You should have understood. What's to
be done? It's all impossible now. I hear their feet on the
gravelled drive and it could be an army, the Sunday invasion
of kith and kin. Do you realize I've never exchanged more
than a greeting with Uncle Tom? He brings food and
presents and Aunty Milly brings silent disapproval. And
Mummy, talking too much and laughing too loudly, and
Dad, talking too little and not laughing at all. Do you know
how many gatherings we celebrate not counting public and
religious holidays? Forty-seven. Almost one a week,
birthdays, anniversaries, engagements, funerals, marriages,
not a week goes by without the pincers coming together to
squeeze blood blisters out of us. Not counting Sundays and
the visits to sick beds, and holidays abroad in rented villas,
exporting across the sea the scandals and gossip, the
censored conversations, the suppressed accusations, looks
avoided, the same jokes, the endless bickering, and we're
sucked in, want it or not –
FREDDIE: Paula, I wish you wouldn't speak to me as if you've
rehearsed everything you're saying. We both know what
you're talking about. You want and you don't want. In that
we are identical twins.
PAULA: No. We're not. I'm not going to end up solitary. I'm not
going to end up wry and defeated. I've read your short
stories. I listen to you and watch you week after week.
You've surrendered, Uncle Freddie, and that I'll never do.
I'm not going to follow the pattern. Look at Audrey. Marries
a Canadian and where do they decide to live? Two streets
away from her parents. And little Danny. Works, studies,
works, why? You know what he told me? That the thought
of us all together suffocates him. A sixteen-year-old boy.
Suffocated. I confided in him what I was going to do today.
And do you know what he said? He said, I envy you. Yes,
suffocated. Well, I'm not buying that we only exist in this
circle. I don't believe that the outside world spins in chaos
and hopelessness and even if it does I'm well able to combat
violence. (*Pause.*) I have to find a balance between myself
and them. Between myself and the world. Between myself

55

and myself. 'Give me but one firm spot on which to stand and I will move the earth.'

FREDDIE: For a girl who can't find the strength to walk out of her own front door, you're very ambitious. (*Pause.*) Solitary, I agree. But wry and defeated? (*Hums.*)

WOMAN'S VOICE: (*Now desperate*) Federico-o-o . . . Federico-o-o . . .

(*Pause.*)

PAULA: As a child I used to day dream of hospitals and of visiting days once a week. No. Once a month.

FREDDIE: (*Sudden rage*) You know what makes me angry? Really deeply angry? That you confided in Danny and not to me. A pimply sixteen-year-old who only knows quantum theories and that E equals MC squared. Why didn't you come to me and ask me to *connive*, you rotten little bitch. Why? Because you thought I wouldn't understand!

PAULA: No, because I didn't want to compromise you –

FREDDIE: Never mind about compromising me, you belittle me and accuse me of believing in darkness. Wry, I don't mind, but defeated? What do you think I've seen in you all these years? Why should I show you, of all people, the rubbish I write, innermost thoughts, confessions? Because I sensed something in you, that's why. And I was right: crazy and devious, you may be, like all the rest of us, but God, no one can ever fault you for lack of imagination. Compromise me? You've compromised my by not confiding in me, by not trusting me. Come to me and say, Uncle Freddie, I need help –

PAULA: I did, I did, that's what I said –

FREDDIE: – I would have given you help, all the help in the world. And why, when we were alone out there in the street, when I was having to use all my force to subdue you, why then didn't you say it was all a sham and I need your help?

PAULA: Because I wasn't any longer in control –

FREDDIE: You talk to me as if I'm an alien, an enemy alien. Yes, Dad's right, you think you live alone, that no one feels what you feel and that's because you're young and can't know, can't imagine how long your elders and betters have lived, how much they've seen. That you should think I wouldn't help –

PAULA: You wanted to be found, you wanted him to fetch you back, what a day, what a place –

FREDDIE: Stop. Stop now. I'm shaking. I'm trembling. Don't go on making of me something I am not. You don't know, you can't imagine –

(*Sound of brass band, singing in celebration. Light on* IVAN, *who is holding a military tunic.*)

IVAN: I even had a uniform made for you in Verona. Put it on, my boy, we'll leave for home tonight.

FREDDIE: I'm not coming.

IVAN: I want you to myself for a day or two. We can come back with presents for all the people who've been so kind to you. But you must think of all this as over now, as a dream, a nightmare.

FREDDIE: I'm going to be married. I'm going to remain here. I'm not coming home.

PAULA: You should have taken me into *your* confidence. How was I to know?

IVAN: You will kill your mother. Is that what you want? A legacy of grief? She's waiting for you.

PAULA: Out go the grappling irons, clawing at our virtues not our vices.

IVAN: I haven't come all this way, gone through what I've gone through, to be denied. Change into your uniform and come home.

(*Love song sounds.*)

PAULA: All it needs is a little strength. Pitiful our cowardice. (*Weeps.*)

IVAN: Go and tell her you're leaving. Tell her at once.

FREDDIE: Why are you crying, Ardella? You mustn't cry. We won't be parted. I won't allow it to happen. I swear it, Ardella. On the lives of our dead comrades. Never. *Mai.* Never.

IVAN: There's nothing wrong with her. The MO says so. It's an old trick. They'll do anything to keep you. She's not dying. She only took eight aspirins. (*He goes.*)

57

FREDDIE: Why did you do it? What good would you be to me dead? I'm not leaving, Ardella. We'll be together always.

WOMAN'S VOICE: (*Desperate*) *Dove vai*, Federico . . . *dove vai . . . ?*

FREDDIE: Where are you going, she called across the valley, but answer came there none.

(*The love song fades. Silence.* IVAN, EMMA, MARGARET *and* MILICENT *re-enter*.)

IVAN: Stop fussing, I feel a new man. My heart is good for a few years yet. Where's Freddie?

MARC: With Paula.

MARGARET: Should I go in?

EMMA: Leave them. He'll put her right. One word from Freddie.

IVAN: I have a good feeling about what's happened. Paula will come through with flying colours. I believe I may have helped her.

EMMA: I'm taking you home, Ivan, I'm getting you to bed.

ivan: I'm not ill.

MILICENT: We must be going, too.

FREDDIE: (*To* PAULA) Get out of bed. Put on your gown and your slippers.

(*She hesitates*.)

Do it.

(PAULA *obeys*.)

IVAN: (*Calling*) We're going, Freddie.

EMMA: Ivan, he's with a patient –

IVAN: Nonsense, he's with Paula. There's nothing the matter with her. An emotional crisis, that's all. And it's over, cured. How? By us. By her own loving community.

FREDDIE: (*To* PAULA) Say nothing. Lean on me. I'll do the talking.

IVAN: (*Calling*) Freddie!

EMMA: Have a little tact –

FREDDIE: (*To* PAULA) Can you cry to order? Tears, real tears, mind. Cry.

(FREDDIE *and* PAULA *come to the others*.)

MILICENT: What now?

FREDDIE: I'm taking her into hospital.

MARGARET: Oh my God, what's happened, what is it?

FREDDIE: She's ill. She cannot remain in this environment.

IVAN: Environment? What is this? A social survey?

MARGARET: Wait, I'll come with you. I'll change.

FREDDIE: No, I want her to be alone.

IVAN: Wait a moment, wait a moment, not so fast. I don't understand, what exactly is the matter with her?

FREDDIE: We are.

IVAN: Don't be so clever, Freddie, it doesn't become you. If she's ill, then her place is here. Here she can be nursed. Here she can be given strength.

FREDDIE: Here she can also die.

MARGARET: Oh, my little girl –

IVAN: Paula, is this what you want? You have a right to refuse. Wouldn't it be better for your mother to nurse you, to be among people you love and who love you? We'll give you all the attention you want.

FREDDIE: She needs attention of another kind. She needs a different environment.

IVAN: Stop using that word environment. This is a home not an environment.

FREDDIE: She needs a separation.

MILICENT: Separation? For how long?

FREDDIE: That's up to her. And up to us.

EMMA: Freddie, please, don't talk in riddles. What will we say? That we've got a child we can't look after?

FREDDIE: I'll let you know when you can visit her –

EMMA: Ivan, stop them –

IVAN: I forbid you to leave this house.

MARC: She's ill. You have no jurisdiction, no mortgage on Paula. We'll do as Freddie says.

TOM: Please, please, don't let's get so excited.

FREDDIE: Come, Paula.

MARGARET: (*Weeping*) I feel such a failure.

(FREDDIE *and* PAULA *begin to go*.)

IVAN: Freddie, what do they know in hospital? She's better off here, among her own. Freddie, what are you trying to do? Leave a legacy of grief? You've no children, so how can you

know what it's doing to Margaret? Think of your sister,
Freddie, the child's mother, it'll break her heart –
MARGARET: I'm coming with you, I'm –
FREDDIE: No visitors.

(FREDDIE *and* PAULA *leave the others. Silence.*)
PAULA: So easy, so quick.
MARGARET: My little girl.
MARC: It's for her own good.
PAULA: I can hear my mother crying –
FREDDIE: Then shut your ears.
PAULA: Perhaps I should go back.
FREDDIE: Let her cry.
PAULA: I feel such pain.
EMMA: No arguments, no discussion, gone, just like that.
TOM: Everything happens for the best, she'll get better.
MILICENT: Perhaps we ought to say she's got something
physically wrong, like – like –
EMMA: No, no, people will think she's pregnant.
MARGARET: We'll say she's – (*Stops.*) What will we say? (*Weeps.*)
IVAN: Whatever we say, let it not be thought she was unhappy.
PAULA: I've stepped into darkness.
FREDDIE: Come.

(IVAN *is left alone in the dark.*)
IVAN: Emmy! Emmy! (*Lights.*) My darling, are you awake? What
time is it? I can't get Paula's face out of my mind. All night
long I've tossed and turned, but she's always there, staring at
me as if I stood accused of crime. Twice I wanted to wake
you but you were fast asleep and you looked so peaceful and
so beautiful. Why should that girl, my own granddaughter,
fill me with confusion and misgiving and guilt? I lay back
and stared at the ceiling and the feeling of alarm persisted.
Why? Why? What is it we've done that's so terrible?

The sun had only just risen and suddenly there was in my
head a tunnel of light. Imagine it. A long bright tunnel of
light narrowing to a distant point. And along the tunnel, like
statues, frozen tableaux, I saw our lives with all the terrible
and wonderful things marked along the road. If I close my
eyes now I can see that tunnel of light again. What a long

tunnel, what a lot of things to remember. And you know what, Emma, my darling? I could never have got from one end to the other without you. People think I'm the strong one. They're wrong. You are the pillar. You are the strength. You are the protector. Along the tunnel, I can see you the first time we met, in your parents' house. I fell for you then and there. Not Romeo, nor Antony, nor Alexander beholding Roxana were so smitten as I was when I first cast eyes on you. Emma and Ivan, Ivan and Emma, there was a ring to it. And I remember how I proposed. I said we would travel together along a road. We'd have children and we'd all travel together, a wonderful new tribe, walking, walking, walking, along the road. And you said, thanks very much, I'll marry someone who can afford a motor car.

And I can see us now. Freddie and Margaret and Milly. I can see this house the first time we walked up the path. And the war, and the telegram, two telegrams, and me, forty-five, in my harness dropping from the sky. And the most wonderful day of my life. Finding Freddie. I can still feel the warmth of his embrace, hear his voice, Dad, what are you doing here? And there's Freddie home and we're a family again. Family. That's what we built. That's what we made. We will be remembered for nothing else. I see one tableau over and over again: Sunday, all of us together, chattering, bickering, laughing, so *lively*. (*Cries out*.) Emma! Emmy!

(EMMA *comes to him; she is wearing a dressing-gown*.)

EMMA: It's all right, sweetheart. I'm here, can't you sleep? Have you had a nightmare?

IVAN: Was I asleep? I – I – get Freddie.

EMMA: Oh my God, what do you feel? Tell me what you feel.
(*He cries out in pain*.)
I'll get him, don't move, breathe easy, I'll get him –
(*She goes*.)

IVAN: Emmy, tell Freddie, I don't want medicine, all I want, tell him, tell him, tell him to bring a blessing.
(*He is still*. FREDDIE *enters followed by* PALLBEARERS. *He covers his father with a sheet and the* PALLBEARERS *take away the body*. FREDDIE *is left standing at the grave. Telephones ring*.

61

EMMA, MARGARET, MILICENT, TOM, MARC *in a circle*.)

EMMA: I've never seen such a crowd.

MILICENT: There were more people than flowers.

TOM: He would have loved it.

EMMA: He loved crowds. Even at a funeral. He loved anything lively.

MARGARET: Freddie took it badly.

TOM: He goes to visit the grave every day.

MARC: Freddie, of all people.

EMMA: I'm sorry Paula couldn't bring herself to be there.

MARGARET: She said she'd go alone.

EMMA: Alone, alone, always alone.

MILICENT: Mum, are you sure you don't want me to sleep at the house tonight?

EMMA: Certainly not. If it's possible to haunt your father will haunt. I'll deal with him on my own. (*Smiles, cries*.) But, children –

ALL: Yes, Mum?

EMMA: Next Sunday, you're all welcome.

MILICENT: We'll be there.

(*They go. Out of the darkness,* PAULA *emerges. Silence*.)

PAULA: Should I feel grief?

FREDDIE: I don't know. You have freedom to feel what you like. I envy you. I only know that I grieve, I mourn. I –

(*He sobs*. PAULA *scatters rose petals on the grave and exits*.
FREDDIE *sobs. The lights fade to darkness*.)

THE DRESSER

for my children,
Antony, Deborah and
Alexandra Harwood

FOREWORD

Because I was Sir Donald Wolfit's dresser for almost five years, it may be thought that the actor-manager in my play is a portrait of Wolfit, and that his relationship with his dresser is a dramatized account of our relationship. There may be other reasons for such a supposition: Lear was Wolfit's greatest performance – so is it Sir's; the grand manner both on and off the stage which Wolfit often employed is also Sir's way; the war did not stop Wolfit from playing Shakespeare in the principal provincial cities and in London; Sir is on tour in 1941, though playing less important dates. But there the similarities, and others less important, all wholly deliberate on my part, end. Sir is not Donald Wolfit. My biography of the actor,[*] with all its imperfections, must serve to reflect my understanding of him as a man and as a theatrical creature.

There is no denying, however, that my memory of what took place night after night in Wolfit's dressing room is part of the inspiration of the play. I witnessed at close quarters a great actor preparing for a dozen or more major classical roles which included Oedipus, Lear, Macbeth and Volpone. I was an observer also of the day-to-day responsibilities which management demanded and, later, as Wolfit's business-manager, partook of those responsibilities. I was a member of the crew who created the storm in *King Lear* which, however tempestuous, was never loud enough for Wolfit, as it never is for Sir. These and other countless memories undeniably fed my imaginings while writing the play.

Sources of another kind were of equal importance. I was

[*]*Sir Donald Wolfit, C.B.E. His life and work in the unfashionable theatre*, (London: Secker & Warburg, 1971).

fortunate, when young, to meet Sir John Martin-Harvey's stage manager; I held two long conversations with Charles Doran, the actor-manager who gave Wolfit his first job; I shared a dressing-room with an old actor, Malcolm Watson, who walked on in Sir Henry Irving's production of *Beckett* at the Lyceum; I worked with several old Bensonians – members of Sir Frank Benson's Shakespearean Company – and I knew Robert Atkins who, for many years, ran the seasons at the Open Air Theatre, Regent's Park. A number of the actors Wolfit employed were what used to be called 'Shakespeareans', men and women who had played with Alexander Marsh, Henry Bainton, H. J. Saintsbury and other actor-managers not of the front rank. There was, too, in Wolfit's company, a wonderfully robust actor called Frank G. Cariello whose greatest professional disappointment was that Martin-Harvey, after after allowing him to play Laertes on tour, re-cast the part for London. Cariello, himself briefly an actor-manager, was a tireless and witty raconteur with a prodigious memory of theatrical times past. The atmosphere engendered by these men, imbibed by me before I was twenty, was much in my mind when writing the play.

The tradition of actor-management made a deep impression on me. I came to understand that from the early eighteenth century until the late 1930s the actor-manager was the British theatre. He played from one end of the country to the other, taking his repertoire to the people. Only a handful ever reached London; their stamping-ground was the provinces and they toured under awful physical conditions, undertaking long, uncomfortable railway journeys on Sundays, spending many hours waiting for their connections in the cold at Crewe. They developed profound resources of strength, essential if they were to survive. They worshipped Shakespeare, believed in the theatre as a cultural and educative force, and saw themselves as public servants. Nowadays, we allow ourselves to laugh at them a little and there is no denying that their obsessions and single-mindedness often made them ridiculous: we are inclined to write them off as megalomaniacs and hams; we accept, too readily I think, that their motto was *'le théâtre, c'est moi!'* The truth of the matter is that many of them were extraordinary and talented men; their gifts enhanced the art of acting; they nursed and kept alive a classical repertoire which is the envy of the world, and created a magnificent tradition which is the foundation of our present-day theatrical inheritance.

I must acknowledge also words written by and about them: Sir John Martin-Harvey's excellent autobiography from which I have quoted in the play, the works of James Agate, the biography of Irving by Laurence Irving and J. C. Trewin's splendid book, *The Theatre Since 1900*.

The play, however, is called *The Dresser*. No actor-manager ever survived entirely through his own efforts. Publicly he liked to proclaim pride in his individuality while acknowledging, in private, his debt to all those who devoted their lives to him and to his enterprise. The character of Norman is in no way autobiographical. He, like Sir, is an amalgam of three or four men I met who served leading actors as professional dressers. Norman's relationship with Sir is not mine with Wolfit. No other character in the play is wholly based on a real person. Her Ladyship is quite unlike Rosalind Iden (Lady Wolfit). I have considered it necessary to make these disclaimers in order to give a truer background to the play. I know to my cost that once a mistaken interpretation attaches to a work of imagination it is difficult, if not impossible, to dispel.

RONALD HARWOOD

CHARACTERS

NORMAN

HER LADYSHIP

MADGE

SIR

IRENE

GEOFFREY THORNTON

MR OXENBY

Two Knights, Gloucester, Kent.

January 1942. A theatre in the English provinces.

Act I: Before curtain-up.
Act II: After curtain-up

The Dresser was first performed at the Royal Exchange Theatre, Manchester on 6 March 1980 with the following cast:

NORMAN	Tom Courtenay
HER LADYSHIP	Isabel Dean
IRENE	Jacqueline Tong
MADGE	Carole Gillies
SIR	Freddie Jones
GEOFFREY THORNTON	Lockwood West
MR OXENBY	Geoffrey McGivern

PLAYERS IN *King Lear*

Gloucester	Rex Arundel
Knight	} Anthony Benson
Albany	
Knight	} Joe Holmes
Gentleman	
Kent	Guy Nicholls

Director	Michael Elliott
Set design	Laurie Dennett
Costumes	Stephen Doncaster
Lighting	Mark Henderson
Sound	Ian Gibson

The play was presented at the Queen's Theatre, London on 30 April 1980 by Michael Codron with the following change of cast:

HER LADYSHIP	Jane Wenham
MADGE	Janet Henfrey
Knight	} Peter O'Dwyer
Gentleman	
Knight	} Kenneth Oxtoby
Albany	
Kent	David Browning
Electrician	Trevor Griffiths

ACT ONE

Sir's dressing room and corridor. Light on NORMAN, *who wears a lost, almost forlorn expression. Light grows to reveal a mud-stained overcoat and crumpled Homburg lying on the floor. Footsteps.*
NORMAN *becomes alert. He rises.* HER LADYSHIP *enters. She stands just inside the doorway.*

HER LADYSHIP: He does nothing but cry.

NORMAN: Are they keeping him in?

HER LADYSHIP: They wouldn't let me stay. The doctor said I seemed to make matters worse.

NORMAN: I shouldn't have taken him to the hospital. I don't know what came over me. I should have brought him back here where he belongs.

HER LADYSHIP: Why is his coat on the floor? And his hat – ?

NORMAN: Drying out. They're wet through, sodden, if you don't mind my saying so. So was he. Drenched. Sweat and drizzle –

HER LADYSHIP: How did he come to be in such a state, Norman? When you telephoned, I thought at first he'd been hurt in the air raid –

NORMAN: No –

HER LADYSHIP: Or had an accident –

NORMAN: No, not an accident –

HER LADYSHIP: No, I know because they said there was no sign of physical injury –

NORMAN: Your ladyship –

HER LADYSHIP: He's in a state of collapse –

NORMAN: I know –

HER LADYSHIP: How did he get like that?

NORMAN: Your ladyship –

HER LADYSHIP: What happened to him?

71

NORMAN: Sit down. Please. Please, sit down.
(*She does so.*)
We have to remain calm, not to say clear-headed.

HER LADYSHIP: The doctor said it must have been coming on for weeks.

NORMAN: If not longer.

HER LADYSHIP: I didn't see him this morning. He left the digs before I woke. Where was he all day? Where did you find him?

NORMAN: What happened was this, your ladyship: after the last 'All-clear' sounded I went into Market Square as dusk was coming on, a peculiar light, ever so yellowish, smoke and dust rising from the bomb craters, running shadows, full of the unexpected. I had hoped to find a packet or two of Brown and Polson's cornflour since our supplies are rather low and the stuff's scarce and you never know. So I was asking at this stall and that when I heard his voice.

HER LADYSHIP: Whose voice?

NORMAN: Sir's, of course. I turned and saw him by the candle-maker who was shutting up shop for the night. He was lit by one tall tallow candle which was guttering and he looked like that painting of him as Lear, all greens and dark blues seen through this peculiar light. He was taking off his overcoat, in this weather. 'God help the man who stops me,' he shouted, and threw the coat to the ground just like Lear in the storm scene. Look at it. I don't know if I'll ever get it clean. And he was so proud of it, do you remember, or perhaps it was before your time? The first Canadian tour, Toronto, raglan sleeves, fur collar, and now look at it.

HER LADYSHIP: What happened after he took off his coat?

NORMAN: Started on the hat, Dunn's, Piccadilly, only a year ago, down on the coat it went and he jumped on it, stamped on his hat, viciously stamped on his hat. You can see. He lifted both hands as he does to convey sterility into Goneril's womb and called out, 'How much further do you want me to go?' His fingers were all of a fidget, undoing his jacket, loosening his collar and tie, tearing at the buttons of his shirt.

HER LADYSHIP: Were there many people about?

NORMAN: A small crowd. That's why I ran to him. I didn't want him to stand there looking ridiculous with people all round, sniggering.

HER LADYSHIP: Did he see you? Did he know who you were?

NORMAN: I didn't wait to find out. I just took his hand and said, 'Good evening, Sir, shouldn't we be getting to the theatre?' in my best nanny-voice, the one I use when he's being wayward. He paid no attention. He was shivering. His whole body seemed to be trembling, and such a trembling.

HER LADYSHIP: You shouldn't have let the public see him like that.

NORMAN: It's easy to be wise after the event, if you don't mind my saying so, your ladyship, but I tried to spirit him away, not easy with a man of his proportions, only just then, a woman approached, quite old, wearing bombazine under a tweed coat but perfectly respectable. She'd picked up his clothes and wanted to help him dress. I just stood there, amazed, utterly amazed. He said to the woman, 'Thank you, my dear, but Norman usually looks after me. I'd be lost without Norman,' so I thought to myself this is your cue, ducky, and said, 'I'm Norman, I'm his dresser.' The woman – she had her hair in curlers – took his hand and kissed it, saying, 'You were lovely in *The Corsican Brothers.*' He looked at her a long while, smiled sweetly, you know the way he does when he's wanting to charm, and said, 'Thank you, my dear, but you must excuse me. I have to make an exit,' and ran off.

HER LADYSHIP: He said, I have to make an exit?

NORMAN: Well, of course, I went after him, fearing the worst. I didn't know he could run so fast. I just followed a trail of discarded clothing, jacket, waistcoat, and thought we can't have Sir doing a striptease round the town. But then I found him. Leaning up against a lamp-post. Weeping.

HER LADYSHIP: Where?

NORMAN: Outside the Kardomah. Without a word, hardly knowing what I was doing, I led him to the hospital. The Sister didn't recognize him, although later she said she'd seen him as Othello last night. A doctor was summoned, short, bald, bespectacled, and I was excluded by the drawing of screens.

HER LADYSHIP: And then you telephoned me.

NORMAN: No. I waited. I lurked, as Edmund says, and heard the doctor whisper, 'This man is exhausted. This man is in a state of collapse.' Then the Sister came out and said I must fetch you at once. That's when I telephoned. And that's how it happened.

(*Pause. 'All-clear' sounds.*)

HER LADYSHIP: He did nothing but cry.

NORMAN: Yes, you said.

HER LADYSHIP: I left him lying on top of the bed, still in his clothes, crying, no, weeping, as though he had lost control, had no choice, wept and wept, floodgates. What are we to do? In just over an hour there'll be an audience in this theatre hoping to see him as King Lear. What am I to do?

NORMAN: Don't upset yourself for a start –

HER LADYSHIP: I've never had to make this sort of decision before. Any sort of decision before. As soon as I came out of the hospital I telephoned Madge and asked her to meet me here as soon as possible. She'll know what to do.

NORMAN: Oh yes, Madge will know what to do. She won't upset herself, that's for certain. Madge will be ever so sensible. Of course, Stage Managers have to be. I had a friend once, had been a vicar before falling from the pulpit and landing on the stage. Ever so good as an Ugly Sister. To the manner born. His wife didn't upset easily. Just as well, I suppose, all things considered. Madge reminds me of her. Cold, businesslike, boring.

(*Pause.*)

HER LADYSHIP: The doctor took me into a little room littered with enamel dishes full of blood-stained bandages. He apologized. They'd been busy after the air-raid. The smell made me faint. He asked me about his behaviour in recent days. Had I noticed anything untoward? I smiled. Involuntarily. Untoward. Such an odd word to use.

NORMAN: What did you say, if you don't mind my asking?

HER LADYSHIP: I lied. I said he'd been perfectly normal. I didn't

want to appear neglectful. I should have been more vigilant.
Only last night I woke –

(*Footsteps.* IRENE *enters the corridor.*)

Is that Madge?

NORMAN: No. Irene.

(IRENE *exits.*)

You were saying. Last night you woke.

HER LADYSHIP: He was looking down at me. He was naked. It
was bitter cold and he was shivering. He said, 'Thank you
for watching over me. But don't worry too much. Just go on
looking after me. I have the feeling I may do something
violent.'

NORMAN: Talk about untoward. I'm glad you didn't tell the
doctor that, they'd have locked him up for good.

HER LADYSHIP: This morning, our landlady reported something
untoward. After breakfast, while I was still asleep, he
listened to the news, she said, and wept. Afterwards, he sat
at the dining table writing, or trying to write, but all he did
was to crumple up sheet after sheet of paper. When I came
down I smoothed them out to see what he'd written. My
Life. My Life. The rest of the page was empty.

NORMAN: He said to me his autobiography would be his only
memorial. 'Have you written much?' I asked. 'Not a word,'
he said. And last night, after Othello, he asked me, 'What do
we play tomorrow, Norman?' I told him *King Lear* and he
said, 'Then I shall wake with the storm clouds in my head.'

HER LADYSHIP: I should have made him rest. The doctor said
he'd come to the end of his rope and found it frayed.

NORMAN: So would anyone if they'd had to put up with what he's
had to put up with. You should've told the doctor all about
the troubles –

HER LADYSHIP: No. Civilians never understand.

NORMAN: That's true. Especially doctors. They never
understand anything. I could kick myself for taking him to
the hospital.

HER LADYSHIP: It was the right thing to do.

NORMAN: I hope so. Doctors. Just imagine trying to explain to a
doctor what Sir's been through. 'Well, you see, doctor, he's

75

been trying to recruit actors for his Shakespearean company but all the able-bodied and best ones are in uniform, and the theatres are bombed to bits as soon as you book them, not to mention the trouble this week with Mr Davenport-Scott.'

Doctors. He'd have had his hypodermic rampant before you could say 'As You Like It'. That's all they know. Hypodermics. If a doctor had been through half of what Sir's been through, his rope wouldn't be frayed, it'd be threadbare.

HER LADYSHIP: What's the latest on Mr Davenport-Scott?

NORMAN: If you don't mind, I'd rather not discuss Mr Davenport-Scott with a lady. I'll tell Madge all about it when she comes in. Suffice to say he will not be making an appearance this evening. Of course, I told Sir. I said, 'Don't, I beg you, don't let your business-manager double as The Fool in *King Lear*.' Now he's lost both in one fell blitzkrieg if you'll pardon the expression.

(*Pause.*)

HER LADYSHIP: Madge is right. There's no alternative. We'll have to cancel.

NORMAN: Oh no, your ladyship, cancellation's ever so drastic.

HER LADYSHIP: He's ill. There's no crime in being ill, it's not high treason, not a capital offence, not desertion in the face of the enemy. He's not himself. He can't work. Will the world stop turning? Will the Nazis overrun England? One Lear more or less in the world won't make any difference.

NORMAN: Sir always believes it will.

HER LADYSHIP: Who really cares whether he acts or not?

NORMAN: There's bound to be someone.

(*Pause.*)

HER LADYSHIP: I never imagined it would end like this. I've always thought he was indestructible. All the years we've been together. Seems like a lifetime.

NORMAN: Even longer he and I. This'll be the first time we've ever cancelled. I want to go to the hospital –

HER LADYSHIP: No, Norman –

NORMAN: I want to sit with him and be with him and try to give him comfort. I can usually make him smile. Perhaps when he sees me –

HER LADYSHIP: They wouldn't even let me stay.

(NORMAN *fights tears. Pause.*)

NORMAN: Sixteen years. I wish I could remember the name of the girl who got me into all this. Motherly type she was, small parts, play as cast. I can see her face clearly. I can see her standing there, platform 2 at Crewe. A Sunday. I was on platform 4. 'Norman,' she called. We'd been together in *Outward Bound*, the Number Three tour, helped with wardrobe I did, understudied Scrubby, the steward. That's all aboard a ship, you know. Lovely first act. 'We're all dead, aren't we?' And I say, 'Yes, Sir, we're all dead. Quite dead.' And he says, 'How long have you been – you been – oh you know?' 'Me, Sir? Oh, I was lost young.' And he says, 'Where – where are we sailing for?' And I say, 'Heaven, Sir. And hell, too. It's the same place, you see.' Lovely. Anyway. 'Norman!' she called. What was her name? She'd joined Sir, oh, very hoity-toity, I thought, tiaras and blank verse while I was in panto understudying the Ugly Sisters. Both of them. 'Are you fixed?' she shouted at the top of her voice. Well. To cut a short story shorter, Sir wanted help in the wardrobe and someone to assist generally, but mainly with the storm in *Lear*. I've told you this before, haven't I? Put me on the timpani, he did. On the first night, after the storm, while he was waiting to go on for 'No, you cannot touch me for coining', he called me over. My knees were jelly. 'Were you on the timpani tonight?' 'Yes, Sir,' I said, fearing the worst. 'Thank you,' he said. 'You're an artist.' I didn't sleep a wink. Next day he asked if I'd be his dresser.

(*Pause.*)

HER LADYSHIP: My father was exactly the same. Always exaggerated his illnesses. That's why I thought it was not very serious, I thought –

NORMAN: Madge. You can always tell. She walks as if the band were playing 'Onward Christian Soldiers'.

(MADGE *knocks on dressing-room door and goes in.*)

MADGE: Any further developments?

(HER LADYSHIP *shakes her head.*)

We had better see the manager. Perhaps you ought to come with me.

NORMAN: Oh, your ladyship, please, let's take our time, let's not rush things –

MADGE: (*To* HER LADYSHIP) There's no alternative.

HER LADYSHIP: Madge is right, he's in hospital. We can't play *King Lear* without the King. No one will pay to see the crucifixion of the two thieves. We have to make a decision.

NORMAN: Forgive me, your ladyship, it's not a decision you have to make, it's the right decision. I had a friend, before one's face was lined, as the saying goes, in a very low state he was, ever so fragile, a pain to be with. You weren't safe from him on top of a bus. If he happened to sit beside you, he'd tell you the ABC of unhappiness between request stops. Someone close to him, his mother, I believe, though it was never proved, understandably upset, made a decision. A little rest, she said, among those similarly off-centre, in Colwyn Bay, never a good date, not in February, wrapped in a grey rug, gazing at a grey sea. Talk about bleak. Mother-dear made a decision but it was the wrong decision. My friend never acted again.

MADGE: (*To* HER LADYSHIP) We have to face the facts.

NORMAN: I've never done that in my life, your ladyship, and I don't see why I should start now. I just like things to be lovely. No pain, that's my motto.

MADGE: But things aren't lovely, Norman.

NORMAN: They aren't if you face facts. Face the facts, it's facing the company I worry about. Poor lambs. What'll happen to them? And the customers? There was a queue at the box office this afternoon, if four elderly spinsters constitute a queue. Pity to give them their money back, they've likely had enough disappointment in life as it is. It's no good Sir talking about responsibility and service and struggle and survival and then you go and cancel the performance.

MADGE: (*To* HER LADYSHIP) It's a disease.

HER LADYSHIP: What is?

MADGE: Hopefulness. I think we should discuss this in private. I'll be in my room.

(*She goes.* HER LADYSHIP *is about to follow.*)

NORMAN: Yes, well, perhaps it is a disease, but I've caught something much worse from Sir.

HER LADYSHIP: What?

NORMAN: A bad dose of Holy Grail.

(*He laughs, but the laughter turns to tears.* HER LADYSHIP *goes to him.*)

HER LADYSHIP: Years ago, in my father's company. The unmentionable Scots tragedy. A new Macduff. Couldn't remember the lines. My father should've sacked him at the end of the first rehearsal. But no, my father said, 'He'll know it, he'll know it.' He never did.

NORMAN: Oh well, that was the Scots tragedy. Everyone knows that's the unluckiest play in the world. That's the one superstition I believe in absolutely. That play would turn a good fairy wicked.

HER LADYSHIP: In the fight scene. The man couldn't remember the fight. He thrust when he shouldn't have and sliced my father's face across. The right cheek seized up in a lopsided grin. The only part left to my father was Caliban.

NORMAN: It's not the same thing –

HER LADYSHIP: I'll be in Madge's room if I'm wanted.

NORMAN: Don't decide yet, your ladyship, let me go to the hospital, let me see how he is, you never know –

HER LADYSHIP: I do know. I realize now I've witnessed a slow running-down. I've heard the hiss of air escaping. We'll call the company together at the half . I'll tell them –

(NORMAN *is suddenly alert.*)

– that tonight's performance is cancelled, that the engagement is to be ended –

(*Heavy footsteps. Both look at each other. Footsteps nearer.* SIR *enters in a dishevelled state. Long pause.*)

NORMAN: Good evening, Sir.

SIR: Good evening, Norman. Good evening, Pussy.

HER LADYSHIP: Bonzo, why are you here?

SIR: My name is on the door.

HER LADYSHIP: Did the doctors say you could leave?

SIR: Doctors? Executioners. Do you know what he told me? A

short, bald butcher, *Il Duce* in a white coat. 'You need rest,'
he said. Is that all? When a doctor tells you you need rest,
you can be certain he hasn't the slightest idea of what's
wrong with you. I discharged myself.

(*He weeps.*)

HER LADYSHIP: (*To* NORMAN) Telephone the hospital.

SIR: Do not telephone the hospital.

(*He continues to weep.*)

HER LADYSHIP: Norman, will you leave us, please?

NORMAN: I'll see Madge and tell her there's an alternative.

(NORMAN *goes. Silence.*)

HER LADYSHIP: (*With real disgust*) You're fit for nothing.

SIR: Please, Pussy, don't.

HER LADYSHIP: Cancel the performance.

SIR: Can't. Mustn't. Won't.

HER LADYSHIP: Then take the consequences.

SIR: When have I not?

HER LADYSHIP: The doctor promised you'd be kept there.

SIR: They tried to inject me. They couldn't hold me down.

HER LADYSHIP: Where have you been all day? Don't tell me you
found a brothel in this town.

SIR: I can't remember all I've done. I know towards evening I was
being pursued but I couldn't see who the villains were. Then
the warning went. I refused to take shelter. I'm accustomed
to the blasted heath. Acrid smell. Eyes watering. Wherever I
went I seemed to hear a woman crying. Suddenly, I had a
clear image of my father on the beach near Lowestoft, plans
in his hands, inspecting the boats his men had built. 'An
actor?' he said, 'Never. You will be a boat builder like me.'
But I defied him and lost his love. Father preferred people to
cower. But I had to chart my own course. I decide when I'm
ready for the scrap-yard. Not you. I and no one else. I.

(*He sits and stares.*)

HER LADYSHIP: The woman you heard crying was me.

SIR: (*Calling*) Norman! Norman!

(NORMAN *comes running down the corridor and goes into the
dressing room, followed shortly by* MADGE.)

NORMAN: Sir.

SIR: Norman, I want you by me.

NORMAN: Yes, Sir.

SIR: Don't leave my side, Norman.

NORMAN: No, Sir.

SIR: I shall want help, Norman.

NORMAN: Yes, Sir.

(MADGE *knocks and enters.*)

SIR: Madge-dear.

HER LADYSHIP: (*To* MADGE) You speak to him. He doesn't hear a
word I say. He's obviously incapable –

MADGE: (*To* SIR) You look exhausted.

NORMAN: That's what I call tact.

MADGE: Are you sure you're able to go on tonight?

NORMAN: He wouldn't be here if he wasn't, would you, Sir?

SIR: (*To* MADGE) How long have you been with me, Madge-dear?

MADGE: Longer than anyone else.

SIR: How long?

MADGE: Twenty years, nearly twenty years.

SIR: Have I ever missed a performance?

MADGE: No, but then you've never been ill.

(SIR *sits and stares.*)

(*Quietly.*) I only want what's best for you.

NORMAN: What's best for Sir is that he's allowed to get ready.

SIR: Ready, yes, I must get ready.

(*He waves them away.*)

MADGE: Ready for what?

(*She goes.* SIR *sits and stares.*)

NORMAN: Excuse me, your ladyship, shouldn't you be getting
ready, too?

(*He puts a kettle on a small gas ring.*)

HER LADYSHIP: I can't bear to see him like that.

NORMAN: Then best to leave us. I've had experience of these
things. I know what has to be done.

(SIR *stifles a sob.*)

HER LADYSHIP: Imagine waking to that night after night.

(*She goes.* NORMAN *secretly takes a quarter bottle of brandy from
his pocket and has a swig. He replaces the bottle and turns to
SIR.*)

81

NORMAN: Right! Shall we begin at the beginning? (*Pause.*) Good evening, Sir. (*Pause.*) Good evening, Norman. And how are you this evening, Sir? A little tearful, I'm afraid, and you, Norman? I'm very well, thank you, Sir, had ever such a quiet day, cleaning your wig and beard, ironing your costumes, washing your undies. And what have you been up to, Sir? I've been jumping on my hat, Norman. Have you? That's an odd thing to do. May one ask why? Why what, Norman? Why we've been jumping on our hat, Sir? Not much fun for me this conversation, not much fun for you either, I suspect. (*Pause.*) Are we going to sulk all evening, or are we going to speak to our servants? (*Pause.*) Shall we play 'I Spy'? I spy with my little eye something beginning with A. I know you won't guess so I'll tell. A is for actor. And actors have to work, and actors have to put on their make-up and change their frocks and then, of course, actors have to act. Zounds, madam, where dost thou get this knowledge? From a baboon, Sir, that wandered wild in Eden. Or words to that effect. I've never known a kettle take so long to boil. Tell you what, have a little brandy. Break the rules, have a nip. A little brandy won't harm as the surgeon said to the undertaker's widow.

(*No response.* NORMAN *has a nip of brandy himself.*)

There's less than an hour to go. You usually want longer. Shall we make a start?

(SIR *looks up at him.*)

Yes, it's me, Norman, the one with the soulful eyes.

(*The kettle boils.* NORMAN *makes tea.*)

I saved my rations for you. I don't mind going without.

(*He hums to himself and then takes a cup to* SIR.)

Drink up. It's tea, not rat poison.

(NORMAN *sits beside* SIR *and feeds him the tea.* MADGE *drinks tea.*)

There. That's better, isn't it? Isn't it?

(SIR *moistens his lips.*)

Would you like a bicky? I saved one from the mayor's reception in Bridlington. No? Then why don't you have one, Norman? Thanks very much, I will. (*He takes a biscuit from*

the tin and eats it.) If you don't mind my saying so, Sir, there
seems little point in discharging yourself from hospital, and
coming to sit here like Niobe prior to being turned into
stone. So. Shall we make an effort?
(SIR *tries to loosen his collar and tie.*)
Let me. That's what I'm here for.
(*He helps* SIR, *who suddenly grabs hold of* NORMAN, *buries his
face in his neck and sobs.*)
I know how it feels. I had a friend, worse than you he was,
and all they ever wanted to do with him was put him away.
And no one wants to go through that. Or so my friend said.
They'll send you to Colwyn Bay and you know you never do
any business in Colwyn Bay. And guess what got my friend
well? Sounds silly this. An offer of work. A telegram, yes,
fancy, a telegram. Can you understudy Scrubby *Outward
Bound* start Monday? He discharged himself, just like you,
my friend did, took the train up to London, found digs in
Brixton and never looked back. What do you make of that?
An offer of work. Meant someone had thought of him and
that's ever such a comfort.
(SIR *disengages himself.*)
So here's something to cheer you up. It's going to be a Full
House tonight. All those people thinking of you and wanting
you to act.
(*Long pause.*)
SIR: Really? A Full House?
NORMAN: Shall we make a start?
(*Long pause.*)
SIR: What play is it tonight?
NORMAN: *King Lear*, Sir.
SIR: Impossible.
NORMAN: Thank you very much, that's nice, isn't it? People
     paying good money to see you and you say impossible, very
     nice indeed, I don't think.
     (*Pause.*)
SIR: I don't want to be seen.
NORMAN: Difficult when you're playing King Lear with the
     lighting you use.

83

SIR: I don't want to see Her Ladyship.

NORMAN: Even more difficult since she's playing Cordelia. You saw her a moment ago. You were alone together.

SIR: Were we? What's the play tonight?

NORMAN: *King Lear*, Sir.

(*Pause.*)

SIR: Madge was wrong.

NORMAN: She often is.

SIR: I have been ill before. Did you ever see me in *The Corsican Brothers?*

NORMAN: Alas no, Sir, before my time.

SIR: I went on with double pneumonia. Apt when you're playing the Corsican Brothers. I'd rather have double pneumonia than this.

NORMAN: Than what?

(SIR *allows* NORMAN *to help him undress.*)

SIR: What prevents me from packing up and going home? Why am I here when I should be asleep? Even kings abdicate.

NORMAN: Well I hope he's happy with the woman he loves, that's all I can say, I hope he's happy. Shall we undress? Talk of undressing, wasn't it a strange light in Market Square this evening?

SIR: I don't remember being in Market Square.

NORMAN: You've been missing the whole day. What do you remember?

SIR: Walking, walking, walking, If only I could find a good, catchy title. I think *My Life* a little plain, don't you?

NORMAN: Still stuck, are we?

SIR: No. I wrote a little today. Two or three sides of an exercise book. But I can't find a title.

NORMAN: We'll think of something.

SIR: See if it's still in my coat. And my reading glasses.

(NORMAN *looks in the pocket of the overcoat, finds the exercise book and a pair of broken spectacles. he takes the book to* SIR *and holds up the spectacles.*)

NORMAN: You won't see much through these.

(SIR *pages through the book.*)

SIR: I thought I'd written today. Look for me. Is there anything?

(NORMAN *flicks through the pages.*)

No. Evidently not. It can't be *Lear* again?

NORMAN: Shall we begin our make-up?

(*He guides* SIR *to the dressing table but* SIR *stops suddenly.*)

SIR: Where's my hat? I'm getting out of here. I'm not staying in this place a moment longer. I'm surrounded by vipers, betrayal on every side. I am being crushed, the life blood is draining out of me. The load is too great. Norman, Norman, if you have any regard for me, don't listen to him –

NORMAN: Who? Who?

SIR: More, more, more, I can't give any more, I have nothing more to give. I want a tranquil senility. I'm a grown man. I don't want to go on painting my face night after night, wearing clothes that are not my own, I'm not a child dressing up for charades, this is my work, my life's work, I'm an actor, and who cares if I go out there tonight or any other night and shorten my life?

(*He sits, buries his face in his hands.*)

NORMAN: I had a friend once said, 'Norman, I don't care if there are only three people out front, or if the audience laugh when they shouldn't, or don't when they should, one person, just one person is certain to know and understand. And I act for him.' That's what my friend said.

SIR: I can't move that which can't be moved.

NORMAN: What are we on about now?

SIR: I'm filled inside with stone. Stone upon stone. I can't lift myself. The weight is too much. I know futility when I see it. I dream at night of unseen hands driving wooden stakes into my feet. I can't move, and when I look at the wounds I see a jellied, leprous pus. And the dream is long and graceless. I wake up, sweat-drenched, poisoned. And the whole day long there is a burning heat inside me, driving all else from my mind. What did I do today?

NORMAN: You walked. You thought you wrote. You were in Market Square. A woman kissed your hand and said you were lovely in *The Corsican Brothers*.

SIR: How do you know all this? Has someone been talking?

(*Pause.*)

NORMAN: I don't wish to hurry you, Sir, no, I lie, I do.

SIR: I hate the swines.

NORMAN: Who?

SIR: He's a hard task-master, he drives me too hard. I have too much to carry.

(MADGE *knocks on the door.* NORMAN *opens it but doesn't admit her.*)

NORMAN: Yes?

MADGE: I'd like to see him.

NORMAN: I'd rather you didn't.

MADGE: It's my responsibility to take the curtain up tonight. There isn't much time.

NORMAN: Things have reached a delicate stage. I don't want him disturbed.

SIR: What's all the whispering?

NORMAN: Nothing, nothing.

MADGE: Has he begun to make up yet?

NORMAN: Not yet but –

MADGE: Do you realize how late it is? They'll be calling the half in a moment.

NORMAN: I know how late it is.

MADGE: Then on your head be it.

(*She goes.*)

SIR: Who was that?

NORMAN: Only Madge to say everything's running like clockwork. (*He looks anxiously at his watch.*) Oh, look! A dressing-gown! Shall we put it on and keep ourselves warm?

(*He helps* SIR *on with his dressing-gown.*)

What's it matter where you were or what you did today? You're here, in the theatre, safe and sound, where you belong. And a Full House. Lovely.

SIR: Really? A Full House?

NORMAN: They'll be standing in the gods.

(NORMAN *guides* SIR *to the dressing table.* SIR *sits and stares at himself in the looking-glass.*)

SIR: Do you know they bombed the Grand Theatre, Plymouth?

NORMAN: And much else of the city besides.

86

SIR: I made my debut at the Grand Theatre, Plymouth.

NORMAN: They weren't to know.

SIR: I shouldn't have come out this autumn, but I had no choice. He made me.

NORMAN: Who?

SIR: I should have rested.

NORMAN: I had a friend who was ordered to rest. He obeyed. That was the end of him. He was ever so ill. Nearly became a Catholic. (*Pause.*) Would you like a little rub-down? (*No response.*)

I'm not surprised you're feeling dispirited. It's been ever such a hard time. No young men to play the juveniles and the trouble with Mr Davenport-Scott.

(SIR *is suddenly alert.*)

SIR: What news of Mr Davenport-Scott?

NORMAN: The police have opposed bail.

SIR: What?

NORMAN: Well, he'd had his second warning.

SIR: How then do we dispose our forces?

NORMAN: Mr Thornton is standing by to play Fool.

SIR: And who as Oswald?

NORMAN: Mr Browne, I'm afraid.

SIR: That leaves me a Knight short for 'reason not the need'.

NORMAN: Ninety-eight short, actually, if you take the text as gospel, so one more or less won't be too upsetting.

SIR: Thornton toothless as Fool. Browne lisping as Oswald. Oxenby limping as Edmund. What have I come to? I've never had a company like this one. I'm reduced to old men, cripples and nancy-boys. Herr Hitler has made it very difficult for Shakespearean companies.

NORMAN: It'll be a chapter in the book, Sir. I hate to mention this but we're going to be short for the storm. We've no one to operate the wind machine, not if Mr Thornton is to play Fool. Mr Thornton was ever so good on the wind machine. Madge knows the problem but she's very unsympathetic.

SIR: You tell Madge from me I must have the storm at full strength. What about Oxenby?

NORMAN: Not the most amenable of gentlemen.

SIR: Send him to me at the half. I'll have a word with him. And I'd better talk to Thornton, too.

NORMAN: You see? That's more like it. You're where you belong, doing what you know best, and you're yourself again. You start making up. I'll go and tell them to come and see you. I've cleaned the wig and beard. I'll see what we can do with these. Jumping on his hat indeed! Shan't be a minute.

(NORMAN *goes.* SIR *looks at himself, then begins to black up.* NORMAN *returns.*)

Oh no, Sir! No! Not Othello!

(SIR *looks at him helplessly;* NORMAN *begins to clean his face with cold cream.*)

SIR: The lines are fouled. Up on your short, down on your long. Do we have a dead for it? Instruct the puppeteer to renew the strings. The stuffing's excaping at the seams, straw from a scarecrow lies scattered down stage left.

(NORMAN *cleans* SIR's *face.*)

NORMAN: I'd have given anything to see the play tonight. There's you all blacked up and Cordelia saying, 'You begot me, bred me, loved me.' Well, you see, ducky, this King Lear has been about a bit.

(SIR *laughs.*)

SIR: We used to have a game when I was with Benson. We called it *Risqué*. You had to turn the line to get a *double entendre*. The best I ever heard was from a character man called Berriton. You know the line, 'What fifty of my followers at a clap? Within a fortnight!'

NORMAN: Yes, I know the line, and the story.

SIR: One day, on the train call between Aberdeen and Liverpool, a journey I recommend as punishment for deserters, Berriton came out with, 'What, fifty of my followers with the clap? Within a fortnight!'

(*They both laugh.* NORMAN *has wiped* SIR's *face.* SIR *falls silent. He looks at himself in the looking-glass.*)

Another blank page.

NORMAN: The time has come, if you don't mind my saying so, to stop waxing poetical and to wax a bit more practical.

(*Pause.* SIR *reaches out for a stick of make-up. Knock on the door.*)

NORMAN: Who?

IRENE: Irene. I've come for the triple crown.

SIR: Enter.

> (IRENE, *dressed as a map-bearer in* Lear, *enters*.)
>
> (*Smiles*.) Good evening, my child.

IRENE: Good evening, Sir.

SIR: All well?

IRENE: Thank you, Sir.

SIR: You've come for the triple crown.

IRENE: Yes, Sir.

SIR: Polish it well. I like it gleaming.

IRENE: Yes, Sir.

SIR: And return it to me well before curtain up. I like it on my head by the quarter.

IRENE: Yes, Sir.

SIR: And when I've used it on stage, see that it's returned to my room after the interval.

NORMAN: She has done it before, Sir.

SIR: I like to be certain. Here it is, my child.

> (*She comes to him. He pats her bottom*.)
>
> Pretty young thing, aren't you?

IRENE: Thank you, Sir.

> (*She goes*. SIR *stares fondly into space*.)

NORMAN: Sir, it's time to age.

> (SIR *looks at his make-up tray*.)

SIR: (*In a panic*) They're all the same colour. Which stick do I use? I can't see the colours.

> (*He looks at* NORMAN *helplessly*. NORMAN *goes to the basin and ewer, pours water, wets a bar of soap, and brings it to* SIR.)

NORMAN: You start with the eyebrows.

SIR: Eyebrows?

NORMAN: Yes, Sir. You soap the eyebrows.

> (SIR *applies soap to his eyebrows so that they are flattened*.)
>
> Good. Now Number Five.
>
> (*He hands* SIR *the stick*.)
>
> Just the mask you always say. Leave clean the upper lip and chin for the moustache and beard. And not too high on the forehead.

(SIR *applies the greasepaint*.)

There. Easy as falling off a tightrope.

(SIR *continues to make up*.)

SIR: In a Pythagorean future life I should certainly take up painting. My palette, a few brushes, a three-and-sixpenny canvas, a camp stool and no one to drive you.

NORMAN: No one drives you but yourself.

SIR: How dare you, how would you know, who says I drive myself? I'm driven, driven, driven –

NORMAN: I'm sorry, I didn't mean –

SIR: You have to believe in yourself and your destiny, you have to keep faith with your aspirations and allow yourself to be enslaved by them, and the bondage is everlasting. How dare you!

NORMAN: I'm sorry I mentioned it –

SIR: You have to learn to wait and wait and wait, and the moment comes when you launch your barque and take the rudder, then, oh my masters! beware. The effort to forget all you are risking, to face a first night audience before whom to lay open your soul, to put your entire life in jeopardy time after time, to bear your back to the stripes of the critics, to go on doing these things year after year, always with the terror increasing, because it's easier to climb than it is to hang on, and now d'you see why Benson wrote me after my first essay into management, 'May you have the health and strength to go on'? On and on and on.

NORMAN: You should put that in the book.

SIR: Do they know what it means? Do they care?

I hate the swines.

NORMAN: Who?

SIR: On and on and on –

NORMAN: All right, Sir, shall we go on and on and on with our make-up?

(*Pause*. SIR *looks helplessly at his make-up tray*.)

Lake for the lines.

(NORMAN *hands* SIR *a stick of lake*. SIR *begins to apply the lines*.)

SIR: There was a time when I had to paint in all the lines. Now I merely deepen what is already there.

(*He continues to make up.* MADGE *comes to the door, and knocks.* NORMAN *answers it.*)

NORMAN: What now?

MADGE: How is he?

NORMAN: He'll be all right if he's left in peace.

MADGE: I want to see with my own eyes.

NORMAN: He is not to be disturbed.

MADGE: And what about the understudies?

NORMAN: He knows all about it, everything's in hand.

MADGE: The manager wants to know if he can let the house in.

NORMAN: Tell him yes.

MADGE: You realize now there's going to be an audience out there.

NORMAN: It'd be silly going through all this if there wasn't.

MADGE: Will he be ready on time? Will he be well enough?

NORMAN: Yes.

(*He closes the door on her.*)

SIR: What is going on, who was that?

NORMAN: Just a minion, minioning.

SIR: Too many interruptions – my concentration – Norman!

NORMAN: Sir?

SIR: How does the play begin?

NORMAN: Which play, Sir?

SIR: Tonight's, tonight's, I can't remember my first line.

NORMAN: 'Attend the Lords of France and Burgundy, Gloucester.'

SIR: Yes, yes. What performance is this?

(NORMAN *consults a small notebook.*)

NORMAN: Tonight will be your two hundred and twenty-seventh performance of the part, Sir.

SIR: Two hundred and twenty-seven Lears and I can't remember the first line.

NORMAN: We've forgotten something, if you don't mind my saying so.

(SIR *looks at him blankly.*)

We have to sink our cheeks.

(SIR *applies the appropriate make-up.*)

SIR: I shall look like this in my coffin.

NORMAN: And a broad straight line of Number Twenty down the nose. Gives strength, you say.

(SIR *adds the line down the nose and studies the result.* NORMAN *pours a little Brown and Polson's cornflour into a bowl.*)

SIR: Were you able to find any Brown and Polson's?

NORMAN: No, but I'm still looking. There's enough left for this tour. Now, we mix the white hard varnish with a little surgical spirit, don't we?

SIR: I know how to stick on a beard. I have been a depictor for over forty years and steered my own course for over thirty. You think I don't know how to affix a beard and moustache? You overstep the mark, boy. Don't get above yourself.

(SIR *begins to apply the gum, and stick on the beard.* NORMAN *turns his back and has a nip of brandy.*)

I shall want a rest after the storm scene.

NORMAN: There's no need to tell me. I know.

SIR: Towel.

(NORMAN *hands* SIR *a towel which* SIR *presses against the beard and moustache.* SIR *looks at himself in the looking-glass, and suddenly goes blank.*)

Something's missing. What's missing?

NORMAN: I don't want to get above myself, Sir, but how about the wig?

(NORMAN *removes the wig from the block and hands it to* SIR.)

And shall we take extra care with the join tonight? On Tuesday Richard III looked as if he were wearing a peaked cap.

(SIR *puts on the wig and begins to colour the join. He stops –*)

SIR: Hot, unbearably hot, going to faint –

(NORMAN *whips out the brandy bottle.*)

NORMAN: Have a nip, it won't harm –

(SIR *waves him away.* NORMAN *has a nip, puts the bottle away, and returns to* SIR, *who hasn't moved.*)

Oh, Sir, we mustn't give up, not now, not now. Let's highlight our lines.

(*Silence.* SIR *continues to add highlights.*)

SIR: Imagine bombing the Grand Theatre, Plymouth. Barbarians. (*Pause.*) I shall give them a good one tonight.

(*Pause.* SIR *becomes alarmed.*) Norman!

NORMAN: Sir?

SIR: What's the first line again? All this clitter-clatter-chitter-chatter –

NORMAN: 'Attend the Lords of France and Burgundy – '

SIR: You've put it from my head. You must keep silent when I'm dressing. I have work to do, work, hard bloody labour, I have to carry the world tonight, the whole bloody universe –

NORMAN: Sir, Sir –

SIR: I can't remember the first line. A hundred thousand performances behind me and I have to ask you for the first line –

NORMAN: I'll take you through it –

SIR: Take me through it? Nobody takes you through it, you're *put* through it, night after night, and I haven't the strength.

NORMAN: Well, you're a fine one, I must say, you of all people, you disappoint me, if you don't mind my saying so. You, who always say self-pity is the most unattractive quality on stage or off. Who have you been working for all these years? The Ministry of Information? Struggle and survival, you say, that's all that matters, you say, struggle and survival. Well, we all bloody struggle, don't we? I struggle, I struggle, you think it's easy for me, well, I'll tell you something for nothing it isn't easy, not one little bit, neither the struggle nor the bloody survival. The whole world's struggling for bloody survival, so why can't you?
(*Silence.*)

SIR: My dear Norman, I seem to have upset you. I apologize. I understand. We cannot always be strong. There are dangers in covering the cracks.

NORMAN: Never mind about covering the cracks, what about the wig join?
(SIR *continues to make up.*)
I'm sorry if I disturbed your concentration.

SIR: 'We both understand servitude, Alfonso.'
What came next? What did I say to that?

NORMAN: 'Was it lack of ambition allowed me to endure what I

93

have had to endure? It depends, your highness, what is meant by ambition. If ambition means a desire to sit in the seats of the mighty, yes, I have lacked such ambition. To me it has been a matter of some indifference where I have done my work. It has been the work itself which has been my chief joy.'

SIR: A fine memory, Norman.

NORMAN: My memory's like a policeman. Never there when you want it.

SIR: That was a play. And a money-maker. Greatly admired by clever charwomen and stupid clergymen. If I was twenty years younger I could still go on acting that kind of rubbish. But now I have to ascend the cosmos. And do they care? I hate the swines.

NORMAN: Shall we finish our eyebrows?

(SIR *combs the soaped eyebrows and whitens them.* IRENE *knocks on the door.*)

IRENE: Half an hour, please, Sir.

(*She goes.*)

SIR: Already?

NORMAN: You were late in tonight, Sir.

SIR: Why hasn't she returned the triple crown? I like it on my head by now. Look!

NORMAN: What?

SIR: My hands. They're shaking.

NORMAN: Very effective in the part. Don't forget to make them up.

SIR: I can't keep them still. Do it for me.

(NORMAN *holds up his own hand, which is trembling.*)

NORMAN: Look, it must be infectious.

(NORMAN *makes up* SIR's *hands.*)

SIR: I can face the division of my kingdom. I can cope with Fool. I can bear the reduction of my retinue. I can stomach the curses I have to utter. I can even face being whipped by the storm. But I dread the final entrance. To carry on Cordelia dead, to cry like the wind, howl, howl, howl. To lay her gently on the ground. To die. Have I the strength?

NORMAN: If you haven't the strength, no one has.

94

SIR: You're a good friend, Norman.

NORMAN: Thank you, Sir.

SIR: What would I do without you?

NORMAN: Manage on your own, I expect.

SIR: You'll be rewarded.

NORMAN: Pardon me while I get my violin.

SIR: Don't mock me. I may not have long.

NORMAN: My father used to say that. Lived to be ninety-three. May still be alive for all I know. There! Albert Dürer couldn't have done better.

(*He rises. He powders* SIR*'s hands.* HER LADYSHIP *enters, wigged and costumed as Cordelia but wearing a dressing-gown.*)

HER LADYSHIP: Bonzo, how do you feel?

SIR: A little more myself, Pussy.

NORMAN: You see? Once he's assumed the disguise, he's a different man. Egad, Madam, thou hast a porcupine wit.

HER LADYSHIP: And you're sure you're able to go on?

SIR: On and on and on.

NORMAN: Don't start that again, please.

SIR: Pussy, I thought it was the Black One tonight.

HER LADYSHIP: My dear.

SIR: Pussy, did I wake in the night? Did I thank you for watching over me? Was there talk of violence.

(*Pause.*)

HER LADYSHIP: No, Bonzo, you dreamt it.

SIR: I still have the feeling.

HER LADYSHIP: Shall I fetch the cloak and tie it on as usual?

SIR: Yes. As usual.

HER LADYSHIP: Mr Thornton and Mr Oxenby are waiting outside to see you. Shall I ask them to come in?

SIR: I don't want to see Oxenby. He frightens me. Mind you, he's the best Iago I've ever had or seen and I include that four-foot-six ponce Sir Arthur Palgrove.

NORMAN: (*To* HER LADYSHIP) That's more like the Sir we know and love.

SIR: *Sir* Arthur Palgrove. He went on playing Hamlet till he was sixty-eight. There were more lines on his face than steps to the gallery. I saw his Lear. I was pleasantly disappointed. *Sir*

Arthur Palgrove. Who advises His Majesty, answer me that?
(*He continues to adjust his make-up, putting the finishing touches.* HER LADYSHIP *draws* NORMAN *aside.*)

HER LADYSHIP: You're a miracle-worker, Norman.

NORMAN: Thank you, your ladyship.

HER LADYSHIP: Here's a piece of chocolate for you.

NORMAN: Thank you, your ladyship.

HER LADYSHIP: It'll be all hands to the pump tonight, Norman.

NORMAN: A small part of the service, your ladyship.

HER LADYSHIP: Thank you.

(*She goes.*)

SIR: Don't suppose I didn't see that because I did. There are thousands of children in this beloved land of ours scavenging the larders for something sweet, and if only they came to me I could tell them of the one person in England who has an inexhaustible supply of chocolate. It is *I* who have to carry her on dead as Cordelia. It is *I* who have to lift her up, carry her in my arms. Thank Christ, I thought, for rationing, but no, she'd find sugar in a sand-dune.

NORMAN: Shall I show the actors in?

SIR: I don't – I don't want –

NORMAN: Sir, you have to see the actors. (*He opens the door and calls*) Mr Thornton!
(GEOFFREY THORNTON, *an elderly actor, enters. He wears a costume as Fool that is much too large for him.*)
Mr Thornton to see you, Sir.

SIR: Well, Geoffrey . . . does the costume fit?

GEOFFREY: Mr Davenport-Scott was such a tall man.

SIR: Mr Davenport-Scott was a worm. You look –
(*He makes a vague gesture.* NORMAN *begins to help* SIR *into his Lear costume.*)
Do you know the lines?

GEOFFREY: Yes.

SIR: Don't keep me waiting for them.

GEOFFREY: Oh no.

SIR: Pace, pace, pace, pace, pace, pace.

GEOFFREY: Yes.

SIR: And keep out of my focus.

GEOFFREY: Yes.

SIR: The boom lights placed in the downstage wings are for me and me only.

GEOFFREY: Yes, old man, I know.

SIR: You must find what light you can.

GEOFFREY: Right.

SIR: Let me hear you sing.

GEOFFREY: What?

SIR: 'He that has and a little tiny wit.'

GEOFFREY: (*Faltering*) 'He that has and – he that has –'

NORMAN: (*Singing*) 'He that has and a little tiny wit . . .'

GEOFFREY: 'He that has and a little tiny wit,
    With hey, ho, the wind and the rain,
    Must make content with his fortunes fit,
    For the rain it raineth every day.'

SIR: All right, speak it, don't sing it. And in the storm scene, if you're going to put your arms round my legs as Davenport-Scott did, then round my calves not my thighs. He nearly ruptured me twice.

GEOFFREY: If you rather I didn't, old man –

SIR: Feel it, my boy, feel it, that's the only way.
    Whatever takes you.

GEOFFREY: Right.

SIR: But do not let too much take you. Remain within the bounds. And at all costs remain still when I speak.

GEOFFREY: Of course.

SIR: And no crying in the part.

GEOFFREY: Oh no.

SIR: *I* have the tears in this play.

GEOFFREY: I know.

SIR: Serve the playwright.

GEOFFREY: Yes.

SIR: And keep your teeth in.

GEOFFREY: It's only when I'm nervous –

SIR: You will be nervous, I guarantee it. There will be no extra payment for this performance. I believe your contract is 'play as cast'.

GEOFFREY: Yes.

SIR: Good fortune attend your endeavours.

GEOFFREY: Thank you, Sir.

(SIR *nods for him to leave*. NORMAN *sees him out*.)

NORMAN: God bless, Geoffrey.

GEOFFREY: I'd rather face the Nazi hordes any time.

(*He goes*.)

SIR: I hope Mr Churchill has better men in the Cabinet.

NORMAN: Mr Oxenby's waiting, Sir.

SIR: Oxenby? What – what – I can't – what does Oxenby want?

NORMAN: It's not what he wants, it's what we want, someone to operate the wind machine –

SIR: I don't want to see Oxenby, I can't bear the man, it's stifling in here –

NORMAN: We'll have no storm without him.

(*Silence*. NORMAN *admits* OXENBY, *dressed as Edmund. He limps. Pause*.)

Mr Oxenby to see you, Sir.

OXENBY: You wanted to see me.

SIR: I – I did I? I – Norman – why – ?

NORMAN: Sir was wondering whether he could ask of you a favour.

OXENBY: He can ask.

NORMAN: You haven't been with us very long but I'm sure you've seen enough to know that we're not so much a company as one big happy family. We all muck in as required. As you will no doubt have heard, Mr Davenport-Scott will not be rejoining the company.

OXENBY: Yes, I've heard. You share a dressing-room with one or two of them, you hear nothing else. It upsets the pansy fraternity when one of their number is caught.

NORMAN: Because Mr Thornton is having to play Fool, and because our two elderly Knights are setting the hovel behind the front cloth during the storm, we have no one to operate the wind machine. We'd ask Mr Browne but he's really rather too fragile. We wondered if you would turn the handle.

OXENBY: In short, no. (*Silence*.) Anything else? (*No response*.) Has he read my play yet?

(*No response.* OXENBY *goes.*)

SIR: Perhaps the Russians have had a setback on the Eastern front. Bolshevism will be the ruin of the theatre.

NORMAN: What are we going to do? Fancy not wanting to muck in.

SIR: He hates me. I feel his hatred. All I stand for he despises. I wouldn't read his play, not if he were Commissar of Culture.

NORMAN: I've read it.

SIR: Is there a part for me?

NORMAN: Yes, but you wouldn't credit the language. The Lord Chamberlain would get lockjaw.

SIR: He was ungenerous about Davenport-Scott. I hold no brief for buggers but where's the man's humanity? A fellow artist brought low and in the cells cannot be cause for rejoicing. I can see exactly what Oxenby's up to. He's writing plays for critics, not people.

NORMAN: Oughtn't we to be quiet for a bit, Sir?

SIR: Where's the girl with the triple crown?

NORMAN: Don't fuss. I'll go and find her.

(NORMAN *goes. Immediately*, IRENE *slips in with the polished triple crown.*)

SIR: Ah, my dear. Norman's just gone to find you.

IRENE: Has he? I must have missed him.

(*She goes close to him, holds out the crown and smiles.*)

SIR: Remind me of your name, my child.

IRENE: Irene, Sir.

SIR: Irene. Charming. Were you at the R.A.D.A.?

IRENE: No, Sir. I went straight into rep.

SIR: Of course. I remember. (*Pause.*) Which rep?

IRENE: Maidenhead.

SIR: Maidenhead. Yes.

(*He takes the crown, puts it down and takes her face in his hands.*)

Next week. In Eastbourne –

(NORMAN *returns.*)

NORMAN: I can't find her –

(*He stops.*)

SIR: Just admiring her bone structure.

99

NORMAN: Run along, Irene.

SIR: Yes, run along.

(*She goes*.)

A born actress. Always tell by the cheek bones.

NORMAN: Put on the crown. It's nearly the quarter. Shall I fetch Her Ladyship and ask her to tie on the cloak?

SIR: How does the play begin, God help me, that child has driven it from my mind –

(MADGE *knocks and enters*.)

MADGE: Quarter of an hour, please, a few minutes late, I'm sorry, that girl, Irene –

SIR: The quarter, I can't, I'm not ready, tell them to go home, give them their money back, I can't, I hate the swines, I can't – I can't –

MADGE: What are you saying, do you want the performance cancelled?

NORMAN: No he doesn't –

SIR: How does it begin?

MADGE: For your own good –

SIR: How does it begin – ?

MADGE: You'll never get through it –

NORMAN: He will, he will –

SIR: How does it begin?

NORMAN: Get out, he'll be good and ready when the curtain goes up –

MADGE: We've run out of time.

NORMAN: There's twenty minutes yet. We'll go up late, if necessary.

SIR: Leave me in peace! I can't remember the lines.

(MADGE *goes*.)

Norman, Norman, how does it begin?

NORMAN: 'He hath been out nine years and away he shall again.' (*Imitates trumpet fanfare*.) 'The King is coming.' (*Silence*.) 'Attend the Lords of France and Burgundy, Gloucester.'

SIR: 'Attend the Lords of France and Burgundy, Gloucester.'

NORMAN: 'I shall, my liege.'

(*Pause*.)

SIR: Yes?

NORMAN: 'Meantime we shall express our darker – '

SIR: 'Meantime we shall express our darker purpose.'
(*Pause*.)

NORMAN: 'Give me the map – '

SIR: Don't tell me, don't tell me, I know it, I'll ask for it if I need it. I have played the part before, You know. 'Meantime we shall express our darker purpose.' (*Long pause*.) Yes?

NORMAN: 'Give me the map there.'

SIR: 'Give me the map there.' Don't tell me, don't tell me. (*Long silence*.) 'What do I fear?'

NORMAN: Wrong. 'Know that we have divided – '

SIR: (*Continuing*) 'Myself? There's none else by. True, I talk of dreams, which are the children of an idle brain.'

NORMAN: Wrong play, wrong play –

SIR: 'I will move storms, I will condole in some measure – '

NORMAN: That's another wrong play.

SIR: 'I pray you all, tell me what they deserve that do conspire my death with devilish plots of damned witchcraft, and that have prevail'd upon my body with their hellish charms? Can this cockpit hold the vasty fields of France? Men should be what they seem. Macbeth shall sleep no more! I have lived long enough!'

NORMAN: Now look what you've gone and done –

SIR: What – ?

NORMAN: Go out, go out, you've quoted the Scots tragedy –

SIR: Did I? Macb – ? Did I? Oh Christ –

NORMAN: Out –

(SIR *goes*.)

Turn round three times. Knock.

(SIR *re-enters*.)

Swear.

SIR: Pisspots.

(SIR *holds his head and stands swaying slightly*. NORMAN *looks at him despairingly*. HER LADYSHIP *enters carrying a cloak and dressed as Cordelia*. SIR *looks at her and takes her face in his hands*.)

'And my poor fool is hang'd. No, no, no life!
Why should a dog, a horse, a rat have life

And thou no breath at all?
Thou'lt come no more.
Never, never, never, never, never!'
(*Silence.*)

NORMAN: Welcome back, Sir, you'll be all right.
(SIR *puts on the triple crown.* HER LADYSHIP *puts the cloak around* SIR's *shoulders. A ritual*:)

HER LADYSHIP: (*Kissing his hand*) Struggle, Bonzo.

SIR: (*Kissing her hand*) Survival, Pussy.
(*Knock on door.*)

IRENE: (*Off*) Five minutes, please, Sir.

NORMAN: Thank you.

SIR: Let us descend and survey the scene of battle.
(*They are about to go when the air-raid sirens sound. They freeze.*)
The night I played my first Lear there was a real thunderstorm. Now they send bombs. How much more have I to endure? We are to speak Will Shakespeare tonight and they will go to any lengths to prevent me.

NORMAN: I shouldn't take it so personally, Sir –

SIR: (*Looking heavenward*) Bomb, bomb, bomb us into oblivion if you dare, but each word I speak will be a shield against your savagery, each line I utter protection from your terror.

NORMAN: I don't think they can hear you, Sir.

SIR: Swines! Barbarians!
(SIR *begins to shiver uncontrollably, and to whimper.*)

NORMAN: Oh Sir, just as we were winning.

HER LADYSHIP: Perhaps it's timely. He can't go on. Look at him.
(*She comforts him.*)
(*To* NORMAN) Fetch Madge.

SIR: Norman!

NORMAN: Sir.

SIR: Get me down to the stage. By Christ, no squadron of Fascist-Bolsheviks will stop me now.
(*He continues to shiver.* HER LADYSHIP *and* NORMAN *look at each other uncertainly.*)
Do as I say!
(NORMAN *and* HER LADYSHIP *help him.*)

HER LADYSHIP: Who'll make the announcement?

SIR: Davenport-Scott, of course.

(*Silence.*)

NORMAN: Oh dear. Mr Davenport-Scott isn't here tonight. Everyone else is in costume.

SIR: You then, Norman.

NORMAN: Me, Sir? No, Sir. I can't appear!

SIR: You, Norman.

NORMAN: But, Sir, I shall never remember what to say –

SIR: Do not argue, I have given my orders, I have enough to contend with –

NORMAN: But, Sir, Sir, I'm not equipped.

SIR: Do it.

(HER LADYSHIP *helps him. As they go.*)

Why can't I stop shaking?

(*Sirens continue loudly. Bombs begin to fall.* NORMAN *swigs deeply from the brandy bottle and finishes it. Sirens. Bomb. Blackout. Sirens and bombs continue. A bright spotlight on* NORMAN.)

NORMAN: (*Softly*) Ladies and gentlemen . . . (*Louder*) Ladies and gentlemen, the – the warning has just gone. An air-raid is in progress. We shall proceed with the performance. Will those – will those who wish to live – will those who wish to leave do so as quietly as possible? Thank you.

(*He stands rooted to the spot. Bombs.*)

(*Blackout.*)

ACT TWO

The wings. Darkness. The air-raid continues. NORMAN's *voice is heard.*

NORMAN: (*Softly*) Ladies and gentlemen . . . (*Louder*) Ladies and gentlemen, the – the warning has just gone. An air-raid is in progress. We shall proceed with the performance. Will those – will those who wish to live – will those who wish to leave do so as quietly as possible? Thank you.

(*Sound of string quartet playing finale of selections from* The Mikado. *Light on* MADGE *in prompt corner. Music ends. Applause.*)

MADGE: Stand by. Stand by on tabs. House lights to a half.

(*She peers through peep-hole at the auditorium. Expectant murmurs from audience.*)

Cue timpani.

(*Timpani starts a steady beat.*)

House lights out.

(*Pause.*)

Cueing grams.

(*A recorded fanfare sounds.*)

Cue drum roll.

(*Timpani breaks into a roll.* MADGE *cues tabs.*)

Stand by on stage. Go Elex. Curtain going up.

(*Light grows to reveal* NORMAN, *who is carrying a whip, a towel and a tray on which stands a glass of stout and a powder puff. He is just entering the wings.*)

(The following continues onstage at the same time as the play begins offstage.)

NORMAN: Geoffrey, was I all right? The announcement. Was I
    effective?
GEOFFREY: Oh yes, old man, damn good.

NORMAN: Your ladyship, was I all right?
HER LADYSHIP: Better than Mr Davenport-Scott.

NORMAN: Really? Do you mean it? I was ever so nervous. Do you
    think anyone noticed the fluff? 'Will those who wish to live.'
    Could have kicked myself. Was I really all right?
HER LADYSHIP: You were fine.
NORMAN: Did he say anything?
HER LADYSHIP: No.

MADGE: Cueing grams.
    (Fanfare.)
    Stand by please, your ladyship, stand by please, Sir.
    (Fanfare. Trumpet sounds from prompt speaker. HER
    LADYSHIP *goes on. Scattered applause.)*
    Cueing timpani, Sir.
    *(*MADGE *flicks a switch. The green cue light goes on.* IRENE
    begins to beat the timpani in a slow rhythm.* MADGE *flicks the
    switch repeatedly, which makes the green light flash.* IRENE
    increases the rhythm of the timpani.)*
    Stand by, Sir. Cueing the King's fanfare.

(Offstage we hear the voices of GLOUCESTER, KENT *and*
OXENBY *(as Edmund) as they begin the play.)*

KENT: I thought the King had more affected the Duke of Albany
than Cornwall.

GLOUCESTER: It did always seem so to us . . .

KENT: Is not this your son, my Lord?

GLOUCESTER: His breeding, sir, hath been at my charge: I have
so often blushed to acknowledge him, that now I am brazed
to it.

KENT: I cannot conceive you.

GLOUCESTER: Sir, this young fellow's mother could; whereupon
she grew round-wombed . . .

GLOUCESTER: But I have a son, sir, by order of law, some year
elder than this, who yet is no dearer in my account . . . Do
you know this noble gentleman, Edmund?

EDMUND: No, my Lord.

GLOUCESTER: My Lord of Kent; remember him hereafter as my
honourable friend.

EDMUND: My services to your lordship.

KENT: I must love you, and sue to know you better.

EDMUND: Sir, I shall study deserving.

GLOUCESTER: He hath been out nine years, and away he shall
again . . .

GLOUCESTER: The King is coming.

(*A great fanfare sounds.* NORMAN *tries to help* SIR *to rise.* SIR *remains seated and continues to shiver.*)

NORMAN: Sir, it's your cue.

(SIR *does not move.* IRENE *continues to drum.*)

Her Ladyship's entered. Quite a nice round, too. Now it's your turn. Come along, Sir.

(*The fanfare ends.* SIR *still does not move.* MADGE *switches off cue light and* IRENE *stops drumming.* MADGE *goes to* SIR *and* NORMAN.)

MADGE: You see? What did I say.

NORMAN: Please, Sir, I implore you.

NORMAN: Sir you're on. You're on.

(*Both* MADGE *and* NORMAN *try to get him on.*)

NORMAN: Please, Sir, it's your entrance. Mr Oxenby's having to extemporize.

(*They try to get* SIR *to his feet. He shivers uncontrollably.*)

NORMAN: Sir, the natives are getting restless (*To* MADGE) Sound the fanfare again.

(MADGE *goes to* IRENE *and whispers instructions.* NORMAN *hoists* SIR *to his feet.*)

(SIR *sits again.*)

(*A bomb explodes quite close.* NORMAN *gets* SIR *to his feet again and guides him towards the stage.*)

(OXENBY *comes into the wings from the stage.*)

OXENBY: Is he coming or isn't he?

NORMAN: Yes!

(OXENBY *goes back on.*)

MADGE: Cue the King's fanfare again.

(*The fanfare sounds. Another bomb explodes quite close.*)

NORMAN: Struggle and survival, Sir, it's a full house.

(SIR *comes to himself.*)

NORMAN: 'Attend the Lords of France and Burgundy,

GLOUCESTER: The King is coming.
>   (*Silence.*)
OXENBY: Methought I saw the King.
KENT: Methought so, too.
OXENBY: Methought I saw him, his procession formed, a
>   hundred knights his escort, sombre they looked, their muted
>   colours of a tone with the bleak heathland which is our
>   kingdom.
HER LADYSHIP: The King, my father, was, methought, behind
>   me. From our camp we marched, a goodly distance, I ahead,
>   as is our custom. Perchance he rested, for age has not the
>   spring of youth.
>   (*Murmurs from the audience.*)

OXENBY: Ah! Methinks I see the King.
OXENBY: No, I was mistook.

OXENBY: My Lord, with thy consent I shall to his majestic side,
>   there to discover his royal progress.

OXENBY: I am assured, my Lord, the King *is* coming.

Gloucester.' (*To* MADGE) Cue the Knights, cue the Knights.

MADGE: (*To the* KNIGHTS) Go on. Go on.

(*She switches off the cue light.* IRENE *stops beating, runs to collect the map and stands by for her entrance.*)

NORMAN: (*To* IRENE) Enter, for God's sake.

(IRENE *goes on.* SIR *stands as if poised on a cliff's edge. Then he marches on. Great applause. Silence.* NORMAN *and* MADGE *watch anxiously.*)

(NORMAN *takes out a fresh quarter bottle of brandy and drinks deeply.*)

(*Blackout.*)

(*Bombs and anti-aircraft guns continue. Dim light.* NORMAN, MADGE, GEOFFREY *and others watch the stage and hear* SIR*'s voice.*)

(*The green light glows and* NORMAN *cracks the thunder sheet. The air-raid continues as* SIR *returns to the wings.*)

(*Lights.*)

MADGE: Stand by the storm.

(*The 'All-Clear' sounds.*)

SIR: (*Looking heavenwards*) Swines! Just when you need them they run away.

MADGE: Go storm.

(*She switches a switch. The red cue light glows.*)

(*Green warning light. The thunder begins,* NORMAN *and* IRENE *managing between them.* SIR *and* GEOFFREY *go on.*)

(HER LADYSHIP *watches the stage.* OXENBY *stands apart, also watching.* HER LADYSHIP *runs to the thunder crew.*)

SIR: Attend the Lords of France and Burgundy, Gloucester.

GLOUCESTER: I shall, my liege.

SIR: Meantime we shall express our darker purpose. give me the
map there . . .

SIR: No, you unnatural hags,
I will have such revenges on you both
That all the world shall – I will do such things –
What they are yet I know not – but they shall be
The terrors of the earth. You think I'll weep;
No, I'll not weep:
I have full cause of weeping, but this heart
Shall break into a hundred thousand flaws
Or ere I'll weep. O fool! I shall go mad.

KENT: For confirmation that I am much more
Than my out-wall, open this purse, and take
What it contains. If you shall see Cordelia . . .
As doubt not but you shall – show her this ring,
And she will tell you who your fellow is
That yet you do not know. Fie on this storm!
I will go seek the King.

GENTLEMAN: Give me your hand. Have you no more to say?

KENT: Few words, but, to effect, more than all yet;
That, when we have found the King – in which your pain
That way, I'll this – he that first lights on him
Holla the other.

SIR: Blow, winds, and crack your cheeks . . .
(*His voice is drowned by the noise of the storm.*)

HER LADYSHIP: Louder! Louder!
> (*She returns to watch the stage as the thunder increases.* HER
> LADYSHIP *returns to the crew.*)

Louder, louder, he wants it louder!
> (*The noise increases.* NORMAN *works frantically.* HER
> LADYSHIP *comes to them again.*)

Louder! Louder!
> (NORMAN *and* IRENE *give all they have.* OXENBY, *who has
> been watching them, takes over the thunder sheet.* HER
> LADYSHIP *takes charge of the wind machine. The sound of a
> mighty tempest is reproduced. And when the sound is
> overpowering and at its loudest: blackout.*)

> (SIR *comes raging into the wings. Lights on* SIR *and* NORMAN.)

SIR: (*Mad with rage*) *Where was the storm?* I ask for cataracts and
hurricanes and I am given trickles and whistles. I demand
oak-cleaving thunderbolts and you answer with farting flies.
I *am* the storm! I am the wind and the spit and the fire and
the pother and I am fed with nothing but muffled funeral
drums. Christ Almighty, God forgive them for they know
not what they do. I am driven deaf by whispers. Norman,
Norman, you have thwarted me.
> (SIR *marches into his dressing room followed by* NORMAN.)

I was there, within sight, I had only to be spurred upwards
and the glory was mine for the plucking and there was
naught, zero, silence, a breeze, a shower, a collision of
cotton-wool, the flapping of butterfly wings. I want a
tempest not a drizzle. Something will have to be done. I
demand to know what happened tonight to the storm!
> (SIR *sinks down on to his couch.*)

NORMAN: I'm pleased you're pleased. I've never known you not
complain when you've really been at it, and tonight, one
could say without fear of contradiction, you were at it. Rest
now.
> (SIR *lies back.* NORMAN *covers him with a rug, mops his brow
> and makes him comfortable. Then he turns gas ring up so that
> kettle boils, makes* SIR *tea and feeds it to him.*)

You've the interval and all Gloucester's blinding before, 'No, they cannot touch me for coining.' Try to sleep. You've been through it, or been put through it, whichever you prefer and you need quiet, as the deaf mute said to the piano tuner. Mighty, Her Ladyship thought you were tonight, she did, that was the word she used, mighty. Of course, I cannot comment on the storm scene but I did hear, 'O Reason not the need'. Tremble-making. Never seen you so full of the real thing, if you don't mind my saying so, Sir. And wasn't Geoffrey agile as Fool? For a man of his age. Kept well down-stage, never once got in your light, much less obtrusive than Mr Davenport-Scott. In every way. And here's something funny. In the storm scene, when we were beating ourselves delirious and I was having to jump between thunder-sheet and timpani like a juggler with rubber balls and Indian clubs, Mr Oxenby came to our aid uninvited. Cracked and clapped he did with abandon. Not a word said, just gave assistance when assistance was needed. Afterwards, just before the interval, I thanked him. 'Get stuffed,' he said which wasn't nice, and added scornfully, 'I don't know why I helped.' And I said, 'Because we're a band of brothers, and you're one of us in spite of yourself.' I did, that's what I said, quite unabashed. He hobbled away, head down, and if he was given to muttering, he'd have muttered. Darkly. (*Pause.*) More tea? Are you asleep, Sir?

SIR: To be driven thus. I hate the swines.

NORMAN: Who? Who is it you hate? The critics?

SIR: The critics? Hate the critics? I have nothing but compassion for them. How can one hate the crippled, the mentally deficient and the dead? Bastards.

NORMAN: Who then?

SIR: Who then what?

NORMAN: Who then what is it you hate?

SIR: Let me rest, Norman, you must stop questioning me, let me rest. But don't leave me till I'm asleep. Don't leave me alone. (*Pause.*) I am a spent force. (*Pause.*) My days are numbered. (*Silence.* NORMAN *watches him, then takes out his brandy bottle but finds it empty. He tip-toes out of the room. In the corridor he meets* HER LADYSHIP, *carrying a sewing-bag.*)

113

HER LADYSHIP: Is he asleep?

NORMAN: I think so.

HER LADYSHIP: I'll sit with him.

NORMAN: Don't wake him, will you, your ladyship. He's ever so
tired.

(*He goes.* HER LADYSHIP *enters* SIR'S *dressing room and
deliberately makes a noise.* SIR *starts.*)

SIR: Is it my cue?

HER LADYSHIP: No. It's still the interval.

(*She sits and begins to darn pairs of tights.*) I have things to say.

SIR: Norman tells me you thought I was mighty tonight.

HER LADYSHIP: I never said anything of the kind. He makes
these things up.

(*Pause.*)

SIR: What have you to say?

HER LADYSHIP: What I always have to say.

SIR: You know my answer.

HER LADYSHIP: You've worked hard. You've saved. Enough's
enough. Tonight, in your curtain speech, make the
announcement.

SIR: I can't.

HER LADYSHIP: You won't.

SIR: I've no choice.

HER LADYSHIP: You'll die. Or end up a vegetable. Well, that's
your affair. But you're not going to drag me with you.

SIR: I am helpless, Pussy. I do what I'm told. I cower, frightened
of being whipped. I am driven.

HER LADYSHIP: Driven, no. Obstinate, yes, cruel, yes, ruthless,
yes.

SIR: Don't.

HER LADYSHIP: For an actor you have a woeful lack of insight.
Use your great imagination, use your inspired gifts, try to
feel what I feel, what I'm forced to go through.

SIR: I do. But I need you beside me, familiar, real.

HER LADYSHIP: I am beside you darning tights. Very familiar,
quite real. All I ask, Bonzo, is that we stop now. Tonight.
The end of the week. But no more. I can't take any more.

SIR: If it were possible –

HER LADYSHIP: It is possible –

SIR: No –

HER LADYSHIP: You deceive no one but yourself.

SIR: If that were true why then am I here, with the bombs falling, risking life and limb, why? Not by choice. I have a duty. I have to keep faith.

HER LADYSHIP: Balls.

SIR: What?

HER LADYSHIP: You do nothing without self-interest. And you drag everyone with you. Me. Chained. Not even by law.

SIR: Would marriage have made so much difference to you?

HER LADYSHIP: You misunderstand. Deliberately.

SIR: I should have made her divorce me.

HER LADYSHIP: You didn't get a divorce because you wanted a knighthood.

SIR: Not true.

HER LADYSHIP: True. You know where your priorities lie. Whatever you do is to your advantage and to no one else's. Talk about being driven. You make yourself sound like a disinterested stage-hand. You do nothing without self-interest. Self. You. Alone.

SIR: Pussy, please, I'm sinking, don't push me further into the mud –

HER LADYSHIP: Sir. Her Ladyship. Fantasies. For God's sake, you're a third-rate actor-manager on a tatty tour of the provinces, not some Colossus bestriding the narrow world. Sir. Her Ladyship. Look at me. Darning tights. Look at you. Lear's hovel is luxury compared to this.

SIR: I'm surprised at you, Pussy. With your inheritance. Your father was of the breed. He donned the purple.

HER LADYSHIP: Donned the purple. The breed. Service. I've heard it all my life. My father also talked as if he were decreeing the apostolic succession.

SIR: I'm not well, I have half of Lear's lifetime yet to live, I have to lift you in my arms, I have howl, howl, howl yet to speak.

HER LADYSHIP: Sir. Her ladyship. We're a laughing-stock. You'd never get a knighthood because the King doesn't possess a double-edged sword. The only honour you'll ever get is when you go on stage and we all bow.

(*Silence.*)

SIR: Do you remember, years ago, one of our Gonerils, a tall dark handsome girl with a Grecian nose –

HER LADYSHIP: Flora Bacon.

SIR: Was it, yes, perhaps it was. Flora. Do you remember the night I was rather hard on Norman because he'd got my tights inside out during the quick change in *The Wandering Jew*? Or was it *The Sign of the Cross*? Whichever. She turned on me. 'He may be your servant,' she said, 'but he's a human being.' Then, to Norman, she said, 'Why don't you leave him? Why do you put up with it?' And Norman said, 'Don't fuss. He only gives as good as he gets. He has to take it out on someone.' He was right. These are the penalties of aspiration and ambition: single-mindedness, intolerance and unspent energy. So awful are they to bear that faith, struggle and duty must stand for them. And so awful are they to bear that others, not so cursed, must suffer in their presence. Norman understands. He knows it is not me but what is given to me, bursting out of me, passed on ruthlessly. Flora Bacon didn't understand. Slave-driver she called me. Why did I ever employ her?

HER LADYSHIP: Her mother was Lady Bacon. She invested £200 in the company.

SIR: I've given work to a good few Bolsheviks in my time. Slave-driver? Me? (*Long pause.*) I thought tonight I caught sight of him. Or saw myself as he sees me. Speaking 'Reason not the need,' I was suddenly detached from myself. My thoughts flew. And I was observing from a great height. Go on, you bastard, I seemed to be saying or hearing. Go on, you've more to give, don't hold back more, more, more. And I was watching Lear. Each word he spoke was fresh invented. I had no knowledge of what came next, what fate awaited him. The agony was in the moment of acting created. I saw an old man and the old man was me. And I knew there was more to come. But what? Bliss, partial recovery, more pain and death. All this I knew I had yet to see. Outside myself, do you understand? Outside myself.

(*He holds out his hand. She does not take it.*)
Don't leave me. I'll rest easy if you stay. Don't ask of me the impossible. Otherwise, I know, without you, in darkness, I'll see a locked door, a sign turned in the window, closed, gone away, and a drawn blind.

HER LADYSHIP: I'll stay till Norman returns.

SIR: Longer. I meant longer. Please. Please, Pussy. Reassure me, I'm sick –

HER LADYSHIP: Sick, yes, so am I. Sick. I'm sick of cold railway trains, cold waiting rooms, cold Sundays on Crewe, and cold food late at night. I'm sick of packing and unpacking and of darning tights. I'm sick of the smell of rotting costumes and naphthalene. And most of all I'm sick of reading week after week that I'm barely adequate, too old, the best of a bad supporting cast, unequal to you, unworthy of your gifts, I'm sick of having to put on a brave face. (*Pause.*) I should have left you in Baltimore on the last American tour. I should have accepted Mr Feldman's offer and taken the 20th Century west.
(*Pause.*)

SIR: Feldman didn't think I'd photograph well. Swine. I hate the cinema. I believe in living things.

HER LADYSHIP: How quickly one's looks go.

SIR: They haven't built a camera large enough to record me.

HER LADYSHIP: I wouldn't have minded a modest success.

SIR: Why they knighted that dwarf Arthur Palgrove I shall never know. 'Rise, Sir Arthur,' said the King. 'But, Sir, I wasn't kneeling.' Not once in his whole career did he put a toe outside London.

HER LADYSHIP: I liked America.

SIR: I hated the swines.
(*Knock on the door.*)

IRENE: (*Off*) Act Two beginners, please, Sir.

SIR: I must rest now, Pussy. I want peace.

HER LADYSHIP: All you want is to have your cake and to eat it.

SIR: I've never seen any point in having cake unless one's going to eat it.
(*He laughs.* NORMAN *re-enters.*)

NORMAN: Everything jolly?

SIR: Don't you know what knocking is?

NORMAN: Please, Sir, not in front of Her Ladyship. I've been
mingling. You should hear what they think out there. I've
never known an interval like it. Michaelangelo, William
Blake, God knows who else you reminded them of. One poor
boy, an airman, head bandaged, was weeping in the stalls
bar, comforted by an older man, once blond, now grey,
parchment skin and dainty hands, who kept on saying,
'There, there, Evelyn, it's only a play,' which seemed to me
no comfort at all because if it wasn't a play 'There-there-
Evelyn' wouldn't be so upset.

SIR: Michaelangelo, did they?

NORMAN: And Blake.

HER LADYSHIP: I'm going to my room.

SIR: Please stay.

HER LADYSHIP: You must rest, Bonzo, mustn't he, Norman?

NORMAN: Yes, he must.

SIR: Pussy –

(*She goes.*)

Be gentle with Her Ladyship.

NORMAN: I'm always gentle with Her Ladyship.

SIR: Especially gentle.

NORMAN: Why?

SIR: Time of life.

NORMAN: You mean hot flushes and dizzy spells.

SIR: She's become very preoccupied with herself.

NORMAN: Sounds like a bad attack of change.

SIR: Be gentle. I don't want her hurt.

NORMAN: Sleep now. Is there anything else you want?

SIR: Only oblivion.

NORMAN: That'll come sooner or later and I hope later. I'll wake
you in plenty of time so you can enter fantastically dressed in
wild flowers. Sleep tight, don't let the fleas bite.

(*He goes.* IRENE, *triple crown in hand, appears and watches*
NORMAN *exit.* SIR *suddenly starts, rises and goes to the door,*
opens it and comes face to face with IRENE.)

SIR: Fetch Madge.

118

(IRENE *runs off.* SIR *finds his exercise book and, straining to see, begins to write. He makes several false starts.* MADGE *enters.* IRENE *waits outside with the triple crown.* MADGE *knocks on dressing-room door and enters.*)

MADGE: Yes?

SIR: It's going well, I think . . .

MADGE: Except for your first entrance.

SIR: Come here.

(*She does so.*)

Hold my hand. Please.

(*She takes his hand.*)

MADGE: It's like ice.

SIR: Cold with fear.

MADGE: What are you frightened of?

SIR: What's to come.

MADGE: You know who you're talking to, do you? It's me. Not someone to impress.

SIR: I'm speaking from my heart. I have never before felt so lonely.

MADGE: Please. I have a show to run –

(*She tries to break free.*)

SIR: Listen to me. I say I'm frightened of what's to come and I mean it. Because for the first time in my life the future is hidden from me. I see no friends. I am not warmed by fellowship. I only know awful solitude.

MADGE: An occupational hazard. (*She breaks free.*) You wanted to see me. About what?

SIR: I look on you as my one true friend –

MADGE: I have to go back to the corner.

SIR: Twenty years, did you say twenty years?

MADGE: Yes.

SIR: Have you been happy? Has it been worth it?

(*Pause.*)

MADGE: No, I've not been happy. Yes. It's been worth it.

(*Pause.*)

SIR: Madge-dear, in my will I've left you all my press-cutting books –

MADGE: I don't want to hear what you've left me in your will –

119

SIR: Cuttings that span a lifetime, an entire career. I've kept them religiously. Good and bad notices alike. Not all that many bad. Talk of me sometimes. Speak well of me. Actors live on only in the memory of others. Speak well of me.

MADGE: This is a ridiculous conversation. You are in the middle of a performance of *Lear*, playing rather less mechanically than you have of late, and you talk as if you're organizing your own memorial service.

SIR: The most wonderful thing in life is to be remembered. Speak well of me. You'll be believed.

MADGE: You'll be remembered.

(*Pause.*)

SIR: Madge-dear, I have something for you. (*He opens a box on his dressing table and finds a ring.*) I want you to have this ring. If possessions can be dear then this ring is the dearest thing I own. This ring was worn by Edmund Kean in a play whose title is an apt inscription for what I feel: *A New Way to Pay Old Debts*. When you talk of it, say Edmund Kean and I wore it.

(*He puts the ring into her hand. She tries not to show her feelings.*)

I once had it in mind to give to to you years ago, but you were younger then, and I thought you would misunderstand.

MADGE: Yes. A ring from a man to a woman is easily misunderstood.

SIR: I know I'm thought insensitive, but I'm not blind.

MADGE: No. I've always known you were aware of what the spinster in the corner felt. (*Pause.*) You were right not to give me a ring years ago. I lived in hope then. (*Pause.*) At least I've seen you every day, made myself useful to you. I settled for what I could get. I was always aware of my limitations.

SIR: You are the only one who really, truly, loves me.

(*She gives him back the ring and goes quickly from the room. He puts the ring on. He turns back to his exercise book and continues to write.* IRENE *knocks gently on the door.*)

Who?

IRENE: Irene. I'm returning the triple crown, Sir.

SIR: Come.
  (*She enters the room.*)
  Put it down.
  (*She does so. He continues to write. Pause.*)
IRENE: Sir, will it disturb you if I say something?
SIR: It depends on what it is.
IRENE: I just wanted to thank you.
SIR: For what?
IRENE: The performance this evening.
SIR: It's not over yet.
IRENE: I felt honoured to be on the stage.
  (*Pause.*)
SIR: Open that drawer you will find a photograph of me.
  (*She does so. He inscribes it.*)
IRENE: I love coming into this room. I can feel the power. And
  the mystery. In days gone by this would have been the place
  where the High Priests robed. I feel frightened. As though
  I'm trespassing.
SIR: A kindred spirit.
  (*They look at each other.*)
  Lock the door.
  (*She does so.*)
  Come nearer –
IRENE: Irene.
SIR: Irene. And you want to act.
IRENE: Yes.
SIR: Passionately?
IRENE: Yes.
SIR: With every fibre of your being?
IRENE: Yes.
SIR: To the exclusion of all else?
IRENE: Yes.
SIR: You must be prepared to sacrifice what most people call life.
IRENE: I am.
  (*Long pause.*)
SIR: Your birth sign?
IRENE: Scorpio.
  (*In the corridor NORMAN enters, comes to the door, tries it gently*

but finds it locked. He listens at the key-hole.)

SIR: Good. Ambition, secretiveness, loyalty and capable of great jealousy. Essential qualities for the theatre. Have you good legs?

(*She shrugs.*)

SIR: Come closer. Let me see.

(*She raises her skirt.*)

Higher.

(*She does so.*)

Too good. All the best actresses have legs like tree-trunks.

(*He feels her thighs.*)

There's not much to you.

(*He feels her hips.*)

Such small bones.

(*His hands wander up to her breasts.*)

Are you getting enough to eat?

(*He takes her face in his hands and seems about to kiss her.*)

So young, so young.

(*Suddenly, in one movement he lifts her bodily into his arms. She cries out.*)

(*A great roar.*) That's more like it!

(*He staggers, lowers her to the ground, then waves her away.*)

Too late, too late.

(*She runs to the door, unlocks it, goes into the corridor and comes face to face with* NORMAN, *who grabs her by the wrist.* NORMAN *shuts the door.* SIR *sits, scribbles, then rests.*)

NORMAN: Well now, my dainty duck, my dear-o.

IRENE: Let go of me.

NORMAN: What was all that about?

(*Pause.*)

IRENE: He seems better.

NORMAN: Better than what or whom as the case may be?

IRENE: I didn't think he'd get through the performance tonight.

NORMAN: He's not through it yet. (*Pause.*) I'm waiting.

IRENE: For what?

NORMAN: A graphic description of events. Out with it. Or I shall slap your face. Hard. You had better know that my parentage is questionable, and that I can be vicious when roused.

IRENE: I thought we were friends.

NORMAN: I thought so, too, Irene. I shall long remember welcoming you into the company in the prop room of the Palace Theatre, Newark-on-Trent, the smell of size and carpenter's glue, the creaking of skips and you locked in the arms of the Prince of Morocco, a married man, ever such a comic sight with his tights round his ankles and you smeared black. I said, 'Don't worry, mum's the word, but don't let it happen again.' We talked, brewed tea on a paint-stained gas-ring, under a photograph of Mr Charles Doran as Shylock, somewhat askew and ever so disapproving. You expressed gratitude and I said, 'Now you're one of the family.' And this is how you repay me.

IRENE: What am I supposed to have done?

NORMAN: You tell me.

IRENE: About what?

NORMAN: About Sir, the Guv'nor, the Chief, Father, Him from whom all favours flow. You know who Sir is, Irene.

IRENE: I'm late. I have to help Her Ladyship with her armour.

NORMAN: Her Ladyship's armour will keep. Perhaps you didn't hear my question. What did Sir do?

IRENE: I'm not telling you –
(He grabs her closer and threatens to strike her.)

NORMAN: I'll mark you for life, ducky.

IRENE: You strike me and I'll tell him, I'll tell Sir, I'll tell Sir, I will, I'll tell Sir –
(He lets go of her.)

NORMAN: Tell Sir? On me? I quake in my boots. I shan't be able to eat my tea. Tell Sir? Gadzooks, madam, the thought of it, you telling Sir on me. Ducky, in his present state, which totters between confusion and chaos, to tell Sir anything at all would take a louder voice and clearer diction than that possessed by the most junior member of this Shakespearean troupe, the assistant stage-manager, dog's body, general understudy, map-carrier and company mattress, namely you. You won't be able to tell Sir you'd let him touch your tits on a Thursday matinee in Aberystwyth. Tell Sir. You think I don't know the game? You think I've dressed the rotten bugger for sixteen bloody years, nursed him, spoiled him, washed his sweat-sodden doublet and hose and his foul underpants night after night without knowing every twist and turn of what is laughingly known as his mind? Never mind tell Sir. I'll tell you. He did something, something unseen and furtive, something that gave him pleasure. 'That's more like it!' More like what, Irene? I have to know all that occurs. I have to know all he does.

(*Pause.*)

IRENE: He lifted me up in his arms.

NORMAN: Lifted you up?

IRENE: And I understood, I understood what he meant. 'So young, so young,' he said, and lifted me up. 'That's more like it,' he cried and I knew, cradled in his arms, that it was youth and newness he was after –

(NORMAN *laughs.*)

– why do you laugh? I was there, it happened, it's true, I felt it. He was trembling and so was I. Up in his arms, part of him, 'That's more like it', and he lowered me, waved me away and I ran off. Youth. And with my eyes closed I imagined what it would be like to be carried on by him, Cordelia, dead in his arms, young.

NORMAN: Never mind a young Cordelia, ducky, he wants a light Cordelia. Light, ducky, light. Look at yourself. Look at Her Ladyship.

IRENE: You don't understand. He needs youth –

NORMAN: Ducky, we tried *The Master Builder* in Leamington Spa. Three performances. We played to absolutely no business at all so don't give me all that wish-wash about youth, I know all about youth knocking at the door, ducky, and audiences stay away in droves, me included. 'That's more like it.' You're lighter than she is, ducky. (*He laughs. Pause.*) You're not the first to be placed on the scales. How do you think Her Ladyship got the job? Her Ladyship, when a slip of a girl, went from map-carrier to youngest daughter overnight. I remember it well. That was the tour the Doge of Venice gave Lancelot Gobbo clap.

(IRENE *begins to cry softly.*)

It's not youth or talent or star quality he's after, ducky, but a moderate eater. (*Pause.*) We could cope with anything in those days. Turmoil was his middle name. (NORMAN *sways a little, then controls himself. He becomes tearful but holds back.*) So. Ducky. Keep well away. The old days are gone, the days of vim and vigour, what's to come is still unsure. Trip no further, pretty sweeting. We can't have any distractions. Not any more. Not if things are to be lovely. And painless. (*Pause.*) Don't disobey me, will you? The fateful words, 'You finish on Saturday' have a decidedly sinister ring –

(HER LADYSHIP *appears.*)

– two rings, and bangles right up to the elbow.

HER LADYSHIP: There you are. You're late with my armour. (*She goes.*)

NORMAN: Off you go, ducky. You have to find another canoe to paddle. Ours, I'm afraid, has holes.

(IRENE *goes.* NORMAN *swigs from his brandy bottle. He goes into Sir's dressing room. Gently, he shakes* SIR *awake.*)

Fantastically dressed in wild flowers.

(SIR *rises. In silence* NORMAN *helps him to change costumes and then bedecks him in wild flowers.*)

SIR: Michaelangelo, did they?

NORMAN: And Blake.

SIR: I knew what they mean. Moral grandeur.

(*Pause.*)

NORMAN: I talked to the girl. She's not as light as she looks. We're none of us strong enough for a change of cast.

(*Pause.* SIR, *suddenly and fiercely, embraces* NORMAN.)

SIR: You cannot be properly paid. *In pectora*, I name you friend. The debt is all mine. And I shall find a way to repay you. I must, must settle all my debts.

NORMAN: Don't, you're making me tearful –

SIR: (*Letting go of him*) God, your breath smells of stale tights. How much have you had?

NORMAN: Not enough.

SIR: Iago, Iago –

NORMAN: Wrong play.

SIR: I have to wake in bliss, I have to carry on Her Ladyship, I
    need you sober.
NORMAN: I am. Sober. Diction perfect. Deportment steady.
    Temper serene.
    (NORMAN *smiles*.)
SIR: It is no laughing matter! (*Pause*.) The final push. I hope
    you're up to it.
NORMAN: (*Under his breath*) And you, dear.
SIR: What?
NORMAN: And you, Lear.
    (*They begin to go. Lights fade to blackout. Drums. Trumpets.
    Clash of swords. Light grows.*)
    (*The wings.* SIR, HER LADYSHIP *and* NORMAN *stand in
    readiness*, IRENE *by the timpani*.)

    (SIR *spits on his hands*.)
HER LADYSHIP: I wish you wouldn't do that. You remind me of a
    labourer.

    (SIR *lifts* HER LADYSHIP *in his arms and carries her on. Those
    in the wings watch*.)

    (*Lights fade to blackout*.)
    (*Lights up again quickly*.)

    (IRENE *drums a slow, sombre rhythm*.)
MADGE: Cue curtain down.

KENT: I am come
        To bid my King and master aye good-night;
        Is he not here?
ALBANY: Speak, Edmund, where's the King? . . .
EDMUND: I pant for life; some good I mean to do
        Despite of mine own nature. Quickly send,
        Be brief in it, to the castle; for my writ
        Is on the life of Lear and on Cordelia.
        Nay, send in time.
ALBANY: Run, run! O run! . . .
        Haste thee, for thy life.
SIR: Howl, howl, howl, howl! O! you are men of stones:
        Had I your tongues and eyes, I'd use them so
        That heaven's vaults should crack. She's gone for ever.
        I know when one is dead, and when one lives;
        She's dead as earth . . .

KENT: Break, heart; I prithee, break.
ALBANY: The weight of this sad time we must obey;
        Speak what we feel, not what we ought to say.
        The oldest hath borne most: we that are young,
        Shall never see so much, nor live so long.

(*Sound of curtain falling. Applause.* SIR *comes into the wings.*)

SIR: (*Looking heavenwards*) We've done it Will, we've done it.

MADGE: Stand by for curtain-calls. Curtain going up.

(*The company take their curtain-calls.*)

Stand by for your curtain-call, Sir.

(SIR *goes on for his call. Thunderous applause and cheers.*
Light change to a solitary light, bright and harsh. SIR *steps into*
the light and NORMAN *stands just behind him in shadow.*
Applause and cheers continue until SIR *raises his hand for*
silence.)

SIR: My lords, ladies and gentlemen. Thank you for the manner
in which you have received the greatest tragedy in our
language. We live in dangerous times. Our civilization is
under threat from the forces of darkness, and we, humble
actors, do all in our power to fight as soldiers on the side of
right in the great battle. Our most cherished ambition is to
keep the best alive of our drama, to serve the greatest poet-
dramatist who has ever lived, and we are animated by
nothing else than to educate the nation in his works by taking
his plays to every corner of our beloved island. Tomorrow
night we shall give –

NORMAN: *Richard III*.

SIR: – *King Richard III*. I myself will play the hunchback king.
On Saturday afternoon my lady wife will play –

NORMAN: Portia.

SIR: – Portia, and I the badly-wronged Jew in *The Merchant of*
Venice, a play you may think of greater topicality than ever.
On Saturday night –

NORMAN: *Lear*.

SIR: – On Saturday night we shall essay once more the tragedy
you have this evening witnessed and I myself shall again
undergo the severest test known to an actor. Next week, God
willing, we shall be in –

NORMAN: Eastbourne.

SIR: – Eastbourne. I trust your friends and relatives there will, on
your kind recommendation, discover source for refreshment,
as you seem to have done by your warm indication, in the
glorious words we are privileged to speak. For the generous

manner in which you have received our earnest endeavours, on behalf of my lady wife, my company and myself, I remain your humble and obedient servant, and can no other answer make but thanks and thanks, and ever thanks.

(*Bows. Applause. He steps out of the light. Applause continues. Light fades.*

Light on SIR's *dressing room and corridor.* SIR *is seated at the dressing table with Scotch and beer.* NORMAN *puts the costume away and starts to clean the moustache and beard which Sir has removed.* SIR *downs the Scotch in one, and sips the beer.*)

SIR: Norman, Norman –

NORMAN: Sir?

SIR: What will happen to you?

NORMAN: Could you be a little more explicit?

SIR: What will happen to you if I can't continue?

NORMAN: Stop it. Nothing ever happens to me. I lead a life quite without incident.

SIR: But if I should be unable to continue.

NORMAN: There's no chance of that so I'm not bothering to answer.

SIR: I worry about you, my boy.

NORMAN: Don't.

SIR: You could become a steward on a ship.

NORMAN: What and give up the theatre?

SIR: I know several ship-owners. They'd help.

NORMAN: I'll trouble you not to trouble them or yourself.

SIR: What will you do?

NORMAN: As best I can.

(*Pause.*)

SIR: What is the play tomorrow?

NORMAN: *Richard III*.

SIR: Slavery, bloody slavery.

(*Knock on the door.*)

NORMAN: Who?

GEOFFREY: Geoffrey.

SIR: Come.

(GEOFFREY *enters, dressed in street clothes.*)

GEOFFREY: Just popped in to say goodnight, old man.

SIR: Goodnight, Geoffrey, Very fine in the storm scene, my boy. Felt your love, that's what matters.

GEOFFREY: Thank you. Fool is by far the most important part I've ever played in Shakespeare. I hope I didn't let you down.

SIR: Offer Geoffrey a small glass of beer, Norman.

GEOFFREY: Thank you.

(NORMAN *pours a small glass of beer and gives it to* GEOFFREY.)

Such an odd feeling tonight, old man, rather exciting to reach my age to prove to others that one can act. That's the wonderful thing about this life of ours. It's never too late. Surprising things happen. But there are disadvantages. One gets the taste for more. Cheers.

SIR: Good health attend you.

NORMAN: Bottoms up, Geoffrey.

GEOFFREY: May I ask you a question, old man?

SIR: Ask.

GEOFFREY: Fool is a curious role. You give your all for almost an hour and a half, then vanish into thin air for the rest of the play. The next one hears of me is you saying that I'm hanged. But why? By whom? It seems awfully unfair.

SIR: My theory is that, in William's day, Fool and Cordelia were played by one and the same person. Must've been a good double. Fool and Cordelia. Saved a salary, too, of course.

GEOFFREY: Well. Things haven't changed. As long as you feel I didn't let you down.

SIR: In no particular.

GEOFFREY: Just one last thing, I won't keep you, I know you're very tired. But when you interviewed me, I said I didn't want too much. Small parts, I said. It may not be thought admirable but I've never put a jot at risk. Never wanted to scale the heights. Played goodish parts, tours of course, never London. I don't complain. Touring's a good life. Enjoyed my cricket in summer, hockey in winter, lovely women, long walks, a weekly change of scene, the English countryside in all weathers. What could be nicer? But never risked a jot. Been lucky. Mustn't complain. I expect I can get

through to the end of the chapter. I've a little put by. My
wife brings in a bit with her singing lessons. I've no right to
expect work, not at my age. War's brought surprising
employment. All the youngsters at front. My grandson, not a
pro, was taken prisoner in Tripoli. Sorry to be so long-
winded. Point is, if at any time circumstances arise, I should
like to be considered for better parts. I shouldn't want an
increase in salary.

SIR: I will keep you in the forefront of my mind.

GEOFFREY: Thank you, old man. Well. Goodnight. Thank you
for the drink.

(GEOFFREY *stumbles.* NORMAN *moves to help him.*)

I can manage.

(GEOFFREY *exits.*)

SIR: Fine fellow. Fine fellow.

NORMAN: Shouldn't we remove our make-up, Sir?

(SIR *stares at himself in the looking-glass.*)

SIR: I hope Will's pleased tonight.

NORMAN: I had a friend –

SIR: Not now, Norman –

NORMAN: I had a friend had ever such a sweet singing voice but
lost it in Colwyn Bay after a bad attack of sea mist. But it
came back to him in the end, and d'you know why? Because
he said to himself they also sing who only stand and serve. Or
words to that effect.

SIR: Are you pissed, Norman?

NORMAN: Me, Sir? Pissed, Sir? Lud, Sir Percy, how you do
tousle me.

SIR: Let me smell your breath.

(NORMAN *gives a short puff of breath away from* SIR.)

NORMAN: There. Told you. Sweeter than Winston Churchill.

SIR: I can't have you pissed.

(HER LADYSHIP *enters dressed in her own clothes.*)

HER LADYSHIP: Not changed yet?

SIR: I've been a little slow tonight, Pussy.

HER LADYSHIP: I'm not waiting. I'll go back to the digs, see if I
can get a fire lit.

SIR: I shan't be long.

HER LADYSHIP: Goodnight, Norman. I'm not certain whether I should thank you or not.

NORMAN: Not. I can't bear being thanked.

(*She goes.*)

SIR: A good woman.

(SIR *applies cold cream slowly and wearily.* OXENBY *knocks on the door.*)

Who?

OXENBY: Mr Oxenby.

(SIR *makes a gesture to imply he doesn't want to see him.* NORMAN *opens the door.*)

NORMAN: What do you want?

OXENBY: My manuscript. He won't read it, I know that.

NORMAN: Keep your voice down. He hasn't gone yet. Wait there. He's a little slow tonight.

(NORMAN *begins to look for Oxenby's manuscript.* OXENBY *waits in the doorway.*)

OXENBY: (*Deliberately loud*) All that struggling and surviving has tired him, no doubt.

(NORMAN *darts back to the door.*)

NORMAN: Please, Mr Oxenby.

OXENBY: (*Hissing*) Outmoded hypocrite.

SIR: What – what – ?

NORMAN: Not now, Mr Oxenby.

OXENBY: Death to all tyrants.

SIR: What, what did he say?

(NORMAN *finds the play and gives it to* OXENBY.)

OXENBY: Tell him from me, I look forward to a new order. I want a company without tyrants.

NORMAN: Who'd be in charge?

OXENBY: I would.

(*He smiles.*)

NORMAN: Don't write him off. Or me. Or Her Ladyship. She has a very fine pedigree. Her father –

OXENBY: I saw her father. As Caliban. A good make-up artist, that's all.

SIR: Close that door.

NORMAN: You'll be lovely with a little success, Mr Oxenby.

OXENBY: Your nose is browner than usual tonight, Norman.
> (*He goes.*)

NORMAN: The little you know –

SIR: What did Oxenby want?
> (IRENE *enters the corridor and pauses at Sir's door.*)

IRENE: Goodnight, Sir. Goodnight, Norman.

NORMAN: If you hurry, you'll catch Mr Oxenby.
> (*She goes.* SIR *begins to smear the cold cream and when the mask is covered and the colours a blur, he lets out a sudden moan and cannot apparently move.*)

NORMAN: Sir, what is it, Sir?
> (SIR *moans.*)

SIR: I'm – I'm tired. Terribly tired. The room is spinning. I – must lie down.
> (NORMAN *quickly helps him to the couch.* SIR *lies back.*)
> See if you can get me a taxi in this Godforsaken place.

NORMAN: All in good time.
> (*No response.* NORMAN *takes cotton wool and begins to clean* SIR's *face.* SIR *begins to cry.*)
> Don't cry. Don't cry.

SIR: There's nothing left.

NORMAN: Stop that at once. I had a friend –

SIR: Oh for Christ's sake, I'm sick of your friends. Motley crew they are. Pathetic, lonely, despairing –

NORMAN: That's nice, isn't it.
> (*Pause.*)

SIR: I beg your pardon. Uncalled for. Count myself as your friend.

NORMAN: Never despairing.

SIR: Have apologized.

NORMAN: Never, never despairing. Well. Perhaps. Sometimes. At night. Or at Christmas when you can't get a panto. But not once inside the building. Never. Pathetic maybe, but not ungrateful. Too mindful of one's luck, as the saying goes. No Duke is more privileged. Here's beauty. Here's spring and summer. Here pain is bearable. And never lonely. Not here. For he today that sheds his blood with me. Soft, no doubt. Sensitive. That's my nature. Easily hurt, but that's a virtue.

I'm not here for reasons of my own either. No one could accuse me of base motives. I've got what I want and I don't need anyone to know it. Inadequate, yes. But never, never despairing.

SIR: I've begun *My Life*.

NORMAN: What?

SIR: Fetch it. The book. I made a start –
(SIR *brings it to him*.)
Find the place.
(NORMAN *pages through the book*.)

NORMAN: You didn't get very far –

SIR: What did I write?

NORMAN: (*He reads*) My Life. Dedication. This book is dedicated to My Beloved Pussy who has been my splendid spur. To the spirit of all actors because of their faith and endurance which never fails them. To Those who do the work of the theatre yet have but small share in its glory: Carpenters, Electricians. Scene-shifters, Property men. To the Audiences, who have laughed with us, have wept with us and whose hearts have united with ours in sympathy and understanding. And Finally – ah Sir – to the memory of William Shakespeare in whose glorious service we all labour.
(*Silence*.)

SIR: *My Life* will have to do.
(*Silence*.)

NORMAN: Wait a moment, wait a moment – (*He re-reads the passage*.) 'Carpenters, electricians, property men . . .' But Sir, Sir –
(NORMAN *looks at him*.)
Sir? Sir?
(*He shakes* SIR *gently. A long pause*.)
We're not dead are we? (*Silence*.) That's your cue. You know the line. 'You lie! Jack Clinton – ' (*He pretends to tear off a moustache. Silence*.) – lives!' Talk about untoward.
(*For the first time* NORMAN's *drunkenness shows physically. He staggers, almost falls*.) You're right. The room is spinning.
(*He regains his balance, stands staring at* SIR, *then is seized by*

terror and panic. He stumbles to the door –) Your ladyship!
Madge! Anybody!

(*He stands in the doorway, whimpering.* MADGE *hurries into the
corridor, then past him into the dressing room.* NORMAN *takes a
step inside and watches her.* MADGE *looks down at* SIR. *She is
perfectly still. She lets out a soft, short cry but then controls
herself. Silence.*)

Wasn't much of a death scene. Unremarkable and ever so
short. For him.

(MADGE *turns away from the body.*)

MADGE: Where's Her Ladyship?

NORMAN: Left before he did. Couldn't wait.

MADGE: I'll telephone her. And I'll get a doctor.

NORMAN: Too late for a doctor, ducky.

(MADGE *leaves the room. As she passes* SIR –)
What's to happen to me?

MADGE: Close the door. Wait outside.

NORMAN: I don't want to wait outside. I never wait outside. I
want to be with him. I know my place.

MADGE: Try and sober up.

(*She goes.* NORMAN, *half-afraid, goes tentatively into the room.
He cannot look at the body. He goes straight to the exercise book
and opens it. He reads to himself.*)

NORMAN: 'Carpenters, electricians, property men?' Cruel
bastard. You might have remembered. (*Silence.* NORMAN
*looks about to make sure he is unobserved. He finds a pencil and
writes in the exercise book. Then, like an angry child he turns on*
SIR's *body and thumbs his nose at it violently. But he begins to
whimper again. He drinks brandy from Sir's drinks tray.* MADGE
returns.)

MADGE: Her Ladyship's coming at once. She took it very calmly.
She asked for him to be covered in his Lear cloak. Where is
it?

NORMAN: Covered in his Lear cloak? Fetch the photographer,
ducky. Covered in his Lear cloak? This isn't the Death of
Nelson, you know.

MADGE: Where is it?

(*He points. She gets the cloak.* NORMAN *looks away. She is about to cover* SIR *but first surreptitiously slips the ring off his finger and pockets it. Then she covers him.* NORMAN *suddenly laughs.*)

NORMAN: There's no mention of stage managers, either.

MADGE: Come out of here.

NORMAN: Are we going to get paid? I mean, is there money in the till after deductions for income tax? We've got to be paid the full week, you know. Just because the man dies on a Thursday doesn't mean we should get paid *pro rata*.

MADGE: Wait outside.

NORMAN: You're nothing now, ducky. He took away your stripes. And mine. How could he be so bloody careless?

MADGE: Come away.

NORMAN: And then where will I go? Where? I'm nowhere out of my element. I don't want to end up running a boarding house in Westcliffe-on-Sea. Or Colwyn Bay. What am I going to do?

MADGE: You can speak well of him.

NORMAN: Speak well of that old sod? I wouldn't give him a good character, not in a court of law. Ungrateful bastard. Silence, ducky. My lips are sealed.

MADGE: Get out. I don't want you in here.

NORMAN: Holy, holy, holy, is it? Are we in a shrine? No pissing on the altar –

MADGE: Stop it.

NORMAN: He never once took me out for a meal. Never once. Always a back seat, me. Can't even remember him buying me a drink. And just walks out, leaves me, no thought for anyone but himself. What have I been doing here all these years? Why? Yes, well, reason not the need, rotten bugger. Beg your pardon, leave the room, turn round three times and come back – come back –

(*He breaks off and turns away from her.*)

Speak well of him? I know what you'd say, ducky. I know all about you. I've got eyes in my head. We all have our little sorrows.

(MADGE *goes but* NORMAN *does not notice.*)

I know what you'd say, stiff upper, faithful, loyal. Loving.

Well, I have only one thing to say about him and I wouldn't say it in front of you – or Her Ladyship, or anyone. Lips tight shut. I wouldn't give you the pleasure. Or him. Specially not him. If I said what I have to say he'd find a way to take it out on me. No one will ever know. We all have our little sorrows, ducky, you're not the only one. The littler you are, the larger the sorrow. You think *you* loved him? What about me? (*Long silence.*) This is not a place for death. I had a friend – (*He turns suddenly as if aware of someone behind him, but realizes he is alone.*) Sir? Sir? (*Silence. He hugs the exercise book. He sings:*) 'He that has and a little tiny wit, With hey, ho, the wind and the rain.'
(*He falls silent. He stares into space.*)
(*Lights fade.*)

J. J. FARR

for
Llewellyn Rees,
to mark thirty-five years of friendship

CHARACTERS

OLIVER BUDE
KENNETH LOWRIE
DENNIS MULLEY
ANDY ANDERSON
AUSTIN PURVIS
J. J. FARR

SET

A house in the country
A courtyard
J. J. Farr's temporary bedroom

The courtyard is formed by one corner of the house and is dominated by a tree giving shade. Under the tree, a table and an assortment of folding chairs. At more than one place steps lead down from a terrace which borders the house on two sides. On each of these sides there are French windows: one leads to the house; the other to J. J. Farr's temporary bedroom which is austere and cell-like with a single bed, a table and chair, a mirror on a chest of drawers. There are two doors in this room: one to the bathroom and one to the house.

Summer

J. J. Farr was first presented by Robert Fox and Memorial Films at the Theatre Royal, Bath, on Tuesday 27 October 1987, and subsequently at The Phoenix Theatre, London, on 18 November 1987 with the following cast:

OLIVER BUDE	Dudley Sutton
KENNETH LOWRIE	Bob Peck
DENNIS MULLEY	Bernard Lloyd
ANDY ANDERSON	Trevor Peacock
AUSTIN PURVIS	Hugh Paddick
J. J. FARR	Albert Finney
Director	Ronald Eyre
Designer	Jocelyn Herbert
Lighting	Rick Fisher

ACT ONE

SCENE ONE

Morning. Just after 9 a.m. In J. J. Farr's room, DENNIS MULLEY *is making the bed. In the courtyard,* OLIVER BUDE, *early fifties, an innocent, stands on a chair, fixing bunting to a tree.* KENNETH LOWRIE, *forty-five-ish, intense, highly-strung, comes out of the house.*

LOWRIE: Is this a good idea?

OLIVER: It has the Warden's blessing.

LOWRIE: What's your name again?

OLIVER: Oliver. Oliver Bude. I answer to anything except Olly.

LOWRIE: Is it a good idea to turn this into a festive occasion?

OLIVER: But it is a festive occasion, Mr Lowrie. The release of
    the hostages is cause for celebration.

LOWRIE: Where's the Warden?

OLIVER: Making the old waiting-room into temporary quarters
    for J. J. No stairs, you see. It has its own bathroom. And if
    the weather holds he can sit out here and recuperate. Do you
    really think the bunting's a mistake?
    (LOWRIE *paces restlessly.*)

LOWRIE: Is there anything I can do to help?

OLIVER: You could stop pacing. I'm quite jumpy as it is.

LOWRIE: Yes, well, I can't help it. I'm nervous of meeting him.
    He's been an important figure in my life – I wish it could be
    under more favourable circumstances –
    (DENNIS *comes out of J. J. Farr's room, stuffing a pillow into a*
    pillow-slip. His age is difficult to guess, mid-sixties, perhaps
    older. When he smiles it signals either self-mockery or secret
    amusement.)

DENNIS: Any good at flowers, Mr Lowrie?

LOWRIE: Flowers?

DENNIS: The coloured things that grow in fields and gardens.

OLIVER: No, no, Warden, Austin does the flowers.

LOWRIE: Warden, I'm not sure about the bunting.

(LOWRIE *turns abruptly and goes back into the house*.)

OLIVER: Mr Lowrie makes me horribly nervous, Warden. He excretes disapproval. I do hope we haven't made a mistake admitting him.

DENNIS: J. J. will calm him down.

OLIVER: I seem to incur his displeasure. He never remembers my name. He reminds me of that dreadful Canadian, Monsignor Hepworth. Whenever he asked for my name, I thought, oh dear, I'm on his list. Another forty-seven thousand years in purgatory.

DENNIS: We must be gentle with Mr Lowrie. He had a particularly difficult time. I haven't really been able to welcome him properly, explain the ins and outs, our little peculiarities –

(*He smiles*.)

OLIVER: How's the room looking?

DENNIS: It needs flowers.

OLIVER: Austin'd be frightfully miffed if anybody else were to do the flowers.

DENNIS: Where is he?

OLIVER: Watching the television. He's been watching since seven o'clock this morning. How a man of his refinement can watch television and eat breakfast at the same time is one of the mysteries of the present century.

(ANDY ANDERSON, *fifty-ish, sad, haunted, always neatly dressed in shabby black, enters. He carries a sandwich tin*.)

ANDY: (*Slightly frantic*) Is he here yet?

DENNIS: Not yet.

ANDY: Any idea when?

DENNIS: Soon.

ANDY: I won't sleep. I'll walk. I'll sleep later. I'll keep awake.

(*He is about to go when* AUSTIN PURVIS, *an exquisite old man, enters, carrying a canvas bag*.)

AUSTIN: I've seen J. J.

ANDY: Is he here?

AUSTIN: No, no, on the television –

DENNIS: You saw J. J.?

AUSTIN: Three times. They show it over and over again.

OLIVER: Why didn't you come out and call us?

AUSTIN: If I'd come out and called you, I'd have missed it.

DENNIS: How did he look?

AUSTIN: (*After consideration*) Not well. In fact, dreadful.

OLIVER: After five months in captivity you'd look dreadful, too.

DENNIS: Did he make a statement?

AUSTIN: No. We saw the aeroplane land. He and the other hostages were taken off but the camera was too far away to see clearly. Ants scurrying, nothing more. They were then escorted through the airport building into a large room where what I believe are called the media were gathered. A Foreign Office man, weedy, adenoidal, said that, under the circumstances, he was sure the media would understand if the released hostages declined to answer questions. But that was wishful thinking on his part because immediately the media started shouting questions with an insensitivity worthy of the Spanish Inquisition. The hostages were hurried out and that's when I saw J. J. He passed close to camera and looked straight at one. A bleak, demented look. (*Silence.*)

ANDY: I'm going to walk. I'll walk up the lane. I'll watch out for him. I've got to stay awake.
(*He goes.*)

OLIVER: Perhaps Mr Lowrie's right. Perhaps the bunting is inappropriate.

DENNIS: Leave it. We want J. J. to feel he's welcome home.
(AUSTIN *sits, takes embroidery from the canvas bag and begins to work at it.* DENNIS *goes back into J. J.'s room and continues with the bed-making.*)

AUSTIN: Television is absurd.

OLIVER: Then why watch it?

AUSTIN: They showed the same pictures of the hostages arriving three times within the hour. On the first occasion, just after 7 a.m. they flashed the word 'Live' on the screen. 'Live'. On the two subsequent showings, they flashed the word

'Recording'. Now, here's the absurdity: it is, in my view, impossible to verify that the first showing *was* live. How would one prove that it was not also a recording? The word 'live' in itself is proof of nothing except, in certain circumstances, the television company's intent to deceive. Even if one stood at the airport watching the aeroplane land while, at the same time, watching a television set showing the pictures of the landing, the one would not, in my view, be verification of the other. I must put that to J. J. That's very much his cup of tea.

OLIVER: I wish they'd make up their minds about J. J. When he was first taken hostage they called him, 'a former Catholic priest' –

AUSTIN: Which is accurate enough –

OLIVER: But during the captivity, when they found out more about him, he became, 'the well-known militant atheist'.

AUSTIN: Interesting. This morning, they described him as 'the distinguished Moral Philosopher'.

OLIVER: That's only since he was released. And I do find that a terrible affectation. One would never dream of describing anyone as an Immoral Philosopher.'

AUSTIN: Yes, one would. Nietzsche.

OLIVER: Our Mr Lowrie watches us, you know. He stares as if trying to see through one. I'd look back at him but I'm frightened of being turned into a pillar of salt.
(*Mischievously.*) I wonder how long it will be before he manages to tell J. J. that he's published a book.

AUSTIN: Under a minute.
(OLIVER *finishes the bunting and climbs down off the chair.*)

OLIVER: You mustn't fuss J. J. with your little games, Austin, the moment he arrives.

AUSTIN: I know how to behave, thank you.
(DENNIS *comes out of J. J.'s room carrying a vase.*)

DENNIS: Austin, be so kind as to arrange some flowers in this vase for J. J.'s room.

AUSTIN: (*Fussed*) Will there be time? He should be here any moment.
(LOWRIE *enters urgently.*)

LOWRIE: Warden, do we want a nurse?

DENNIS: What are you talking about?

LOWRIE: The telephone was ringing in the hall so I answered it.
A Foreign Office official – difficult to understand, very
nasal – speaking from the airport, wants to know if we need
a nurse for Mr Farr or can we manage ourselves?
Apparently he's not at all well. The Foreign Office bloke
says he's a complete wreck, but they forgot about a nurse,
and Mr Farr's on his way –

OLIVER: We don't need a nurse. Andy can cope –

DENNIS: Is he still on the telephone?

LOWRIE: Yes –

OLIVER: Warden, tell them we don't need a nurse.

(DENNIS *goes into the house, followed by* LOWRIE.)

LOWRIE: (*As he goes*) He should be here any second, he said.

OLIVER: I hope Dennis is firm with them. Andy is very capable.
Unless there's blood, of course. He's had so much
experience of hospitals, poor man. And, anyway, it would
be quite unpractical. Where would we put a nurse? If it
were a female she and J. J. would have to share a room and
that would never do.

AUSTIN: Oh, don't be such a prude, Oliver. We're talking about
a member of the medical profession.

OLIVER: Let me remind you that the medical profession is not
above having unsavoury habits just like the rest of us. I
trust you have not forgotten my little contretemps –

AUSTIN: Imagination –

OLIVER: It was not imagination. Dr Tomelty interfered with
me.

AUSTIN: You were examined intimately, nothing more.

OLIVER: Allow me to be the judge of that.

AUSTIN: Certainly not. You're the least capable person of
judging such things. You're a natural celibate. You've
always said that celibacy was the least of your problems.

OLIVER: That doesn't alter the fact that Dr Tomelty told me to
drop my trousers and the moment my back was turned she
interfered with me.

(LOWRIE *enters, carrying a couple of books.*)

LOWRIE: Do you think Mr Farr will mind if I ask him to sign a couple of his books?

OLIVER: Not the moment he arrives.

LOWRIE: No, no, no. I'll just put them down – the opportunity may – they're both a bit battered –

AUSTIN: So I see.

LOWRIE: I've read them. Countless times. All his works, really. I know whole passages – they've meant a lot to me. There are books that mean – a lot.

AUSTIN: Which particular ones do you want him to inscribe?

LOWRIE: *Seeing, Not Believing* and *After God*.

OLIVER: I never got through *Seeing, Not Believing*. Much too intellectual for me. But even I managed to read *After God*.

AUSTIN: Yes, you would. The doubting man's guide to certainty. Such a vulgar little work. The title page summed it all up. *After God. J. J. Farr*.

OLIVER: It did a lot to popularize his thought.

AUSTIN: Precisely. And do you remember, Oliver, all those cheap little jokes so beloved of those cheap little reviewers? Not Farr enough. Farr too Farr. Farr Off. Farr Out. We did tease him.

OLIVER: Farr Better. Farr Worse.

AUSTIN: He doesn't like being teased.

LOWRIE: Is he very forbidding?

AUSTIN: Distant. Not forbidding.

OLIVER: Can be fierce. He sometimes looks at people as though he's come to arrest them.

AUSTIN: Boyish. He reminds me of a lad who was at school with me. Brainbox, we called him. J. J.'s like that. A clever little boy who can explain away fear of the dark.

OLIVER: Andy's the only one who can make him laugh. He tells J. J. dirty jokes and sings him obscene ditties. Odd, isn't it?

LOWRIE: *Seeing, Not Believing* – at the time of my – my crisis – contorted my mind.

OLIVER: (*With genuine concern*) Was that a good thing?

AUSTIN: I used to be able to do the opening sentence. 'In the dying years of the present century, no reasonable person can be reasonable and religious.' I've always thought those words very striking.

148

LOWRIE: That's in the *Oxford Book of Quotations* now, you know.

AUSTIN: Well, yes, I remember it all caused quite a stir at the time.

OLIVER: Did it not. Cardinal Bingham described J. J. as the devil incarnate.

AUSTIN: But then Cardinal Bingham was always given to understatement.

OLIVER: What's the opening sentence of your book. Mr Lowrie? I do think opening sentences are frightfully important, don't you? I like all books to begin, 'A shot rang out!' How does your book begin?

LOWRIE: 'Faith in the supernatural is a neurotic device to deaden fear of death.'

AUSTIN: You and J. J. should get on well.

LOWRIE: I tell you this: if he is a complete wreck it'll be physical not mental. Farr has the sort of intellect that's not easily intimidated. There was one report that struck me as particularly telling. The go-between, that obscene little lawyer, Dr Fawzi, when asked by a reporter how J. J. Farr was bearing up, said, remarkably well, except that he was extremely unpopular with his fellow Christians. I thought to myself, I bet he is. And when Fawzi said in that smug, cigarette-choked voice, 'God is not mocked, you know', I thought, he is by J. J. Farr.

(*He laughs.* ANDY *rushes in.*)

ANDY: He's here, he's here, J. J.'s here, he's coming round the side, I'm going to fetch him –

OLIVER: How does he look?

ANDY: Get Dennis –

(ANDY *exits hurriedly.*)

OLIVER: Where is he?

LOWRIE: On the telephone –

AUSTIN: (*Overlapping*) Somewhere in the house.

(J. J. FARR *enters, helped by* ANDY, *who carries* J. J.'*s suitcase. J. J. could be anything from mid-forties to mid-fifties. He is pale, drawn. He is wearing clothes that are obviously brand new, a hat, but no jacket. He walks with difficulty. His struggle to appear in control is immense. Awkward silence.*)

OLIVER: Welcome home, J. J.

J. J.: I thought of you all often.

AUSTIN: Dear J. J.

J. J.: I'm rather tired.

OLIVER: Oughtn't you to sit?

LOWRIE: Would someone introduce us?

OLIVER: Yes, of course. J. J., this is a new resident, Kenneth
Lowrie.

(LOWRIE *offers a hand but* J. J. *doesn't respond.*)

J. J.: Have we met before?

LOWRIE: No, but you did once review a book of mine in the
TLS. Favourable. *The Externalization of Demons.*

J. J.: I don't remember.

AUSTIN: (*Quietly to* OLIVER) And such a catchy title.

(OLIVER *suppresses a nervous giggle, like a child, hand covering
the mouth.*)

ANDY: I have to sleep now. Pleased to see you, J. J. We thought
about you an awful lot, too. A minute of silent thought every
morning for the whole five months. Oliver's idea.

J. J.: Where's Dennis Mulley?

OLIVER: He'll be here presently –

J. J.: And David Ingham? Why have we got a new resident?
What's happened to David?

OLIVER: David was taken ill some weeks ago. He collapsed
suddenly here in the garden. He went very peacefully and
quietly. He didn't suffer.

(J. J. *removes his hat and crosses himself.*)

ANDY: (*Alarmed and astonished*) J. J. –

(*They all watch* J. J., *amazed. His eyes are closed and his lips
move. Then he opens his eyes.*)

J. J.: I ought to warn you of something. I don't know what
you've been told but it's best you hear the facts from me. I
was examined in Cyprus by doctors. They came to the
conclusion that I'm mentally deranged –

(*He tries to laugh but is dangerously near tears.*)

OLIVER: Now, now, J. J., oughtn't you to go straight to bed?

J. J.: You mustn't treat me like a naughty boy. Which I am – (*He
forces a smile.*) Here's the problem. My memory, at the

moment, is selective. I recall some events with burning clarity. Other things – It's a mild form of hysteria, a blocking out. Understandable. In the circumstances. That's what's so fascinating to me. I can see myself but the self I see is blind. I'm rational and irrational. I seem to be suffering – according to these doctors – from some sort of reversion – I've reverted – (*He stops himself.*) – that's not quite right – well, well, all in good time – I can, like now, talk about myself as if I were someone else. But when I am that someone else I can't talk at all. It's the crying that deceived the medical men – I'm going to cry at any moment now – the doctors take it to be a sign of mental and emotional instability. But it's the residual pain of an unwanted experience, the pleasure of a joyous struggle, and the certainty of a glorious victory in which I want you all to share –

(*He fights tears.* DENNIS *enters.*)

DENNIS: J. J. Welcome home. Welcome home. Let me look at you. You're pale. I thought you'd have a splendid suntan. Anyway, you look ten years younger than when I last saw you. Come, let's be un-English and embrace.

(DENNIS *hugs* J. J., *who screams out in pain, almost faints. He whimpers pitifully.* ANDY *dashes to hold him.*)

ANDY: Better get him to his room –

(ANDY *escorts* J. J. *to his room and helps him on to the bed.*)

J. J.: (*In terror*) Don't touch my back – not my back –

(J. J. *lies face down on the bed.*)

ANDY: (*Shying away*) You're bleeding.

J. J.: (*Barely audible*) Domine, non sum dignus –

ANDY: What's wrong with your back? Should I get Dr Tomelty?

J. J.: They punished me – pills – pills in the bag.

(ANDY *finds the pills, and goes into the bathroom.* J. J. *cries.* ANDY *returns with a glass of water and helps* J. J. *to take the pills. During this,* DENNIS *turns, ill at ease, to the others.*)

DENNIS: You make an effort to be welcoming and that's the thanks you get.

(*He smiles. Silence.*)

OLIVER: He's dreadfully ill.

DENNIS: Apparently.

OLIVER: But you didn't see what we saw. He crossed himself and prayed.

(DENNIS *tries to smile.*)

He asked after David and when I told him that David had died –

(*Silence.*)

AUSTIN: I was much more perturbed by his language. 'A joyous struggle, a glorious victory' does not bode well. He seems broken.

(*Silence.* ANDY *comes back into the courtyard.*)

ANDY: He's got some sort of wound on his back. He says they punished him. Better get Dr Tomelty. She'll clean it, dress it. I've given him a sedative. Valium-based. Think he'll sleep.

AUSTIN: I shall pick flowers for his room.

J. J.: (*Crying out*) Charlatan! *Hic est, hoc est!* Open the cage! Open the cage! Hey presto, we have blood! Wants a priest – he wants a priest! *Ce n'est pas nécessaire, il est mort –*

ANDY: Never thought to hear night-noises at this time of the morning.

(ANDY *goes back into the room and watches over him.*)

J. J.: (*Moaning again*) *Allahu Akbar, Allahu Akbar. Pater noster, qui es in coelis, sanctifecetur nomen tuum. Adveniat regnum tuum. Fiat voluntas tua –*

(*His words become mumbled; the mumbling turns into moaning.*)

LOWRIE: Crossing himself, J. J. Farr, incredible.

DENNIS: You obviously have a gift, Mr Lowrie, for the economical turn of phrase.

(*He goes. Silence. Lights fade to blackout.*)

SCENE TWO

Noon. Eight days later. In his room, J. J. *is putting on his shirt with great care. There is a dressing covering a wound in the small of his back. When he finishes, he exits into the bathroom.* LOWRIE, *seated at the table under the tree, is writing furiously, referring to two or three books.* ANDY *sleeps in the shade.* DENNIS *enters.*

DENNIS: Mr Lowrie, would you mind, now?

    (LOWRIE *begins to gather up his papers.*)

LOWRIE: And how's the hostage getting on?

DENNIS: Slowly.

LOWRIE: Still praying, is he? (*No response.*) I want to ask you
    something, Warden. I'll be blunt.

DENNIS: When are you anything else?

LOWRIE: Are you equipped to deal with him? (*No response.*) You
    let him talk to you. He's been talking every day for over a
    week. Is your conversation structured in any way? Do you
    know about the trigger words? He shouts at night. He keeps
    me awake. I've been making notes of what he says. They
    may be helpful. Put them to him, take him off guard,
    surprise him, shock him. Do you know anything about
    confrontation techniques? (*No response.*) You just let him
    ramble on, do you? I mean, what's the burden of your
    conversation?

    (*Pause.*)

DENNIS: I was once, years ago, for a short while, his confessor.

LOWRIE: (*Backing off*) All right, all right, all right. Because I've
    done some work in this area –

DENNIS: Have you?

LOWRIE: You've not read my book?

DENNIS: No.

LOWRIE: I deal in some detail with the relationship between
    psychosis and religion.

DENNIS: Sounds fascinating.

LOWRIE: I have a chapter on Farr's sort of strategy. It's a hysteric
    manoeuvre. A touch of aggression can be remarkably
    effective therapy. I don't suppose you'd let me have a go at
    him?

DENNIS: No.

LOWRIE: Patients find it difficult to maintain the psychotic-
    religious mode when attacked. It's in my book.

DENNIS: When I have time I must give it a whirl.

LOWRIE: (*Exploding*) Stop disparaging me, I'm not someone to be
    disparaged.

DENNIS: I never disparage anyone except myself –

LOWRIE: I'm not one of your relics, Warden. My disgrace wasn't closet queenery or altar boys or piss artistry. My struggle was intellectual –

DENNIS: Calmly, Mr Lowrie, I didn't mean to upset you –

LOWRIE: The only indecency of which I was guilty was trying to expose an ancient, debilitating psychosis. Not an opiate. An illness. My bishop told me this was a place 'to hang up my collar' for a while, a place where one could contemplate, a community which was meant to re-educate not embalm, a place to recover, to take stock. I told him I'd prefer the hostel in the Holloway Road, where there were *real* people. No, he said, this was the place for me. And what do I find? The air fetid with the smell of stale bread and sour wine. It needs fumigating. You want to get rid of the male spinsters, Warden, the crypto-or-not-so-crypto-homosexuals. The world has changed –

DENNIS: I know you've had a bad time, Mr Lowrie, but I want to assure you that –

LOWRIE: (*Cutting in, almost continuous, embattled*) – Yes, yes, a bad time, yes, because how do you make it clear that man has to learn to love himself not God? Yes, I had a bad time trying to bring reason to bear on a dead mythology, trying to make others understand that the only paradise we'll ever know is on this earth and of our making. We have to work, not pray. You, me, all of them, should be out there working, doing socially useful work. If they really want to know what hell's like –

DENNIS: (*A smile*) I'm not sure they do –

LOWRIE: (*Continuing*) – let them visit the inner cities, let them put their energies into alleviating poverty in this world, now. They're parasites, behaving as though they were still priests, poncing off the community –

DENNIS: So are you, Mr Lowrie, so am I, still priests, I mean, technically at least –

LOWRIE: No. Not me. Well, technically, perhaps, but in no other way.

DENNIS: (*A smile*) And I'm not sure I approve of the word

'poncing'. We are beneficiaries of a Trust, set up a hundred years ago, to provide a home where men like us may learn to ease the pain of loss –

LOWRIE: You see? You see? Loss, the pain of loss. What loss? We're free. We've broken our compulsions and doubts. We've lost nothing. But you and the others still seem to cling involuntarily to your superstitions and tribal rites. I can't identify any one thing, but I have the impression that you behave not like ex-priests but failed priests. And if there are to be houses like this, Trusts set up 'to ease the pain of loss', let them be filled with men of real distinction who can point us in other directions, help us to find a new heaven. On this earth. Now. Philosophers, logicians, psychologists, sociologists. This place could become a centre of excellence, instead of a genteel geriatric clinic. Put the present bunch out to work, Warden. They'll soon stop feeling the pain of loss.

DENNIS: And J. J. Farr?

LOWRIE: Ah, yes, former Father Farr. He shouldn't be here. He needs proper treatment and I don't think you're equipped to give it. I can let you have the name of someone –

DENNIS: Thank you, I appreciate it but let's see, shall we? No, don't go. (*Pause.*) You may be able to help.
(DENNIS *takes a letter from his pocket. In his room,* J. J. *returns. He goes down on all fours and rests his hands and head on the bed. From time to time he straightens and seems to sway.*)
You say you've heard him crying out at night –

LOWRIE: My notes, you're welcome to them –

DENNIS: Thank you. But – have you ever heard him mention the name Magee?

LOWRIE: Magee?

DENNIS: A Jesuit. Father Liam Magee. It's important.

LOWRIE: No, I don't think so. Why?

DENNIS: (*Scanning the letter*) This Father Magee was held in the same place as the hostages, although not one of them. Apparently, J. J. was with him when he died. The Irish Embassy want to know what happened. And so, of course, does the priest's mother. So, if he ever mentions the name

Magee, in any context, will you let me know?

(DENNIS *goes to* J. J.'s *room but, seeing* J. J. *on his knees, returns to the courtyard. Meanwhile,* LOWRIE *has made a note of something.*

He's – he's at prayer.

LOWRIE: And I used to think J. J. Farr peed eau-de-Cologne.

DENNIS: Well, perhaps now a more appropriate metaphor would be holy water.

(*He smiles.*)

LOWRIE: He shouldn't be here.

(*He goes.* ANDY *rises.*)

ANDY: That man's in pain. Terrible pain.

DENNIS: You were awake, you ought to have made it known.

ANDY: Difficult to sleep with him banging about. Why are people always so aggressive in the face of conviction? I wonder if he was a convert. (*Quietly, to* DENNIS.) Dr Tomelty says J. J.'s wound is still festering.

DENNIS: Did she say what happened?

ANDY: I forgot to ask her. I'm not at ease in her presence. She's so awfully well-endowed. I wish there were something really wrong with me, she could do me a terrible injury.

DENNIS: Go back to sleep, Andy. In your room.

ANDY: (*With an appropriate gesture*) She's – colossal. I mean, have you ever seen such bazonkers?

DENNIS: Seldom.

(*In his room* J. J. *finishes his prayers.* DENNIS *begins to arrange two chairs under the tree.*)

ANDY: There was a nurse in St. Augustine's. Molly, her name was. She had big bazonkers, too. When she came to give me my medicine, I'd pretend I couldn't sit up. She'd bend over me. Then, as she said, 'Now, be a good boy,' I'd grab 'em. Oh, what a fondle was there, my countrymen. Joyous, truly joyous. She fell for it every time, did Molly. She probably enjoyed it. 'Now, be a good boy,' and all hands on breasts. Joyous, joyous. 'And you a man of the cloth,' she'd say.

(J. J. *comes out of his room.*)

(*To* J. J.) Talking about bazonkers, J. J.

(J. J. *smiles faintly.*)

Now, be a good boy –
(*He goes.* J. J. *nods to* DENNIS, *then sits. The chairs have been arranged in an odd way:* J. J.'s *chair is placed sideways on to the other. The effect of this will be that* J. J. *will look at* DENNIS *while he talks, but* DENNIS *will not look at* J. J. *A long silence.*)

J. J.: I'm still in the cage.

DENNIS: Literally a cage?

J. J.: Literally. Shouting abuse. What happened while I was in the cage, on the eighteenth Sunday of our captivity, is, I know, crucial. But I can't seem to – I can't – or won't – or don't want to –
(*He begins to pant in panic.*)

DENNIS: In your own time, J. J., in your own time –

J. J.: Why did I shout abuse, I'll get to it, I'll get to it, but why – ?

DENNIS: Don't force it. Let the wind blow, let the wind take the dry, dead leaves.
(*Silence.*)

J. J.: Did I tell you about the lecture?

DENNIS: No.

J. J.: I remembered last night. On the day we were taken, I'd given a lecture. The title was: 'Faith and logic: the continuing conflict'. The usual drivel. I talked for an hour without notes. Afterwards, the Professor who introduced me said that it was a dangerous subject 'in this day and age'. I went back to the hotel, showered, changed, and then heard a commotion in the corridor. I opened my door and that's when I came face to face with a gunman wearing a black hood. Have I told you that?

DENNIS: About the gunman, yes.

J. J.: Have I told you that twelve of us were kept in one hotel room for two days and nights in squalid conditions?

DENNIS: Yes, and that blindfold you were taken to a prison. But you didn't want to talk about the prison.
(*Silence.*)

J. J.: Old, foul-smelling, airless. Nine of us are put there to a cell. The remaining three men are given separate cells. That, we all know, is ominous because one's an American – a travel

157

agent; the second, an Israeli television producer; the third, a
Jew, a French economist. We are guarded by men and, I
think, women, whose faces we never see. To keep our spirits
up, one of my cell-mates, Jimmy Martin, a freelance
journalist from Melbourne, sings.
(*Pause; he sings softly.*)

> 'O dear, what can the matter be?
> Three old ladies locked in the lavatory,
> They were there from Monday to Saturday,
> Nobody knew they were there.'

(*Pause.*)
But that soon stopped. He was beaten. Our guards were high
on hash or coke, which of course licensed their brutality. (*He
shudders. With a puzzled look.*) I remember something from
my lecture. 'What are we to make of terror? Gangster ethics
born of a single resentment. Revenge feeding revenge.
Helplessness and rage. Continuous defeats and small
victories. How are we to understand nihilism – the dive into
nothing? How are we to understand it?'

DENNIS: I thought, from what I've seen and heard, that you
might again have found the way.
(*Silence.*)

J. J.: On the third Sunday, a strange thing occurred. We were
visited by a priest, Macnee or Magee, it was never clear. Our
captors, being themselves believers, encouraged belief in
their captives, which was oddly symmetrical.

DENNIS: (*Smiles*) Can something be oddly symmetrical?

J. J.: Perhaps not, perhaps. This priest had been inside for over
eighteen months, a prisoner of the old regime, but not freed
in the general amnesty, forgotten, weak, ill, shivering with
fever. There were six Papists among us including the
American travel agent and my cell-mate, Jimmy Martin –

DENNIS: Do you count yourself in that number?

J. J.: Yes, Father Macnee or Magee heard their confessions
through the iron bars of their cells, absolved them and gave
them the Eucharist out of a tin or enamel mug, a stale crust
on a battered plate. He recognized me. He said, 'I know
you.' And I said, 'Leave me alone. I don't want anything to

do with you.' He nodded sadly and passed on. Each Sunday thereafter he came to us but ignored me. Then, there were dreadful events. On successive days, the American, the Israeli and the French Jew were taken out and shot. When the priest next appeared I began shouting abuse at him, obscenities, as if blaming him for what had happened. I can't explain that yet.

DENNIS: Not everything can be explained.

J. J.: The more I tried to stop myself shouting, the more vehement I became.

DENNIS: What sort of things?

> (J. J. *shakes his head, refusing to speak. Silence.* DENNIS *takes the letter from his pocket.*)
> And this Father Magee died, did he?

J. J.: (*Alarmed*) What?

DENNIS: They say you were with him when he died.

J. J.: Who says? Where did you get that from? What's that got to do with anything? Who says I was with him?

DENNIS: Easy, J. J., easy –

J. J.: Easy, easy, what you are talking about? Why do you ask about Macnee out of the blue, where do you get it from?

DENNIS: Some inquiry or other, his mother wants to know about his death –

J. J.: What about his death? Is she doubting my credentials, what's it about, I was there, it was all right – ?

DENNIS: Tell me, then –

J. J.: (*Savage*) He died and they desecrated his body, that's all, easy, easy.

> (*Silence.* DENNIS *puts away the letter.*)

DENNIS: Tell me about the cage, the literal cage. (*No response.*) Is this the block? (*No response.*) Is this where memory selects? Is this the cage in which the memory is also imprisoned? (*No response.*) If the cage is literal, who put you there and why?

J. J.: (*Suddenly*) Is the local man going to come and see me?

DENNIS: No.

J. J.: Why not?

DENNIS: His bishop has forbidden him to visit this house.

J. J.: That's criminal.

DENNIS: Bishops often are.

J. J.: How long have I been back?

DENNIS: Eight days. Eight days today.

J. J.: I want to go for a walk tomorrow –

DENNIS: Yes, fine – (*Silence.*) Why did they put you in the cage?

J. J.: (*Slightly aggressive*) All right, I'll tell you, if you're so
interested, of course I'll tell you, nothing very terrible, if you
feel obliged to know –

DENNIS: Only if it's important –

J. J.: You be the judge of that, you tell me how important it is –

DENNIS: (*Smiling*) The old ways, the old days.

J. J.: The Papists.

DENNIS: Yes?

J. J.: After the third execution, after the French Jew died, our
captors stopped the priest visiting the cells.

DENNIS: Why?

J. J.: Difficult to say. The theory was that he'd been with the
American when the American was executed and they didn't
want us to learn the details, there was no rational
explanation, there never is –

DENNIS: Why the cage?

J. J.: I'm getting there, I'm getting there.

DENNIS: (*Smiling*) Dry, dead leaves.

(LOWRIE'*s face appears at a window, watching them, secretly.*)

J. J.: One of the Papists put in a request that we be allowed to
attend Mass on Sunday. There were days of negotiation. In
the end, on Sundays, we, the five remaining Papists, were
led to a tunnel, dark and low. Jimmy Martin said, 'This leads
to an arena and we're going to be eaten by lions.' But at the
end of the tunnel we found ourselves in a cage. Like in a
circus. An animal cage. Iron bars on wheels, used a long time
ago to transport criminals from place to place. And, in this
cage, we were wheeled into the prison yard.

DENNIS: The literal cage.

J. J.: Yes, yes, I said, I objected. I didn't want – I had no interest
– but my complaints were disregarded. So. On Sundays we'd
be wheeled into the prison yard and the priest would come in
tattered, stained vestments, and those of us who wanted to

attend were let out of the cage. On all but one occasion I
remained behind the bars. Shouting my abuse.

DENNIS: During his Mass?

J. J.: Oh yes, during his Mass, of course, when else? Yes, yes,
during his Mass, all right.

DENNIS: But he ignored you. (*Smiles.*) Or tried to.
(*Silence.*)

J. J.: Someone complained.

DENNIS: The priest?

J. J.: No, no, not the priest, not the priest. I must go for a walk
tomorrow –

DENNIS: Yes, yes. (*Pause.*) Who complained?

J. J.: I don't know. Never found out. But I was punished and
told not to do it again.

DENNIS: Punished how?

J. J.: I was told God is not mocked. No. God is not mocked. Help
me with my dressing –

DENNIS: No, J. J., not now – let Dr Tomelty –

J. J.: Yes, now. I want to show you –
(*He takes off his shirt, an obviously painful task. He manages to
remove the dressing.* LOWRIE *sees* J. J.*'s wound first, and recoils
from the sight.* J. J. *turns to show* DENNIS. *On his back is a
festering sore.*)
Can you see what it is?

DENNIS: (*Very calm*) No.

J. J.: It's a cross.

DENNIS: Is it? I can't tell. Did they cut that into you?

J. J.: No. They branded me.
(*He stands, showing* DENNIS *the wound on his back. Lights fade
to blackout.*)

SCENE THREE

Two days later. 4 p.m. J. J.*'s room is empty.* LOWRIE *sets up a table
and puts a tablecloth on.* OLIVER *and* ANDY *carry cushions on from
the house.* AUSTIN *enters.* DENNIS *brings on a tray of food for the
picnic.* LOWRIE *exits.*

OLIVER: (*When* LOWRIE *is out of the way*) He didn't really say we should have sociologists here, did he?

ANDY: Yes, and philosophers and logicians.

OLIVER: But sociologists. Can you think of anything more boring?

ANDY: Yes. Nuclear physicists, they're more boring. Very tiresome people, nuclear physicists.

AUSTIN: Her late Majesty the Queen of Portugal was a very tiresome person.

OLIVER: Oh, do concentrate, Austin. She's not likely to come here, is she? In the first place she's dead. In the second, we don't take old queens.

DENNIS: I'm not sure Mr Lowrie would agree.

(ANDY *laughs intensely but stops just as* LOWRIE *enters from the house with a plastic bucket. They all become faintly embarrassed. He puts down the bucket and goes back into the house.*)

OLIVER: Of course, if he said he wants us to do useful work, that, you may depend on it, was a dig at me. I make no secret of the fact that I have capital. It'd be immoral for me to work. I'd be taking a job from somebody who really needed one. But I visit prisons. That's useful. At least, to the prisoners. One hopes. And you, Dennis, nobody works harder than you. Where would we all be without you? And Andy. It can't be much fun being a nightwatchman. But it's useful. It's guarding society against criminals.

ANDY: And fires. That's my chief worry. Fires.

(LOWRIE *returns with four or five ice trays, and proceeds to empty the cubes into the plastic bucket.* DENNIS *helps him.*)

LOWRIE: And will Mr Farr be joining us?

DENNIS: I hope so.

LOWRIE: He's going for walks now, isn't he? Twice a day. I followed him.

DENNIS: I hope the exercise did you both good.

LOWRIE: You know where he goes, don't you? (*No response.*) The illness is easily identified. I call it in my book 'Waferitis'.

DENNIS: The *bon mot* as ever, Mr Lowrie. (*To* ANDY.) Time to fetch him.

(ANDY *goes round the side of the house.*)

When J. J. joins us, let's keep things jolly.
(LOWRIE *goes back into the house*.)

AUSTIN: My mother used to say that to me annually, each
birthday, just as the guests were about to arrive. 'Austin-
dear,' she'd say, 'you mustn't mind if the other children play
with the presents they bring you. We must keep things jolly.'
It always ended in tears, but never mine.
(ANDY *escorts* J. J. *into the courtyard. He seems more rested*.)

J. J.: When I was in captivity, the heat was unbearable and I used
to daydream about the English weather, longing for grey
skies, and scattered showers. Instead I come back into a
heatwave. Typical.

DENNIS: Here's your chair, J. J. –

OLIVER: Don't you look well, J. J.?

ANDY: Dr Tomelty gives him his pills lying down, that's why –
(*Uneasy silence*.)

AUSTIN: Did I ever tell you my story about the pearls and the
Queen of Portugal, J. J.?

OLIVER: Of course you did, dozens of times.
(*Pause*.)

AUSTIN: The Queen of Portugal was on a private visit to London.
After attending Mass, she invited me to have breakfast with
members of her household and some female friends. At
Claridges. In her suite. I was the only male present and,
therefore, seated on the Queen's right. Presently she turned
to me and said, 'Isn't it terrible, Monsignor, how standards
have declined? I've looked around this table,' she said, 'and I
see only four gals wearing real pearls.' 'Forgive me, ma'am,'
I replied – (*He unbuttons his shirt to show that he is wearing a
string of pearls*.) – 'five.'
(LOWRIE *returns with three or four bottles of hock, which he
puts in the plastic bucket*.)

DENNIS: The wine's on, Oliver.
(*Murmurs of thanks.* LOWRIE *pulls the first cork to cheers*.)

ANDY: Festivities are about to commence.

OLIVER: And, Andy, don't drink too much. You know it makes
you weep.

DENNIS: Tuck in. Mr Lowrie will do the wine. I'll do J. J.

(*They all help themselves.* DENNIS *brings a plate to* J. J.)

OLIVER: What fun this is. Isn't this fun?

ANDY: (*About to eat*) *Benedic, Domine, nos et haec tua dona quae de tua largitate sumus sumpturi. Per Christum Dominum nostrum.*

(*He crosses himself.* J. J. *puts a hand to his forehead as though beginning the sign the cross, but lets it rest there. Then all, except* J. J., *begin to eat in silence.*)

J. J.: Did I tell you, Andy, we used to sing dirty songs in the prison? (*He hums the tune of 'Three Old Ladies'.*) But I've forgotten the words –

ANDY: (*Singing*) 'Oh dear, what can the matter be?
   Three old ladies locked in a lavatory –
(J. J. *begins to cry silently.*)

DENNIS: All right, Andy, not now –
(ANDY *suddenly moves round to* J. J.)

ANDY: J. J., old chap, dear old chap, I don't know the details, but I can guess. I don't envy you. I wouldn't have survived as you've survived. A chap doesn't expect to travel the Damascus road twice in a lifetime. I can't remember what faith was like, it was so long ago. And I was always a fallen angel. I've only really thought about one thing all my life. And what's it matter? It may all soon be over at any moment for all of us. (*He looks skyward.*) Now. Now. What price *Pacem in terris*? No good watching for fires, then. The fire will be too big. It can happen at any moment. Now. Now. When that chap wrote 'the horror! the horror!' he was still sucking at his mother's nipples.

J. J.: It's unbearably hot, I'm burning –

OLIVER: Really, Andy, what's the point of giving you a party if you're going to be so depressing?
(J. J. *mops sweat from his face.*)

ANDY: Dear J. J., dear old chap, you seem to have walked through unwanted fire back into the sun. And that's an unenviable thing.
(*Silence.*)

OLIVER: (*Almost a sigh*) Yes, yes, yes, yes, yes.
(DENNIS *starts a round of 'Happy Birthday'. Silence.* LOWRIE

watches J. J.*and comes near to him, calculating, determined.*)

LOWRIE: There's something I've been longing to ask you, Mr Farr –

J. J.: Yes?

LOWRIE: It's about this change of mind or heart you seem to have suffered.

DENNIS: No, Mr Lowrie, not now, this is meant to be Andy's party.

LOWRIE: (*Overlapping*) Is that what the doctors meant when they said – (*In the clear.*) – you'd suffered a reversion?

J. J.: We are what we have always been.

AUSTIN: (*Trying to lighten the atmosphere*) Oh, good, J. J., you must be on the mend. I've been waiting for one of your little aphorisms. I've always enjoyed your lecturettes on logic and rationality. They seemed to me quite as absurd as anything else. But there's a puzzle I want to put to you about television –

LOWRIE: Hold on a minute, what did you mean, Mr Farr? We are what we've always been?

DENNIS: Go on about television, Austin –

LOWRIE: No. I'd like to hear what Mr Farr has to say. That's a provocative statement, we are what we've always been. Did you mean that in a general sense, or were you being specific, about us?

J. J.: Specific. About you, about me, about all of us here.

LOWRIE: Then we're entitled to an explanation –

DENNIS: No, we're not, Mr Lowrie –

LOWRIE: Stop protecting him, Warden. Let's hear what he has to say. He's vocal enough at night, keeping us all awake –

DENNIS: Mr Lowrie, I forbid this –

LOWRIE: Why do you shout out, Mr Farr? Why do you talk in code?

J. J.: What d'you mean, code? I don't shout out –

LOWRIE: Oh yes, you do. The messages are in code but we don't have the key, only you have the key –

OLIVER: Isn't it time for J. J.'s rest?

LOWRIE: No, it isn't time for his rest, he's only just joined us –

OLIVER: Another time, then, another time –

LOWRIE: *Hic est*, abracadabra, we have blood, what's it about, Mr Farr?

J. J.: Where did you hear this?

LOWRIE: That's not wine, that's urine –

J. J.: Where do you hear these things?

LOWRIE: From you, crying out at night, crying out for help –

J. J.: When, when, when do I cry out?

ANDY: I don't hear you, J. J., I'm at work –

LOWRIE: We hear you, we hear you –

OLIVER: Yes, we hear him, but what's it matter, not now, please not now –

LOWRIE: (*Overlapping*) Wine, urine, blood, you keep us awake at night –

J. J.: I'm drugged, I don't know what I' saying. I'm drugged –

LOWRIE: He wants a priest –

J. J.: What?

LOWRIE: Charlatan –

J. J.: I was in the cage –

LOWRIE: Open the cage, open the cage, *hic est*, hey presto –

J. J.: I don't want to hear –

LOWRIE: Who's Father Macnee?

J. J.: Magee –

LOWRIE: Magee, Macnee, who is he – ?

J. J.: A priest –

DENNIS: This must stop –

LOWRIE: *Allahu Akbar* –

J. J.: No, no. That was later, later –

LOWRIE: Hey presto –

J. J.: No, no –

LOWRIE: *Ce n'est pas nécessaire* –

J. J.: (*Involuntarily*) *Il est mort* –

LOWRIE: *Hic est* –

J. J.: *Hoc est* –

LOWRIE: Hey presto –

J. J.: We have blood –

LOWRIE: Charlatan –

J. J.: Abracadabra –

LOWRIE: He wants a priest –

J. J.: I'll come, I'll come –

LOWRIE: Tell us, Mr Farr –

J. J.: (*A cry*) What would *you* have done?

LOWRIE: About what? About whom?

J. J.: About Father Magee.

LOWRIE: Tell us about Father Magee –

J. J.: He wants a priest –

LOWRIE: Who wants a priest – ?

J. J.: No, no no, *once* a priest –

LOWRIE: Did you say wants a priest or once a priest?

J. J.: Dennis, Dennis –

   (DENNIS *goes to him.*)

   – once a priest –

DENNIS: Yes, yes, I know –

LOWRIE: Once a priest, he said once a priest –

DENNIS: Let me take you to your room –

LOWRIE: Were you called on to act as a priest? Is that it, is that it –? Were you called on to act as a priest?

J. J.: Yes, yes, yes, I left the cage – and was a priest again – a priest – (*Turning on* LOWRIE.) What would have you done? (*He weeps, all defences gone; sobbing.*) What would you have done?

AUSTIN: (*After a moment; distressed*) Yes, weep. J. J., weep for all of us here. What would we have done? It could happen to any of us. The nightmare. To be called on. How would we have answered? How would you have answered, Mr Lowrie, once a priest?

LOWRIE: I'd have stayed in the cage. That's what Mr Farr should have done. Stayed in the cage. Where he belongs.

   (*He goes.*)

ANDY: At least our Mr Lowrie's not a hypocrite.

   (J. J. *weeps. Lights fade to blackout.*)

ACT TWO

SCENE ONE

Two days later. Dusk. In the courtyard, DENNIS, ANDY, OLIVER *and* AUSTIN *are grouped around* J. J. *in silence. They are waiting. Then* LOWRIE *emerges from the house.* DENNIS *indicates somewhere for him to sit, but he prefers to be apart from the others, and hardly looks at* J. J. *when they are settled:*

J. J.: A Sunday, the eighteenth of our captivity. The hundred and thirtieth day. In the eye of the sun, the heat of a blowtorch. Father Magee appears. Emaciated and threadbare. Like his vestments. This was after my punishment. After they branded the cross on my back for shouting abuse during Mass. But I still keep up my derision, mumbling my insults, eyes closed. They think I'm praying now. 'Charlatan, abracadabra, *hic est, hoc est*, hey presto, we have blood.' Here's the scene. Blinding heat. Prison yard. Five of us in a cage. A hooded guard, armed, high on hash, dangerous. Enter the priest. *Et introibo ad altare Dei*. He carries a tin mug and an enamel plate he uses as chalice and paten. Only one of our number asks to be let out that day. My cell-mate, Jimmy Martin. Out he goes, kneels before Magee. From me, a constant mumbled commentary. 'Get it right, Father, strike your breast, *Domine, non sum dignus*, what, no bells?' And so on and so forth. Quietly, cowardly, until whatever he was using for wine and bread are placed under the magic spell. The priest crosses himself with the tin mug. *Sanguis Domini Nostri*. At this precise moment, he collapses, struggling not to spill the contents of his makeshift chalice. Somehow, Jimmy manages to get hold of it as the priest falls. The guard sniggers. Jimmy places the mug on the priest's chest and leans close to hear him. Minutes pass. Then, Jimmy hurries to the cage. Someone asks, 'Is he dead?' 'No,' Jimmy says, 'but near. His mind's wandering.' 'Listen,' says Jimmy, 'I'm going to say something now, something he's asked me to say. I'm just going to say it because it's what he asked. He wants a priest. I told him there wasn't one here. He was the only priest. But he said to say, "Once a priest, always a priest," and one of you would come.' 'So. I'm going to say it,' says Jimmy. ' "Once a priest, always a priest." ' And so from me: 'All right. I'll come.' I call to the guard, *'Mon frère, ouvrez la porte. Je veux aider le prêtre.'* He lets me out. He sniggers again. I go to Father Liam Magee, who lies dying in the prison yard. 'Thank you,' he says, 'I knew you'd come. Hear my confession.' I say, 'You've nothing to confess, you're a good man.' But he begs me. I take his worn, grease-stained stole and put it round my neck. I do what's required of me. When I come to give him the sacrament I find the chalice empty. The contents must have spilled in his fall. He reaches under his cassock, into his soiled underpants and produces a small phial of yellowish liquid. 'Please, please,' he says. I take the phial and empty the contents into the tin mug. He hands me his missal. I consecrate the yellow liquid and, as I finish, the priest dies. Jimmy, witness to all this, asks the question, 'What do we do with the consecrated wine?' 'It's urine,' I say. 'It's white wine,' he says, 'and you consecrated it.' I say, 'If you believe it's now blood, drink it.' I turn to the guard. *'Le prêtre est mort.'* The guard laughs crookedly, then raises his gun, takes aim at the priest's body and fires. The shot goes wild. Jimmy says, 'He's trying to hit the chalice.' So, I call to the guard, *'Ce n'est pas nécessaire. Il est mort. Je veux rentrer dans la cage.'* But he fires again in the direction of the corpse. And then, coolly, detached, ice in a blast-furnace, I walk back to the body, take the mug and gulp the contents. The guard cracks me with the back of his hand across my face. I bleed from the nose and taste my own blood. He puts Jimmy and me back in the cage and locks us in. He fires a couple of shots into the priest's corpse. From somewhere far off, the muezzin begins calling the faithful to prayer: *'Allahu Akbar, Allahu*

Akbar.' God is greater. There is no God but God.
(*Silence.*)

ANDY: I would have done what you did, J. J.

OLIVER: Yes, yes, I suppose so, perhaps I would. I don't know, I
don't know.

AUSTIN: There was no choice.

LOWRIE: What about the Warden?

DENNIS: (*Smiles*) You know me. Anything to oblige.

LOWRIE: You all belong in small rooms with rubber walls.

AUSTIN: With rubber what?

LOWRIE: Walls, walls, padded cells –

ANDY: Why?

LOWRIE: What you've described, Mr Farr, this so-called
rediscovery of faith and priesthood is, well, the word that
springs most trippingly to the tongue, is 'grotesque'.

DENNIS: Take no notice, J. J., he does it to provoke.

LOWRIE: Still protecting him, are you. Warden? Still afraid I
might damage your penitent, I mean, patient?

J. J.: Why do you talk about me as if I weren't here?

LOWRIE: It goes deep, the withdrawal, the fantasy. I know very
well where you are, and I'll fight you on your own ground.

DENNIS: Don't rise, J. J. It's a game.

LOWRIE: Yes, yes, all right, a game, let's play a game.

OLIVER: Must we turn everything into a game? Serious issues
have been raised. Oh, don't let's turn it into a game.

AUSTIN: The English turn everything into a game. Their excuse
is that anything enjoyable is more salutary than anything
salutary. It's absurd, of course, but then it's English. It's the
pride they take in their lumpy scepticism.

LOWRIE: Aren't you English?

AUSTIN: I? Of course. My scepticism is lumpier than most.

J. J.: (*To* LOWRIE) I'll play your game.
(*He covers his eyes with one hand.*)

LOWRIE: Calling for reinforcements? Bringing up the big guns?
Asking for guidance from GHQ?
(J. J. *looks at him.*)
Right. (*To* AUSTIN.) Mr – I'm sorry. I don't remember
your name –

AUSTIN: Purvis –

LOWRIE: What is the opening sentence of *Seeing, Not Believing* by J. J. Farr?

AUSTIN: 'In the dying years of the present century, no reasonable person can be reasonable and religious.'

LOWRIE: (*To* J. J.) Your words.

J. J.: Yes.

LOWRIE: Are we then to understand that you are now no longer a reasonable person?
(*Groans from the others.*)

ANDY: Unfair. That was written ages ago. He's somebody else now.

AUSTIN: Quite. You have to forgive him, Mr – You see, J. J.'s an intellectual. He's allowed to change his mind.

J. J.: Until the eighteenth Sunday of my captivity, I'd never before had a direct experience of – (*He can't find the words.*) Neither as layman nor as priest. I followed a course expected of me. But on that Sunday, in the prison yard, I faced – I met – (*He falters.*)

LOWRIE: Go on, say it: 'God'.

J. J.: God, then.
(*The light is fading fast now.*)

LOWRIE: You say you met God. And you want me to take your word for that. Well, there's a difficulty here. Because for some curious reason your god doesn't allow all his creatures to meet him. So, I'm afraid, Mr Farr, you're going to have to prove him more conclusively. Prove this god who revealed himself to you, then we may be able to accept your experience of him. Prove your creator of space and time, existing beyond both.
(*Again the others groan.*)

DENNIS: Come Mr Lowrie, you have to do better than this. You're dealing with old pros here. We all know there's no satisfactory proof of God. If it were otherwise, we none of us would be in this house. We would still be priests.

LOWRIE: Right. And, as it's impossible to prove He exists, it's also impossible to accept any experience of Him. Therefore, He does not exist –

OLIVER: May not exist, surely, may not, there's the hell of it, may not –

LOWRIE: All right, may not exist and, therefore, any experience of something that may or may not exist, may or may not be a lump of shit.

ANDY: Disprove God.

OLIVER: Good, good, Andy, that's my point. That's impossible too, isn't it, Mr Lowrie? There's doubt for you –

LOWRIE: (*Quite unruffled*) All right. Proof or no proof, surely Mr Farr's beliefs ought still to be reasonable. Because if they're unreasonable, they're total gibberish. We can test it. Let's test your creed, Mr Farr. You would now say, presumably, that you believe in one god who may or may not exist, the maker of heaven and earth – just consider these words – the maker of heaven and earth and of all things visible *and* invisible. The maker of invisible things? It's gibberish. You may as well say you believe in haberlacky domotribble transcombasculation.

AUSTIN: I couldn't follow that –

DENNIS: You weren't meant to –

LOWRIE: Gibberish, mumbo-jumbo. Like your story, Mr Farr. These words. Cage. Was there a cage? Or are you describing an inner state? Priest. Was there a priest? Or were you projecting a fantasy of your own past? Tin chalice, the eye of the sun, *Allahu Akbar*, the grease-stained stole, *le prêtre est mort*. Jumbled fragments of mounting hysteria. I'll tell you what happened during your captivity. You grew fearful of death, of eternal nothingness. You were terrified of dying.

ANDY: Not true. You said you'd test his creed but you stopped short. 'I believe in the Resurrection of the Dead and the Life of the World to come.'

LOWRIE: Resurrection? What's that if it isn't an opiate to counter the fear of death? Death shall be conquered, et cetera, et cetera. Why should death need to be conquered if it isn't fearful? Why not just let it be?

ANDY: (*Edgy*) He's secure. You are floundering.

(J. J. *has been, and is, alert during all this. The arguments buzz round him, over him, through him.*)

172

LOWRIE: Secure in what? In the life hereafter? Do you honestly
   believe that in the dying years of the present century it's
   possible for a reasonable being to believe in a life after death?
   Take a sampling, any section of the population you like, at
   random. Walk into any university and ask, 'Do you believe
   in life after death?' Ask surgeons gathered around the
   operating table, looking into the blood and mess of human
   beings. 'Do you believe that if your patient dies he or she will
   enjoy a life hereafter?' Ask lawyers, teachers, men of
   business, artists. Ask a biologist if he has evidence of life
   beyond the grave. Stop people in the street and you know
   very well what their answer will be. We all know, the rational
   side of us knows, what the answer must be.
OLIVER: That's very naughty of you, Mr Lowrie. When I was
   being trained that's what my moral tutor would have called
   'gross generalization'. Surely there will be individuals,
   doctors, lawyers –
ANDY: Sociologists –
OLIVER: Yes, even sociologists, scientists and, most obvious of
   all, people in the street. Individuals, Mr Lowrie, who will
   say they expect life after death.
LOWRIE: The most extreme form of wishful thinking known to
   the human animal. Lip-service, historical excreta heaped on
   us, generation after generation, humbug and hypocrisy,
   endless, untreated shit.
   (*Darkness*.)
AUSTIN: I should like to say something. Will you, Mr Lowrie,
   permit an old man to ask why you, who make so much of
   reason, should argue so unreasonably?
DENNIS: It's his game, Austin –
AUSTIN: Game or not, it's very disagreeable. Weren't you ever
   taught at school or university or at your seminary that
   argument is best when devoid of abuse? Argument in a
   civilized world must be polite, reasoned and rational,
   otherwise chaos results.
LOWRIE: Yes, yes, yes, in your old-fashioned, ideal, embroidered
   world, yes. But these things matter to me. It's all that
   matters to me. The unmasking of the lies.

173

AUSTIN: Stop lecturing and hectoring –

   (DENNIS *turns up the light over the door to the house, and to*
   J. J.*'s room.*)

LOWRIE: And do you know what breeds the lies? Fear, fear of
   death. That's what Mr Farr experienced, and that's what
   holds him hostage, nothing else.

ANDY: Is that what being alive feels like to you? Like a hostage
   taken at random? Is that how existence seems to you?
   Violent, cruel, without reason? Is that how you've come to
   view your own life?

LOWRIE: Don't turn this on me, it's him we're talking about.

ANDY: I begin to see. To you life corresponds exactly to his
   experience in that prison, in that cage. Meaningless, an
   animal existence, devoid of purpose and spirit.

LOWRIE: Any other interpretation in the dying years of the
   present century and in the light of modern scientific
   knowledge would be fanciful.

DENNIS: Science, science, the new religion, the old religion. You
   allow scientists to ask, 'How did this or that come about?
   Why does this or that occur?' After all, science itself thrives
   on the questions 'how' and 'why'. Only when J. J. – and
   others – ask, 'How does it come about that we exist or why
   should we be here at all? only then do you say, 'There is no
   answer.' In every other aspect of life we search for reasons
   why things occur, so to ask the ultimate questions about
   existence is nothing more than the most logical, reasonable
   thing we could do. Aristotle said we look for reasons why
   things exist because they are not self-explanatory. He said
   that everything in motion must be moved by something else,
   that everything in the world is motivated by some inner
   energy to become something greater than it is. Going
   backwards, man grows out of the child, the child from the
   embryo, the embryo from the ovum, and so on, and so on,
   and so on, until what? *Primum mobile immotum,* a prime
   mover unmoved, incorporeal, indivisible, spaceless, sexless,
   passionless, changeless, perfect, eternal. God. Science
   encourages us to seek ultimate explanations which,
   incidentally, it is itself unable to provide. You allow it in

science, but not, as it were, in life. (*Smiles*.) I take no view, you understand, I simply make the point.

LOWRIE: But why should there be an ultimate explanation of the universe? Why should we assume anything at all? Science obliterates Aristotle. Facts, verifiable facts, that's what I'm interested in. These are the facts: the world has no purpose, no inherent spiritual power, no beauty, no morality, no rationale. Those are all interpretation. We are cogs in a mechanical process. Facts. The universe is a result of accident. There is no ultimate explanation. No one has, or had, or ever will have, immortality. Nature is purposeless. Facts. We live, we endure, we die.

OLIVER: But that's also a set of beliefs, isn't it? Weren't we taught that? I do believe we were. You can't prove your set of beliefs either.

DENNIS: You want facts and logic and reason. Faith, absolute faith in a creator, with all its spiritual implications, is not something that needs to be proved or disproved. Surely they taught you that in your seminary. That's what they taught me. Faith is something beyond dispute. You either have it or you don't. Faith is. Or is not.

AUSTIN: That's very good, Dennis. No help whatsoever, but very good.

OLIVER: And what about the poor people who took J. J. hostage? There's no point in saying to the terrorists, prove your faith. They have faith and believe it to be the only faith, their cause the only cause. That's a question of their belief, isn't it, a matter of fact, not open to argument? In Dennis's sense, their faith is beyond dispute. Am I right? Andy, am I right?

ANDY: But that's Mr Lowrie's position, too. I said you saw your life as hostage to misfortune but I was wrong. You are at the other end of the telescope. You're not the hostage, you're the terrorist. The man with the gun who imprisons all opposing thought in a damp, crowded cell. You believe your interpretation is the only interpretation. But if it's facts you're after, Mr Lowrie, then you had better come to terms with the fact of J. J.'s experience –

LOWRIE: His experience is a series of random events initiated by

madmen which in turn made him mad. A mosaic of which he
remembers only the most striking shapes and the most
glaring colours. The prison cell, the tunnel that leads to the
Roman arena, the branding of a cross on his back, the priest
dying in his arms. The shapes and colours not of faith but of
fear. And 'All faith in the supernatural is a neurotic device to
deaden the fear of death.'

ANDY: You're deaf, you don't hear him, it wasn't any of those
things, certainly not the dying priest or the torture or the
pain. It wasn't fear of his own death –

LOWRIE: What, then?

J. J.: It was taking God, or piss, into my mouth.
(*Silence. Exasperated,* LOWRIE *suddenly storms back into the
house.*)

AUSTIN: Anyone else being bitten to death?
(*He exits.*)

OLIVER: Time for bed.
(*He exits.*)

DENNIS: I think we could have done without that, J. J.
(*He exits,* J. J. *covers his face with his hands. Slowly,
deliberately,* ANDY *places a chair at the odd angle, sideways on
to* J. J. ANDY *sits. He doesn't face* J. J. *but* J. J. *faces him.
Silence.* ANDY *quietly hums 'Three Old Ladies'.* J. J. *lowers his
hands,* ANDY *smiles.*)

ANDY: I'm here, J. J. I won't look at you. I won't say a word.

J. J.: (*Searching*) Yes, word, word, words. Words won't stretch.
Words fall short – go so far and disintegrate. Before the
word, before the beginning, there has to be a death, I think,
then sleep, and the – dream, and the waking – inside the
dream – even birth is not the word. It's a kind of coming into
being, isn't it, a kind of intuition of being? Here, then, now,
there. I want to use the word union, but that's misleading.
There was a union certainly, no doubt of that, I and – this –
this – No, no, not light, but light of a sort – two selves – one
so low as to be worthless, but knowing itself to be the other –
higher – nameless –
(ANDY *slowly turns to look at him.*)
Simply. This may be something. Peacefulness because there

was no connection with time. The terrorists worship time, the past and the future and so they persecute and make wars. It's dark but radiantly clear. There is no – separateness of anything – it's beyond understanding. I was able to hear the softest sounds loudly, see a distant point as though to touch it. And it was *in* me. In me. In my mouth, my gullet, my intestine, my bowels. And there were beautiful things, too. The making of beds and the cleaning of the cell and eating the dry, glutinous rice. It didn't matter what happened to me then. I was free. And it was in me. Outside me. Nameless. (*Silence.* ANDY *rises quickly.*)

ANDY: (*Hurrying away*) And I'll be late for work –
(*And as he goes, lights fade to blackout.*)

SCENE TWO

Later that evening. 10 p.m. *In his room,* J. J. *is eating from a tray: a simple meal of yoghurt and an orange. His concentration on each mouthful is absolute.*

In the courtyard, a stab of torchlight as DENNIS *enters from around the side of the house. As* DENNIS *turns,* LOWRIE *comes out of the house. He carries a carrier bag with something in it. He is crossing towards* J. J.*'s room when he sees* DENNIS. *He hides the carrier bag behind his back and stops.*

DENNIS: Taking the air, Mr Lowrie?

LOWRIE: (*Slight hesitation*) No – I – I thought I left a book out here – I'm working – I need – I –

DENNIS: I don't know how you can work in this weather. Clammy, like Rome in midsummer.

LOWRIE: Rain's forecast.
(*He goes back into the house.*)

DENNIS: Is it? (*He goes to* J. J.*'s door, knocks once and opens it.*) Sorry to disturb you, J. J., but you won't forget to lock this door, will you?
(J. J. *is barely aware of him. He continues to eat.* DENNIS *checks the windows. As he does so there is a knock on* J. J.*'s inner door.*)

J. J.: Yes?

(LOWRIE, *with the carrier bag hidden behind his back, enters* J. J.'s *room*.)

LOWRIE: I'd like to see you, but if it's not convenient –

J. J.: Sit. I won't be a moment.

    (J. J. *finishes eating.* LOWRIE *surreptitiously places the carrier bag near the foot of the bed so that* J. J. *can't see it.* DENNIS *exits, going on his rounds. When* J. J. *finishes, he turns to* LOWRIE *and gazes at him.* LOWRIE *becomes uncomfortable.*)

LOWRIE: I've come to apologize.

J. J.: No need.

    (LOWRIE *laughs nervously. Pause.* LOWRIE's *manner is now, for the most part, conciliatory: he is up to something.*)

LOWRIE: (*A sort of smile*) I can't explain why I become so obnoxious. It's a kind of showing-off. I think it's because I need to demonstrate my sincerity. Adolescent, really. I'm sorry.

J. J.: Nothing wrong with that.

    (*He smiles.*)

LOWRIE: I need to demonstrate my absolute freedom from faith. You see, my priesthood became fraudulent.

J. J.: Tell me.

LOWRIE: Basic stuff. Instead of feet, I saw hooves. Instead of hands, claws. People, a herd. Music, an algebraic formula, poetry, the accident of alphabet. And all the glory of the world a misunderstanding by a self-regarding species. (*Smiles.*) The animal kingdom. Not uncommon, I believe.

J. J.: Was it sudden – ?

LOWRIE: Not sudden, no, intermittent. Nightmares at first. Then, in waking hours, mental skirmishes, raids on my consciousness. For example, when I tried to pray. Or during Mass. Then, more and more frequently. Until it was unbearable.

J. J.: What did you do?

LOWRIE: I cut my wrists. (*He shows the scars; again the smile.*) You see, I know all about cries for help.

J. J.: And were your cries answered?

LOWRIE: Yes. By you, for one.

J. J.: Me?

LOWRIE: Your books. While I was recovering, I began to read you. When you dismantled God, you gave me the confidence I needed. That seemed to be important then, while I was still a priest. I was a convert, you see. I've always been a convert.

J. J.: But I left room for doubt.

LOWRIE: I didn't see that at the time.

J. J.: What did you do?

LOWRIE: I had to find a way of earning my living again. Most of all, I wanted to continue my studies. I'd read psychology before becoming a priest and needed to bring myself up to date. And then, I wanted to write a book. I found a publisher. He gave me a small advance. I studied and wrote by day. At night I worked in a bakery. It was a kind of nether world. I'd use the word purgatory in its true sense. The book was published. It was well reviewed –

J. J.: By me, you said –

LOWRIE: Yes, by you. Among others. Then my bishop asked to see me, to discuss my future. He advised me to take time to reflect on what I was doing. I resisted, of course, but then he suggested this house. 'A place to hang up your collar for a while,' he said. And when I learned that you lived here, I decided it was where I wanted to be.

J. J.: You must be disappointed.

LOWRIE: It's also why I want to help you. I owe you a debt. You showed me the way to truth.

J. J.: But the ground's shifted, hasn't it? Hasn't it?

LOWRIE: I want to help you, Mr Farr –

J. J.: I know –

LOWRIE: (*Flaring*) Don't mock me.

J. J.: I don't. Believe me. I know you have this need –

LOWRIE: You say – you say now – that you left room for doubt, a safety-net, a silver-plated agnosticism engraved with your initials. Give me the benefit then, of viewing your present state in exactly the same half-light. Allow yourself room for doubt now.

J. J.: I'll allow anything.
(*Pause.*)

LOWRIE: I'm going to be blunt. You don't have to be a trained

179

psychologist to know that what happened to you was a
psychotic transference –

J. J.: You may well be right –

LOWRIE: – the moment of revelation, the comfort you gave a
dying man –

J. J.: Yes, yes, odd thing, the psyche –

LOWRIE: That was the moment, wasn't it? The priest dying in
your arms, and you became that priest? Shaman. Witch
doctor. Tragic hero and intermediary.

J. J.: I think you've got the wrong man. These words, you see.
Not sure about these words –

LOWRIE: No, no, listen to me. I don't deny that you were put
through a savage, horrifying ordeal. As a result of this
admittedly intense experience, in which you are obliged to
revert to your priestly function, you now claim to have
regained faith in a god in whom you once said it was
impossible to believe. I am asking you to question the
validity of your experience. In the face of irrational forces
you ran for shelter. Now, when was your life most sheltered
and most ordered? When were you most respected,
unquestioned? In your priestly habit. What you describe is a
classic pattern, a retreat into familiar territory, an escape to
safety. All I ask is that you admit this possibility and seek
treatment. What can you lose? At best it will save you pain,
unhappiness and despair.

J. J.: Shall I tell you what it feels like? It's as though you insist on
talking about someone who isn't here. But here I am. I know
it's hard to grasp – I was there – now I'm here – being taken
hostage, being branded, the communion – everything, had
one meaning then – but not –

LOWRIE: Well, now, I was waiting for that word. Meaning. The
god-tyrant directing our lives in ways too complex for us to
comprehend. Was there also meaning for those who were
taken out and shot?

J. J.: Yes, if you believe that death isn't an end. No, if you
believe that death is the worst thing that can happen.

LOWRIE: I do believe that, that's precisely what I do believe.

J. J.: But what difference does death make?

LOWRIE: What?

J. J.: Fear of death may be your prison.

LOWRIE: Don't turn it on me. I know how the priestly mind
works. You believe there was meaning in what happened to
you. Don't you? Don't you? You think the whole bloody
event was organized by your god to bring you back into the
priesthood. You think that the murder of three innocent
men was simply part of some divine plan for the salvation of
J. J. Farr.

J. J.: I don't know the meaning for them, I don't know the
meaning for me –

LOWRIE: There was no meaning –

J. J.: You may well be right –

LOWRIE: – not for you, not for the dead. What was the purpose
of their being taken out and shot? Are they now looking
down on you, cheering you on, rejoicing in their
martyrdom, is that what you believe – ?
(*Silence.*)

J. J.: The nights are drawing in.

LOWRIE: What?

J. J.: Can't you smell it? The slightest chill. The day's gone. Or
going. The earth's a good stand-by. It's our one sure
footing.

LOWRIE: You see? You avoid answering. You won't face what's
happened. You're ill.

J. J.: (*Vigorous; pointing at the orange on the tray.*) Look – look –
(*Touches the orange.*) touch – (*Sniffs it.*) smell – (*Places the
orange in* LOWRIE'*s hand.*) feel. How can I – ? What can I
– ? (*He begins to remove his shirt.*) Take off the dressing. Go
on, go on. Put your hand on the scar, don't say anything,
just feel this cross –
(LOWRIE *doesn't move.* J. J. *manages to remove the dressing.*
LOWRIE *gazes at the scar.*)
Feel it.

LOWRIE: But that's not a cross, it's a crescent moon.
(J. J. *looks at him in disbelief, twists and turns in an effort to
see the scar, then goes into the bathroom. After a second, his
laughter can be heard.* LOWRIE *picks up the carrier bag and*

takes from it a bottle of wine and a corkscrew. He opens the wine.
J. J. *becomes aware of what he is doing.*)
(*Calling to* J. J.) I'm going to help you whether you want to be helped or not.
(J. J. *returns.*)
God didn't mark you, terrorists marked you. The sign you were given was not the one you wanted. And when you say you took God into your mouth, you took urine.

J. J.: Urine, wine, sand, blood, God, stuff, of my own making –

LOWRIE: (*Jumping on it*) Of your own making, precisely. Could it be of my making, then, since I, Kenneth Lowrie, duly ordained a Catholic priest, who saw faith as a sham, who tried to take his own life, who knows, as a rational human being, that there is no god, that there is no life after death, still have the same magical power as you have to transform wine into the blood of your Lord, Jesus Christ?

J. J.: Is it important?

LOWRIE: I know a believer when I see one.
(*From his back pocket* LOWRIE *takes a small missal and opens it. He places the bottle of wine on the table and proceeds to consecrate it.*)

J. J.: What are you doing?

LOWRIE: Latin for you, I think, Father. (*Reading from the missal.*)
Simili modo postquam coenatum est –

J. J.: Don't – don't – please – don't do that –

LOWRIE: (*Continues*) – *accipiens et hunc praeclarum Calicem in sanctas ac venerabiles* –

J. J.: Stop. Stop, for your own sake –
(*He seems about to go for* LOWRIE *but turns away.*)

LOWRIE: (*Continues*) – *manus suas: item tibi gratias agens, bene* –
(*He makes the signs of the cross over the bottle of wine.*) – *dixit, deditque discipulis suis, dicens: Accipite, et bibite ex eo omnes. Hic est emin calix sanguinis mei, novi et aeterni testamenti: mysterium fidei: qui pro vobis et pro multis effundetur in remissionem peccatorum.* (*He genuflects.*) *Haec quotiescumque feceritis, in mei memoriam facietis.* (*Silence.*) Is that now the blood of Jesus Christ? If so, what shall we do with it?
(*He holds up the bottle.*

Stillness.
Very deliberately, slowly, J. J. *takes the bottle from* LOWRIE *and pours some of the wine on the carpet.* LOWRIE *recoils, shocked. Then* J. J. *begins to swig from the bottle.*)
(*Involuntarily.*) You've been eating, you should have made yourself sick.

J. J.: (*Swigging*) I'l be sick, I'll be sick –
(J. J. *starts to sway, continuing to drink. He finishes the bottle.*)

LOWRIE: There's some on the floor, you spilled some on the floor –
(J. J. *drops to his knees and starts to lick the floor.*)
(*Barely audible.*) You're insane – look, look at you, you're licking wine stains from the carpet – stop it, stop it –

J. J.: (*Almost unable to rise*) Oh my God –

LOWRIE: There was no intention – it can't be valid – how can it be anything but wine?
(J. J. *tries to stand.*)

J. J.: Did you say, was there – did you – *in vaetam aeternam – Amen, amen,* let me see your hands – let me – you're not a priest, you're an alchemist –
(*He lunges clumsily towards* LOWRIE.)

LOWRIE: Don't touch me –

J. J.: – and you're not the first. A bishop told me that once, while paddling at Blackpool, he held out his hands over the waves and consecrated the Irish Sea. And this madman now believes whenever it rains the earth is being drenched in God's blood. But every millimetre of sea and land, every leaf and pebble was consecrated long before that, before him, before you, before me, before let there be light. You think it needs you to do it, but it doesn't, it's been done. So let's drink to that, let's drink this wine, let's have a party, let's be drunk –

LOWRIE: You need treatment –

J. J.: (*Overlapping*) – the heat –
(*He makes for the door and staggers out into the courtyard.* LOWRIE *comes to the door and watches him gasping for breath.*)
The world is spinning – I am – I am – extremely – I have –
(*Triumphant.*) I have seen a new heaven and a new earth –

(*Shouting.*) Hic est – hoc est – Allahu Akbar – (*He falls to the ground. Shouting.*) Charlatan. (*Then, quietly.*) I see three of you. (*Laughs.*) Don't tell the Warden –

(LOWRIE *goes.* J. J. *sits grinning.*)

Good old Jimmy Martin. I remember the naughty verses –

'The first lady's name was Elizabeth Porter,
She was the Bishop of Chichester's daughter,
There on account of some overdue water,
Brought on by a half-pint of beer.'

(*A spill of light from the house.*)

'The second lady's name was Dorothy Humphrey,
She sat down but then could not get her bum free,
She said, "Never mind, for I'm perfectly comfy,
Nobody knows that I'm here."'

(DENNIS, *trying the cord of his dressing-gown, comes out from the house and goes to* J. J. *He draws back at the smell of wine on* J. J.'s *breath.*)

'The third lady's name was Virginia Wender,
There on account of a stocking suspender,
Caught in the hair of her feminine gender,
A terribly painful affair.'

(*Near to passing out.*) A terribly painful affair –

(*He falls back, moans, and begins to retch violently.* DENNIS *goes to him. Lights fade to blackout.*)

SCENE THREE

Eight hours later. Just before 7 a.m. In the courtyard, LOWRIE *stands, eyes closed, still as a statue. After a little time he opens his eyes and breathes rhythmically as if summoning strength – a preparation for something. Slowly he looks around, at the house, at the sky. Then from his pocket he takes an envelope. He goes to the door of* J. J.'s *room and slips the envelope under the door.*

J. J. *sleeps.* ANDY *enters from inside the house in a state of some agitation.*

ANDY: J. J., J. J. – (*Sees* LOWRIE.) Mr Lowrie, I've got to talk to someone –

LOWRIE: Not now – I don't want – I can't – not now –

ANDY: (*Overlapping*) I'd have woken Dennis, but you'll do, you'll do –

LOWRIE: (*Overlapping*) You're supposed to be at work –

ANDY: (*Overlapping*) This business has upset me –

LOWRIE: Why are you back from work?

ANDY: I didn't get to work –

LOWRIE: I have something I must do –

ANDY: (*Grabbing hold of* LOWRIE) I've got to talk to you –

LOWRIE: I can't – this is not the time – let go of me –

ANDY: Listen to me –

LOWRIE: You'll wake the house.

ANDY: Listen to me –

LOWRIE: I don't want to listen to you –

ANDY: Bastard, bastard, you and Farr, you're both bastards, you masturbate thoughts and feelings like cheap whores in a massage parlour, it's upset me, it's upset me, it's upset the whole house –

LOWRIE: Let go – let go –

ANDY: I don't think she could have been more than seventeen –

LOWRIE: What – ?

ANDY: (*Holding on to* LOWRIE's *arm with both hands*) Please listen, but don't look at me, turn away, don't look at me –

LOWRIE: (*Anguish increasing*) Please, let go, please, please – I won't be here much longer –

ANDY: (*Overlapping*) You and Farr, wine, blood, Jesus, we've got lives to lead, lives to lead, I've been such a good boy for so long – what's faith and God and – just listen – just listen. Don't look at me.
(*Pause. He lets go of* LOWRIE, *who manages to slip away unnoticed.*)
She was young. Old routine. Used to do it even when –
(*Pause.*) Tonight. Revivalist meeting. Sat at the back. Drunks, druggies, derelicts, me. She came round with the collection. No make-up, rosy cheeks, damp eyes, spotlessly clean fingernails cut short. I put a fiver in the box. Afterwards, I followed her. She walked quickly, humming a hymn. So, I hummed it, too. She looked around. She

remembered me. She remembered the fiver in the box. Old
trick. Got talking. Talked of revelation, redemption, I
know the game, got her going, it always does, God is love, I
said. She began to pant. Held her hand. Down the alley,
God is love. Relax, relax, I said, And before you could say
Armageddon we were at it like Seventh Day Adventists.
Then at the moment of ecstasy, she cried, 'Hallelujah!' and
that's the best compliment I've had from any girl. It's all
right, isn't it, Mr Lowrie, no harm done, it's all right?
(J. J. *rises and puts on his dressing-gown. He discovers the
envelope near the door.*)
No it isn't, is it? No. Wish I could break the umbilical.
Know I'm going to be punished, know it. The fire, the
bloody fire – Say it's all right. What's it cost you?
(ANDY *turns and realizes that* LOWRIE *is not there.* J. J. *comes
out into the courtyard.*)

J. J.: Where's Mr Lowrie?
ANDY: He was here a moment ago.
J. J.: Find him.
(ANDY *starts to go but stops dead.*)
ANDY: (*Seeing* LOWRIE *offstage*) Oh hell, no, no –
(LOWRIE *enters bleeding, having cut his wrists. He staggers,
then stumbles, and is unable to rise.* ANDY *does not move.*)
J. J.: (*Severe*) Get Dennis.
(ANDY *goes.* J. J. *fetches a cloth or towel from his room. He
returns to* LOWRIE *and attends to him.*)
LOWRIE: Leave me alone – don't come near me –
J. J.: (*Tough*) Lie still –
(J. J. *applies tourniquets above* LOWRIE's *elbows.*)
(*While applying the tourniquets.*) You stupid sod. In all the
months of captivity, no one, not one single hostage, when
the bluntest, rustiest, dirtiest razor might have seemed like
salvation, not once did anyone whisper the possibility of
suicide. What do you want me to feel? Sympathy? Alarm?
Responsibility?
(LOWRIE *whimpers.*)
Shall I tell you what I really feel? Disgust. So easy, isn't it,
so privileged, just take your own life, put an end to it, duck

out, just look at you, look at you –
(DENNIS, *tying the cord round his dressing-gown, comes from
the house, followed by* ANDY, *who hovers in the background*.
DENNIS: Is he all right?
J. J.: Yes, of course he's all right.
(OLIVER, *also in a dressing-gown, appears*.)
OLIVER: What's happened, is Mr Lowrie hurt?
J. J.: (*To* OLIVER) Make tea, hot and sweet.
(OLIVER *exits*.)
ANDY: Will he be all right?
J. J.: Shock, that's all, he's lost some blood, but not serious, not
at all serious –
ANDY: (*Helping* J. J.) Why, Mr Lowrie, why?
DENNIS: Not now, Andy, not now –
ANDY: Why should he do this to us? I thought he was beginning
to like it here –
DENNIS: Leave him be, Andy.
J. J.: I'll tell you why. Because he's like all of you here, Andy.
You don't live in this world, you never have. Too much
thought, not enough heart. You, Lowrie, all of you. I wish
I could feel sorry for all of you, but the problem is you all
get on my bazonkers.
(ANDY *hovers*.)
ANDY: Should we get a doctor?
J. J.: Andy, stop standing around like a spare prick at a
wedding. Find some disinfectant, towels, bandages, go on –
(ANDY *goes, passing* OLIVER, *who returns with tea. He kneels
beside* LOWRIE *and helps him to drink*.)
OLIVER: Mind, it's very hot. Slowly, slowly. (*To* J. J.) What a
dreadful thing. I've brought a couple of my tranquillizers.
They're rather strong. Do you think it a good idea?
J. J.: Yes, yes, why not, yes, yes.
DENNIS: I'll telephone the doctor –
(*He exits*.)
OLIVER: (*Quietly, to* LOWRIE) I am very sorry you were driven
to such despair. Perhaps when you feel stronger you might
want to have a little chat with me. I'm rather a woolly
person, punctured by doubt. But I may be able to give

comfort, who knows?

(ANDY *returns with a tray on which there is a bowl, cotton wool and a bandage. He puts them down beside* J. J.)

(*Feeding* LOWRIE *the tea.*) That's the way. (*Giving him the tranquillizers.*) Just put these on your tongue and down they go. I made the tea very sweet, very sweet indeed. Swallow. Swallow.

J. J.: (*To* LOWRIE) I'm putting on disinfectant. It'll remind you of incense. It may sting.

OLIVER: (*To* LOWRIE) There, good boy, all gone. You'll feel better. Bless you.

(DENNIS *returns.* OLIVER *rises and* DENNIS *takes his place beside* OLIVER.)

DENNIS: Do you want me to let anyone know what's happened? Do you want to see anyone? Your parents? (*No response.*) Have you brothers and sisters? A friend, perhaps?

(LOWRIE *tries not to cry.*)

We'll look after you. I think you'll agree we're equipped to do that, and when you feel better –

(AUSTIN *enters, dressed, carrying his canvas bag.*)

AUSTIN: Where is this rain we've heard so much about? On television a moment ago they talked about water rationing. And then they showed pictures of famine. Why do they always show pictures of famine at meal times?

OLIVER: Guilt, old chap, guilt.

AUSTIN: Ah, that rings a bell. (*Seeing* LOWRIE.) What's the matter with Mr Lowrie? Has he taken to sleeping out of doors?

(OLIVER *takes* AUSTIN *aside to explain, just as* LOWRIE *suddenly erupts, trying to tear off his bandages. All, except* J. J. *and* AUSTIN, *rush to attend him and then* DENNIS *turns on* J. J.)

DENNIS: (*Suddenly, deeply-felt anger*) I lay this at your door, J. J. You've burst in, shattered our peace, and brought nothing but turmoil. I don't know where you are, J. J., in some rarefied turret. When do you ever talk about pain and misery and joy and despair and pleasure and beauty and love and the terrible glory of just being? In this house we are moderate men or we are nothing. Mr Lowrie's right. You don't belong here any more. You can't go on living here. I shall speak to the trustees. No, no, no, I'm sorry, I'm sorry, I'm sorry. It was hasty of me. Forget I said it, we'll talk about it, there's no need to do anything now –

(J. J. *goes quietly into his room, then quickly into his bathroom, out of sight. Silence.*)

ANDY: I'll walk. I'll keep awake. I'll walk.

OLIVER: Should you? Shouldn't we all be together, for Dennis's sake? Moral support, that sort of thing –

ANDY: (*Flaring*) All right, I'll stay, I won't walk. Now, now, now. (*Silence.*)

DENNIS: It'll all be over soon. And so will the day and the night and the struggle for sleep. (*Pause.*) Did I say terrible things to J. J.?

OLIVER: No, no, no, you were quite right.

AUSTIN: Oughtn't you to get Mr Lowrie indoors?

OLIVER: He's asleep.

AUSTIN: (*Enjoying it all*) When was the last time we had to get rid of a resident?

(*He sits and works on some embroidery.*)

OLIVER: Poor old Francis Barnaby.

ANDY: So it was. A dear fellow. But in this case we were either blind or naïve. When I cleared out his room, the empty bottles under his bed filled three sacks. And I never saw him pissed. (*Pause; to* DENNIS.) Sorry it fell on you, old chap. Unpleasant thing to have to do. But quite right, quite right. This chap needs help. But not J. J. Never J. J.

DENNIS: Francis Barnaby. Yes. I remember. Autumn leaves gusting. A chill wind. A chill room. (*Smiles.*) Chill-dren. (*Silence.*)

OLIVER: What a twelvemonth this has been. David dying and my prostate. Now this.

AUSTIN: The Greeks ordered things so much better. They had the ostracon.

ANDY: The what?

AUSTIN: The ostracon. A piece of pottery, a chard, a flake of limestone on which it was possible to write a name. That was in the golden age, in Athens, when everything was lovely.

(*Smiles.*) Some say in mid-winter, others a month or two later, the assembly was asked whether or not it would hold an ostracism. If the answer was yes, at the next convenient meeting each citizen took the flake of limestone, the ostracon, and wrote on it the name of a person he believed threatened the stability of the state. No specific charges were brought. A valid ostracism required six thousand votes. The man against whom these votes were cast had, within ten days, to leave the city for ten years.

ANDY: In this house, it seems, they have to leave at once. Well, I suppose, all of us here have been through it in another place, at another time. In my case, twice. I've always believed my name was inscribed on an ostracon the day I was born. That was the first time.

DENNIS: It's what the terrorists feel who took J. J. hostage. What the hostages felt, too, no doubt. What, perhaps, Mr Lowrie feels. They believe the gates of the city are locked against them, but the gates of the city are of their own making.

ANDY: I always thought we were wrong to get rid of Francis. He never endangered the state. And, funny, his breath never smelt.

(J. J. *returns to his room; he is dressed. He starts to pack.*)

AUSTIN: Does anyone know why our Mr Lowrie tried to take his own life?

(*Silence.*)

OLIVER: In my worst moments I never despaired. It's Mr Lowrie's one act of humanity since he's been here. Poor, dear man.

DENNIS: Some nights, after my fall from grace, after my wife died, I used to wake and think of suicide. In a mysterious way, I found it a powerful solace. Thoughts of suicide got me through many a bad night.

(*He smiles. Silence.*)

AUSTIN: (*In his own world*) A profound loss of faith is not cause enough for despair. I remember this. A long time ago. At the time of my greatest anguish. Someone I loved told me that when I made the sign of the cross, ballerinas all over Europe turned green with envy. That cheered me up. Too ridiculous. And, after all, who knows, faith may return? I've always thought that would be a lovely thing. And life is such an absurd sorrow. If there were no world and one was told to imagine it, how impossible that would be.

ANDY: I'll give you all one crumb of comfort. If God is dead, as the philosophers say, then it follows that the devil must have died, too. And that's an enormous relief.

LOWRIE: (*Barely audible*) I want to see Mr Farr.

OLIVER: What, Mr Lowrie?

LOWRIE: Warden –

(DENNIS *goes to him.*)

LOWRIE: I want to see Mr Farr.

DENNIS: It can wait, Mr Lowrie. Let's get you into bed –

LOWRIE: Ask him if he'll see me.

(*The others watch as* DENNIS *goes to* J. J.'s *door and knocks. No response. He knocks again and goes in.*)

DENNIS: Mr Lowrie wants to see you.

J. J.: (*A short sound*) Ah.

DENNIS: He tried to kill himself before, you know.

J. J.: Yes, I know.

DENNIS: Perhaps we shouldn't have admitted him.

J. J.: Who can say?

DENNIS: I'm sorry about my outburts –

J. J.: We both understand why it's impossible for me to go on living here, don't we?

DENNIS: Can't we talk it over? I didn't mean it – (*Pause.*) Though I admit, it would be particularly difficult for me, having you here. I envy you, J. J. I'd give anything to escape from this – this subsidized limbo. To stand on my own two feet again. What will you do now?

J. J.: Stand on my own two feet again.

DENNIS: Will you – will you ask to go back?

J. J.: I have no plans.

(*He packs the orange in his suitcase.*)

DENNIS: I know a man, in Scotland, Archie Craig, takes in all sorts – even married priests. Would you like me to write to him?

(J. J., *taking his case, goes into the courtyard. He puts down the case then goes to* LOWRIE's *side.*)

J. J.: You wanted to see me.

LOWRIE: (*Quietly*) Warden –

(DENNIS *goes to him.*)

– ask everyone to leave us, please –

ANDY: Good, I can sleep now –

(*All go, except* DENNIS.)

DENNIS: (*To* J. J.) Can you cope? (*No response.*) Call us if –
(*He follows the others. For the most part* LOWRIE *now speaks as
if from a dream, the effect of the sedative.*)

LOWRIE: Turn away, don't look at me.

(J. J. *does so.*)

J. J.: I'm not looking.

LOWRIE: You were god to me. But now I know you don't exist.
And that's a relief. Do I make myself clear? Am I coherent?
I've had to go through a lot to prove you don't exist. Now I
can get some peace and peace is what I'm really after.

J. J.: What did you mean in your note – 'Both things are acts of
defiance'?

LOWRIE: What did I mean? What did I mean? Yes, yes, yes. Both
things. The wine and my own blood. When I consecrated the
wine. When I cut my wrists. Both acts of defiance.

J. J.: Who were you defying? Me?

LOWRIE: Not only you.

J. J.: Who?

LOWRIE: Who do you think? (*Silence.*) Know there isn't one.
Know neither of you exist. Know there's nothing. Know
death is death. Certain of it. Death is death. But have to –
have to test that certainty. Need proof. A need to go – to the
edge. Faith was like that. Edge of faith, priesthood. Bleak
world, mine. And yours. Don't say anything. Don't want
arguments. Or comfort. Or help. Or forgiveness. Or creeds.
Or salvation. Please, please, don't say you'll pray for me.
Just want you to know that I, I acknowledge a need for
treatment. Now, leave me in peace. I'm free of you.
(*Silence.*)

J. J.: You're not free of anything.

LOWRIE: Charlatan –

(J. J. *goes to* LOWRIE *and holds him.*)

J. J.: In a cage, an animal tortured by animals, I had this – I don't want to make too much of it – but this – this image: in the world, with all its terror and pain and horror, there are scales tipped in favour of harmony, beauty, love, goodness, all the things you affect to deny. You can't put your faith in facts and reason. There's no logic in it, is there? Without those scales, so precariously weighted, the world would have disintegrated a hundred million years ago. The balance of goodness is slight but it exists outside of us, not our making –

LOWRIE: You talk shit. Untreated shit.

(J. J. *lets go of him.*)

This world, this world, one truth, *Allahu Akbar*, one truth, one truth, *Domine, non sum dignus*, one truth, this world, one truth –

(J. J. *gets his suitcase.* LOWRIE *continues to mumble.*)

J. J.: (*Calling*) You can come back. We're finished.

LOWRIE: (*Continuing, but losing consciousness*) – this truth, this world, charlatan, *hic est, hoc est,* hey presto, we have blood, *il est mort,* this world, *Allahu Akbar,* one truth, this truth –

(*The others return,* DENNIS *leading.*)

J. J.: Look after him.

(J. J. *takes the orange out of the suitcase and leaves it behind him. He exits.*)

LOWRIE: (*Continuing*) – one world, one truth, now, hey presto, wants a priest, *ce n'est pas nécessaire,* this truth, this world, this now, this now, now world, this truth, now world, now truth, now, truth –

(*His words become sounds, like a murmured prayer, as the others gather round to lift him.*
Lights fade to blackout.)

ANOTHER TIME

CHARACTERS

IKE LANDS, *aged sixty-one*

LEONARD LANDS, *aged sixteen and fifty-one*

BELLE LANDS, *aged forty-nine and eighty-four*

PROFESSOR ZADOK SALT, *aged fifty-four and eighty-nine*

ROSE SALT, *aged fifty-one and eighty-six*

JEREMY LANDS, *aged eighteen*

TWO TECHNICIANS

NOTE:
The actor who plays IKE in Act One plays LEONARD in Act Two.
The actor who plays LEONARD in Act One plays JEREMY in Act Two.

ACT ONE
Early 1950s

The small ground-floor flat belonging to Belle and Ike Lands in
Sea Point, Cape Town.

Scene One: The hall, 6.30 p.m. on a winter evening in June.
Scene Two: Belle's bedroom, at approximately the same time
              on the same evening.
Scene Three: The hall, a moment later.
Scene Four: Belle's bedroom, a week later.

ACT TWO
Thirty-five years later

A recording studio in Maida Vale, London.

Scene One: The studio, shortly before 1 p.m.
Scene Two: The control booth, at approximately the same
              time on the same day.
Scene Three: The studio.
Scene Four: The control booth.

Another Time was first presented by Duncan C. Weldon and Jerome Minskoff for Triumph Theatre Productions Ltd. at the Theatre Royal, Bath, on 22 August 1989, and subsequently at Wyndham's Theatre, London, on 25 September 1989 with the following cast:

ACT ONE
Early 1950s

IKE LANDS	Albert Finney
LEONARD LANDS	Christien Anholt
BELLE LANDS	Janet Suzman
PROFESSOR ZADOK SALT	David de Keyser
ROSE SALT	Sara Kestelman

ACT TWO
Thirty-five years later

LEONARD LANDS	Albert Finney
JEREMY LANDS	Christien Anholt
BELLE LANDS	Janet Suzman
PROFESSOR ZADOK SALT	David de Keyser
ROSE SALT	Sara Kestelman
Director	Elijah Moshinsky
Designer	Saul Radomsky
Lighting	Paul Pyant

ACT ONE

Early 1950s. The pentagonal hall of a small ground-floor flat.
The hall is used as a dining room but is also a thoroughfare. There is a
front door, which leads to a path that leads to the street; a door to
Belle's bedroom; a short passage off which there are other doors (not
necessarily visible) to Ike and Leonard's bedroom, the bathroom,
living room and kitchen. There is a dining table in a polished dark
wood with four matching chairs, and a modern desk-cum-bookcase.

SCENE ONE

The hall. 6.30 p.m. IKE LANDS, *aged sixty-one, sits at the table*
reading a volume of an encyclopaedia. He is a handsome man with a
lame left hand on which he wears a brown leather glove. He turns the
pages with the third finger of his right hand which he first moistens on
his tongue. He occasionally reacts audibly to what he reads: a tuneless
whistle or clucking his teeth. After he has turned a page or two, his
son, LEONARD LANDS, *aged sixteen, enters, carrying a music case*
and a satchel. He is dressed in school uniform: a black blazer, white
shirt and tie, and grey flannels.

IKE: Leonard!

LEONARD: Hello, Dad.

    (LEONARD *is about to go into his bedroom.*)

IKE: Don't I get a kiss?

    (LEONARD *kisses him on the cheek.*)

    And how's Arthur Rubenstein this evening?

LEONARD: Dad, I'm not Arthur Rubenstein.

IKE: Did you have a good lesson?

LEONARD: Fine. Mom and Aunty Rose were on the bus. I came
    back with them. They're outside talking to Miss Anna Katz.

IKE: A very cultured woman. You going to practise now?

LEONARD: No. I've some homework to do first –

(He goes to the desk and starts to unpack his satchel. BELLE LANDS enters. She is forty-nine years old, a once beautiful woman, but now tired and anxious.)

Where's Aunty Rose?

BELLE: Still talking to Anna Katz. I'm too tired to stand and listen. *(She crosses to her bedroom door.)* Leonard, ask your father if he's in for supper.

LEONARD: *(As a matter of course)* Dad, Mom wants to know if you're in for supper.

IKE: Tell her of course I'm in for supper, when am I out?

LEONARD: Yes, he's in for supper.

BELLE: I'm going to make a cup of tea for Rose and me. Ask your father if he wants tea or coffee.

LEONARD: Dad, do you want tea or coffee?

IKE: *(A shrug)* Anything.

(BELLE goes into the kitchen.)

Leonard, before you start on your homework, will you do me a favour?

LEONARD: What?

IKE: Don't say what like that. I'm not going to ask you to climb Table Mountain.

LEONARD: I'm sorry, what's the favour?

IKE: Will you cut my fingernails for me?

LEONARD: *(After a slight hesitation)* Yes, of course.

(IKE removes his glove from his lame hand. LEONARD finds a pair of nail scissors, sits by his father and starts to cut his fingernails.)

IKE: People think I should be able to cut the nails of my bad hand myself. But I can't. I don't know why. I can't.

(ROSE SALT enters. She is fifty-one, a spinster, energetic and intelligent. LEONARD continues to cut his father's nails.)

ROSE: Good evening, Ike –

IKE: Hello, Rose, how goes it?

ROSE: I'm fine. Is Belle in her room?

LEONARD: No, she's making tea.

IKE: So, Rose, I've been meaning to ask you, what do you hear about this new book?

ROSE: What new book?

IKE: This American *Naked and the Dead* business by this fellow, what's-his-name?

ROSE: Mailer, Norman Mailer. Ike, it's filth. Have nothing to do with it. Don't have it in the house.

(BELLE *returns with a tray with a pot of tea, two cups and a glass of water. She puts the glass of water in front of* IKE.)

IKE: Ask your mother what's this.

LEONARD: What's this, Mom?

BELLE: I asked him if he wants tea or coffee and he said anything, so I brought him a glass of water.

ROSE: (*Laughing*) Belle, you're a cow –

IKE: (*Under his breath*) God Almighty –

BELLE: (*Also laughing*) Well, he said anything –

IKE: (*Louder; dangerous*) God Almighty –

BELLE: Tell him to keep his shirt on. Get a cup from the kitchen –

ROSE: I'll go –

(*She exits into the kitchen.*)

BELLE: (*To* LEONARD) Leonard, you need a haircut.

LEONARD: Mom, I have to talk to you –

BELLE: So, come and talk.

LEONARD: I want to look at some maths first.

(ROSE *returns with a cup and saucer. She pours* IKE *a cup of tea.*)

BELLE: Leonard, why don't you work in the lounge or the bedroom, what d'you want to work in here for?

LEONARD: I prefer it here –

BELLE: You prefer it here, it's like a railway station and you prefer it here. I don't know how you can concentrate –

ROSE: Milk and sugar, Ike?

IKE: Sugar, no milk, thank you.

(BELLE *goes to her bedroom door and opens it.* ROSE *gives* IKE *his tea and then follows her.*)

BELLE: I'll be in my room –

LEONARD: I won't be a moment –

ROSE: Belle, you'll never guess what Ike just asked me –

BELLE: That's true –

(*They go, closing the door.*)

IKE: What did I just ask her? I asked her about a book. What's the fuss? Do they think I don't know what goes on in this world?

(LEONARD *continues to cut* IKE's *nailes*. IKE *sips his tea*.)

LEONARD: Dad, if you don't keep still I'll cut you.

IKE: Worse things can happen.

(LEONARD *cuts*, IKE *reads*. *From* BELLE's *room, laughter*.)

Thick as thieves, those two sisters, thick as thieves. The whole Salt family was very close-knit. Like an island. Very independent. Well, look at your mother and Rose. Your Uncle Zadok's the best of the bunch. Their father, old Leopold Salt, Leonard, was a Freethinker. Enough said. Your other grandfather, my father, was a wonderful whistler. I often think that's where you get your musical talent. Don't tell your mother.

(*He reads*. LEONARD *cuts*.)

The stuff they put in these books. Listen to this, d'you know what procaine hydrochloride is?

LEONARD: No.

IKE: An anaesthetic introduced in 1905 under the trade name Novocaine.

(*Belle's door opens a crack*. *Neither* IKE *nor* LEONARD *notice*.)

Things like that are interesting. You should read these, Sir John Hammerton's *Book of Knowledge*, Leonard, I bought them for you –

BELLE: *I* bought them for him.

(IKE *and* LEONARD *look round and* BELLE *closes the door*. *Silence*.)

IKE: What a bad hand I was dealt.

LEONARD: You mean this hand, your paralysed hand?

IKE: No, I mean a hand of cards, the shuffle of life, the deal, the deal, the cards you get, the hand you're given to play in the game of life. You, you've been dealt a Royal flush, thank God, unbeatable, a great musical talent, you play the piano like Franz Liszt and you're not seventeen yet, a genius, what a hand you've got, but me, I got a hand with fours high. You know why I say this? Because I think by nature I could have been a scholar. I love books, Leonard, like your mother and your Aunty Rose. I love learning. But what chance did I have? What chance did any of my generation have? We were refugees, immigrants, if we had talents or gifts or inclinations no one knew, no one cared. We had only one obligation. To make a living. To survive. We were never allowed to be what we really were. That's an accident of history, a rotten shuffle, a hand fours high. No, no, no. I love learning. (*Silence. Lowering his voice.*) Leonard, are you smoking cigarettes?

LEONARD: No, Dad –

IKE: Tell me the truth, Leonard –

LEONARD: No, Dad –

IKE: I'm not going to get cross –

LEONARD: I'm not smoking, Dad –

IKE: I'm desperate for a cigarette, Len. (*Pause.*) I just want one of your cigarettes.

(*Pause.* LEONARD *takes a packet of ten cigarettes from his music case and gives* IKE *one.*)

IKE: (*Noting the packet*) Sir Seymour, eh?

LEONARD: (*An urgent whisper*) Don't tell Mummy.

(IKE *lights up and puffs deeply.*)

IKE: I wonder how much they paid him.

LEONARD: Who?

IKE: Sir Seymour, Sir Seymour Hicks.

LEONARD: You should know, you sold the cigarettes –

IKE: They never told me. People like me don't get told things like that. That kind of information is all Head Office. They never tell the commercial travellers anything. And anyway, it was never a good line. People like the old brands. New brands are difficult. But they must have paid him something. I mean, a famous actor gives his name to cigarettes, he's got to be paid a few bob. (*Looks at the packet.*) Can't be a bad deal. You give your name, they put your photograph on the packet and he's not even in Sir John Hammerton's *Book of Knowledge*. He was dealt a good hand, that's all, and he never looked much of an actor to me. Now, Ronald Colman, that's a different story. Perhaps they would have liked to have named a cigarette after Ronald Colman, but there's

already the mustard, so you're in trouble. Still, I bet Sir
Seymour was well paid. And du Maurier. And that singer
fellow, De Reszke. One day, please God, you'll have a
cigarette named after you. No, no, Leonard, plastic hangers
is the coming thing. I'm telling you, there's a fortune in
plastic hangers. If I could just bring off this one deal, get the
agency for these plastic hangers, we'd never have to worry
again. (*Puffs deeply.*) I was dying for a cigarette. (*Pause.*)
Len, you haven't got a couple of bob on you, have you?

LEONARD: No, I spent all I had on the cigarettes, I'm sorry.
(*Pause.*)
Dad –

IKE: What?

LEONARD: I've got something to tell you.

IKE: Bad news?

LEONARD: I had my lesson with Professor Kinski this afternoon –

IKE: And?

LEONARD: He thinks I ought to go overseas to study. To Vienna.
(*Silence.*) You think there's any chance? (*Silence.*)

IKE: (*A sigh*) Money, money, money, money.

LEONARD: Yes, I know, never mind, Dad –

IKE: Len, it's like I always say, it's not what you know, it's who
you know –
(*Silence.*)

LEONARD: I better talk to Mummy about Vienna.
(*Silence.*)

IKE: You know where I'd like to go?

LEONARD: Where?

IKE: Pompeii, Pompeii and Herculaneum. I was reading about
them this afternoon. According to Sir John Hammerton you
can see the ruins of both cities on the same day. What a trip
that would be, eh? Destroyed by a volcano. Just imagine it,
Len, you're sitting there having your breakfast or reading a
book or practising the piano, and suddenly no warning,
whooosh! Gone. And it's all preserved for you to see. That's
history for you. That's being in the wrong place at the wrong
time. I sometimes feel –
(*Silence.*)

LEONARD: I must do my homework.

    (*He goes to the desk and starts to unpack his satchel.*)

BELLE: (*Off*) Leonard, come and talk to us, your maths can wait –

    (LEONARD *rises. As he crosses to Belle's door the front doorbell rings.*)

LEONARD: (*Putting his head into Belle's room*) There's someone at the door –

BELLE: (*Off*) It'll be Uncle Zadok, your father can let him in.

    (LEONARD *hesitates for a moment but goes to the front door and opens it to* PROFESSOR ZADOK SALT, *aged fifty-four.*)

ZADOK: Maestro!

    (*he squeezes* LEONARD's *cheeks with grunts of pleasure.* LEONARD *hates this.*)

    Ike, good evening.

IKE: Hello, Zadok, I'm pleased to see you. Your sisters are in there.

ZADOK: But it's you I've come to visit.

IKE: Me?

BELLE: (*Off*) Leonard, is Uncle Zadok there?

LEONARD: (*Calling*) Yes, he's here –

ZADOK: I'm not staying long – (*He crosses to Belle's door, knocks and opens it.*) Sisters mine, it's your brudder.

BELLE: (*Off*) Hello, Zadok –

ROSE: (*Off*) Hello, Zadok –

BELLE: (*Off*) Tell Leonard to come and see me –

ZADOK: (*Shutting the door*) Maestro, your mother wants to see you –

LEONARD: Coming, Mom –

ZADOK: Ike, I'm starving –

IKE: So, go into the kitchen, open the fridge and find something. It's the maid's night off.

    (ZADOK *goes into the kitchen.* LEONARD *considers for a moment, then goes to his music case, takes out the packet of cigarettes and slips two of them to* IKE. IKE *shudders, controlling tears.*)

LEONARD: For God's sake, don't cry, Dad –

IKE: (*Crying*) You've got such a good heart – I'm sorry – I'm sorry – God Almighty, what a life – (*Recovering.*) Go and see your

mother. Don't put her in a worse mood than she's in already.
(LEONARD *goes into Belle's room as* ZADOK *returns, eating a chicken leg. He puts his head into Belle's bedroom.*)

ZADOK: I've stolen a chicken leg. (*He closes the door.*) So, Ike, how are you?

IKE: So-so. I get these pains in my stomach.

ZADOK: Take a laxative.

IKE: I take but nothing happens. So, what d'you want to see me about?

ZADOK: I want to talk to you.

IKE: It's not my birthday, you know.
(ZADOK *sits.*)

ZADOK: Ike, how's the hand?

IKE: It gets cold in this weather.

ZADOK: And the leg?

IKE: The same.

ZADOK: Listen, Ike, just listen to what I've got to say. As you well know, I'm a dry, dusty, unemotional man, so I'm going to put this in a dry, dusty and unemotional way.

IKE: I'm listening –

ZADOK: I happened to meet David Figg the other day, he's the best GP in town, the top man, and we had a chat about you. He said to me, 'With Ike Lands, it's mind over matter.'

IKE: What's mind over matter?

ZADOK: Your hand.

IKE: My hand's mind over matter?

ZADOK: According to Dr Figg, if you wanted to use it, you'd use it.

IKE: (*Showing him the gloved hand*) I want to use it, Zadok.

ZADOK: I'm only quoting Dr David Figg. What's your own doctor say?

IKE: Simons? Nathan Simons, round the corner? What does Dr Simons say about my hand? He says, 'I've never seen a hand like this', that's what he says. That man Simons, I'd like to see his certificate, I don't think he ever qualified. Simons, what does he know? He knows 'take two aspirin' and 'come and see me when your temperature's down.' Simons, I'd be better off with a vet.

ZADOK: David Figg says your hand is mind over matter. And he says the same is probably true of your bad leg. Consider the facts, Ike. Your mother dies, you have a – a crisis –

IKE: It was a breakdown, call a spade a spade. I'm not ashamed, it was a nervous breakdown. I grieved until my heart broke – (*He shudders with tears.*)

ZADOK: Now that was before the war –

IKE: 1935, just after Leonard was born, 7 January 1935, that's the anniversary of her death, fifteen years ago, God rest her soul. They were difficult times. But then the war came and I liked it in the army –

ZADOK: Ike, I never understood how you got into the army. What did the army doctor say when you showed him your hand?

IKE: I didn't show it to him. He didn't ask so I didn't show. Army doctors, doctors. (*Waves them away.*) No, but I liked the army. The pay was regular. They sent Belle some money each month. Back pay, they called it. She was happy then. Happier. And then, with my luck, I'm demobbed a year and I have to go and get knocked down by a car.

ZADOK: And your leg goes lame. Now, what David Figg is saying is that there may be a psychological cause. You get these terrible shocks, your mother's death, the accident, and they manifest themselves physically. That's what he means by mind over matter.

IKE: Is that what you came specially to tell me, mind over matter?

ZADOK: Look, Ike, we've been friends since before you became my brother-in-law. David Figg says the best man to have a look at you is Norman Hurwitz, this man is the top psychiatrist in the country, he's a professor –

IKE: A psychiatrist – ?

ZADOK: A professor of psychiatry –

IKE: You think I should see a psychiatrist?

ZADOK: Why not? It's not shameful, a paralysed hand isn't the plague, it's not catching, it's not syphilis –

IKE: Please, Zadok –

ZADOK: Go and see him, what can you lose?

IKE: (*After a moment*) What can I lose? Only a paralysed hand, I suppose.

ZADOK: And a gammy leg.

IKE: Is that what you wanted to see me about?

ZADOK: Should I arrange an appointment with Professor Hurwitz?

IKE: You know him?

ZADOK: Certainly.

IKE: You know everybody, eh, Zadok?

ZADOK: As you've always said, Ike, 'It's not what you know –'

IKE: (*Joining in*) – 'It's who you know.'
(*They laugh quietly.*)
I'm glad you came tonight, Zadok.

ZADOK: Ike, it's always a pleasure to see you.

IKE: You've got a moment?

ZADOK: A moment.

IKE: You can't stay for supper?

ZADOK: No, I've got to give a lecture tomorrow, I have to prepare –

IKE: I don't see a lot of people these days. So, tell me, you like being a professor?

ZADOK: Too much administration, not enough teaching. I'm a better teacher than administrator but, yes, I like it.

IKE: Such a wonderful title.

ZADOK: What?

IKE: Professor of Moral Philosophy.

ZADOK: I'm glad you're impressed.

IKE: I'd have given anything to be a Professor of Moral Philosophy. Tell you what, I'd have given anything just to have gone to a university. I'm not cut out for commerce, Zadok. Tell you the truth, I would never say this to Belle, I'm not a businessman –

ZADOK: Things will turn the corner, Ike –

IKE: Yes, turn the corner, I'll turn the corner and what'll I find? Another cul-de-sac. Like the fish shop. What bad luck we had there. Everybody before and since has made a fortune out of that fish shop, but not me. I don't know, somehow, I just can't seem to – to –

ZADOK: Everything's going to come out right, mark my words.

IKE: From your mouth into God's ear.

ZADOK: You've got something going?

IKE: I might get an agency for plastic hangers.

ZADOK: Sounds good. (*Silence.*) And that son of yours, that Leonard, I could eat him –

IKE: You honestly think he's the real thing, Zadok?

ZADOK: I know it. I've talked to people, people who understand music, expert people, everyone's agreed that Leonard has genius.

IKE: Genius, really?

ZADOK: People who've heard him play and, incidentally, I don't know how much he tells you, but you know Miss Anna Katz, she went to his recital and she says he plays like Rachmaninoff.

IKE: Kinski, you know his teacher, Otto Kinski, he's also a professor, Viennese, a refugee from Hitler –

ZADOK: I know him –

IKE: He thinks Leonard should go overseas to study.

ZADOK: I'm not surprised.

(*Laughter from Belle's room.* IKE *suddenly heaves with suppressed crying.*)

Ike, what's the trouble – what's the matter – ?

IKE: I don't want to let that boy down –

ZADOK: What are you talking about, why should you let him down?

IKE: How can I afford to send him to Vienna? I can't afford a packet of cigarettes –

(IKE *cries.* ZADOK *is horribly embarrassed.*)

God Almighty, what a life –

ZADOK: We'll find a way, we'll all club together.

(*Silence.*)

IKE: It's cruel, Zadok, it's cruel –

ZADOK: What is?

IKE: Life, history, it's cruel –

ZADOK: You know what, Ike? You would have made a good Professor of Moral Philosophy.

IKE: Don't I know? My head is full of knowledge and no way to use it. Did you know, for example, that procaine hydrochloride is an anaesthetic introduced in 1905 under the trade name Novocaine?

ZADOK: No, I didn't know that –

IKE: You see what I mean? Take this hand of mine – (*Holds up his gloved hand*) – I understand this to be a symbol of my life, I understand things like that –

ZADOK: Don't be a bloody fool, Ike, symbols of life aren't that easy to come by –

(*The sound of* BELLE *laughing*.)

IKE: She's happy tonight. But listen to me, Zadok, I've got this useless hand, useless, I can't move it, not a finger, it's like my life, a bum hand, you can't win the game with a bum hand of cards, you can't have a life –

ZADOK: We're all dealt bum hands, Ike –

IKE: Nonsense, that's nonsense –

ZADOK: Ike, we all have our tragedies, our hardships. You think I asked for my wife to die three months after we were married?

IKE: That's different, death's entirely different, I'm talking about struggle. I've had to struggle like no one else I know – I've had such bad luck – the world's been against me, Zadok –

ZADOK: Ike, I'm going to talk to you straight, the world's not against you. 'The fault, dear Brutus – '

(LEONARD *returns, closing Belle's door, goes to the desk and takes books out of his satchel*.)

(*Without interruption*.) – is not in our stars, but in ourselves', ourselves, Ike, the fault is in us, in me, in you –

IKE: I'm responsible for my bad hand?

ZADOK: Listen to me, Leonard, you listen to me, too. I've got something important to say. There is no justice in this life. Remember that. There is no justice.

(LEONARD *exits. Silence*.)

IKE: Failure. Yes. It's a terrible thing to be a failure. That's what Belle holds against me.

ZADOK: Nonsense. You know what's a terrible thing? Self-pity, that's a terrible thing. Giving in, that's a terrible thing. Doing nothing, that's a terrible thing. Thinking the world's against you, that's a terrible thing. Not knowing that only you yourself is against you is a terrible thing.

IKE: You think that ending up here at the bottom of the world, a refugee, an immigrant, you think that was my doing?

ZADOK: It's irrelevant, Ike. It's not where you are it's *who* you are. Who you really are. You've been dealt a hand and all you're obliged to do is play the best game you can. That's all you can do, that's all any of us can do.

IKE: You mean to say, Zadok, a clever man like you, you mean to say that history, events not of our making, persecutions, wars, they don't make a mess of our lives?

ZADOK: Only if we let them.

IKE: You mean the Jews in Europe let the Nazis put them to death? You mean my grandfather allowed the Cossacks to behead him?

ZADOK: But you're not dead, Ike. You're alive and you had better live as though you're alive. And I speak as a dry, dusty, unemotional man.

IKE: I can't help feeling what I feel, Zadok –

ZADOK: (*Exploding*) You can, you can help feeling what you feel, that's the whole point. We're not blighted, we're not cursed, we're not immobile, we have this ability to take our lives into our own hands, we can move or we can stand still, we can accept or we can reject, and we can *change*!

IKE: Zadok, give me a chance to explain. I can't help feeling that history spat me out here, that's what I feel –

ZADOK: All right, so it spat you out. History spits out people all the time. And some die, yes, and the world is cruel and relentless and savage. As I always say, there's no justice. But for those who live there's one obligation and that's life itself, Ike. Do me this favour, don't give into misfortune. At least do something about it. Let me make an appointment for you to see Norman Hurwitz –

IKE: I'll think about it.

ZADOK: Please, I beg you, Ike, go and see him, and who knows? Your life could be transformed.

IKE: So, what else is new?

ZADOK: Things could be worse, Ike.

IKE: That's always true. But what about tomorrow, Zadok, do you worry about the future?

ZADOK: I have my qualms. We've got a government here, they

behave like Nazis, they *are* Nazis. Of course, I worry about the future –

IKE: You know what I say when I read about the government? I say thank God it isn't us they're picking on. It makes a nice change. Yes, the future, God help us.

ZADOK: Let me tell you something, Ike. You're blessed. And you know why? Because you have Leonard and Leonard is the future –

IKE: From your mouth into God's ear. (*Silence.*) Sometimes I feel I could do with procaine hydrochloride, an anaesthetic called Novacaine in 1905. One favour, Zadok, don't mention that psychiatrist to Belle –

ZADOK: If you'd rather I didn't – (ZADOK *goes to Belle's door and opens it. Into the room*) I have to be going –

ROSE: (*Off*) From 'Pippa Passes,' by Robert Browning.

ZADOK: Make it snappy.

ROSE: (*Off*) 'From without is heard the voice of Pippa singing –
　　　The year's at the spring
　　　And day's at the morn;
　　　Morning's at seven;
　　　The hillside's dew-pearled;
　　　The lark's on the wing;
　　　The snail's on the thorn:
　　　God's in his heaven –
　　　All's right with the world!'

ZADOK: Touch wood. I'm off –

ROSE: (*Off*) What time is it?

ZADOK: Quarter past.

ROSE: (Off) I'm off, too –

BELLE: (Off) Must you?

ROSE: (Off) Yes, I must.
　　　(ZADOK *withdraws, closing Belle's door.*)

ZADOK: So, Ike, you'll keep your promise?

IKE: What promise?

ZADOK: If I make an appointment for you to see Norman Hurwitz, you'll see him?

IKE: I made no promise. I'll think about it, that's what I promised. And that's what I'll do. I'll think about it. And

Zadok, you can call in to see me without having a purpose, you take my meaning?

ZADOK: I take your meaning –

IKE: Because, for me, talking to you is better than listening to poetry.

(ROSE *comes out of Belle's room.*)

BELLE: (*Off, calling*) Len, here a moment –

ROSE: Where's Leonard?

ZADOK: (*Bellowing*) Leonard!

ROSE: So, Ike, did you have a nice chat with Zadok?

IKE: We had a chat.

ROSE: That's nice

(LEONARD *enters from the living room.*)

ZADOK: Leonard, your mother wants you. We're just off.

(LEONARD *tries to skirt past him.*)

Where you going? Don't I get a kiss?

(LEONARD, *reluctantly, goes to him.* ZADOK *stares at him for some seconds and smiles in a sickly way. Then, suddenly, he grabs* LEONARD's *cheeks and squeezes them, making grunts of pleasure.*)

I love this boy.

(ROSE *kisses* LEONARD.)

ROSE: Goodnight, Len, Ike. See you soon (*Calling.*) Goodnight, Belle –

ZADOK: Goodnight, Belle –

BELLE: (*Off*) Goodnight –

(ZADOK *and* ROSE *exit.* LEONARD *goes into Belle's room.* IKE *returns to his encyclopaedia.*)

(*Off*) Ask your father if he wants cold chicken or eggs for supper.

(LEONARD *returns.*)

LEONARD: Dad, do you want cold chicken or eggs for supper?

IKE: Eggs.

LEONARD: (*To* BELLE *in her room*) Eggs. I'll have eggs, too.

(*He comes back into the hall, closing the door.*)

IKE: Len.

LEONARD: Yes?

IKE: Did you talk to your mother about what Professor Kinski said? About Vienna?

213

LEONARD: Yes.

IKE: What did she say?

LEONARD: She said she'd think about it.

> (IKE *nods.* LEONARD *goes to his satchel and searches for a book.*
> IKE *stands for the first time. He drags his left leg and moves
> slowly across to Belle's door.* LEONARD *watches him.* IKE
> *knocks on the door.*)

BELLE: (*Off*) Who is it?

IKE: Me.

> (*Silence.* IKE *opens the door, goes into Belle's room and closes the
> door.* LEONARD *stands perfectly still, waiting, in dread. After a
> moment,* IKE *storms back into the hall.*)

> God Almighty, God Almighty – (*He sits at the table, angry,
> tormented. Shouting at Belle's room.*) Why do you treat me like
> this? What have I done that's so terrible?

> (*Silence.* LEONARD *busies himself with his homework. Lights
> fade to blackout.*)

SCENE TWO

*Belle's bedroom, just after 6.30 p.m., approximately the same time as
the previous scene. The room is furnished with little taste. There is a
single bed, a dressing table, an armchair, a built-in wardrobe and
Degas prints of ballet dancers on the wall. The window has bars. The
door opens.*

BELLE: (*Off*) I'll be in my room –

LEONARD: (*Off*) I won't be a moment –

ROSE: (*Off*) Belle, you'll never guess what Ike just asked me –

BELLE: (*Off*) That's true –

> (BELLE *and* ROSE *enter.* BELLE *carries a tray with teapot and
> cups.*)

> I wonder what Leonard wants to talk about. I'm always filled
> with such terrible foreboding –

> (ROSE *sits.*)

ROSE: Listen to me, Belle, I think Ike's an amazing man –

BELLE: Yes, amazing.

ROSE: No, he is. I mean, he always knows what's going on. You know what he just asked me? About *The Naked and the Dead* –

BELLE: That American novel?

ROSE: Yes, filthy, you've no idea –

BELLE: Have you read it?

ROSE: Certainly. It's filth. Mind you, Belle, I laughed, there's one thing there, the soldier, when he hates someone, he puts them on what he calls his 'shit list'.

(*They laugh.*)

Such words in a book –

BELLE: Has Ike read it?

ROSE: No, I told him not to. He's such an innocent, he wouldn't sleep for a week.

BELLE: He'd sleep. Ike sleeps through anything. Worse, he'd snore.

ROSE: How does Leonard cope with the snoring?

BELLE: He's like his father, he'll sleep through anything too. And when you're young –

ROSE: Sometimes I don't think it's right, a son shouldn't share a bedroom with his father.

BELLE: What d'you want me to do in a two-bedroom flat, you want me to sleep in the same room as Ike, you want me to be kept awake all night?

ROSE: Keep your hair on, Belle, I only said I wondered –

BELLE: I heard what you said. (*Sits on the bed.*) God, I'm tired. I'm tired of working.

ROSE: I brought something nice to read to you tonight.

BELLE: What?

ROSE: Robert Browning.

BELLE: Oh, my favourite. (*She rises and goes to the door.*) What do they talk about, Leonard and his father?

(*She opens the door a crack.*)

IKE: (*Off*) – things like that are interesting. You should read these, Sir John Hammerton's *Book of Knowledge*, Leonard, I bought them for you –

BELLE: *I* bought them for him. (*She closes the door.*) He bought them for him, he bought them for him –

(*Silence.*)

ROSE: Belle, I want to talk to you.

BELLE: Talk.

(*She sits down.*)

ROSE: About Ike.

BELLE: I don't want to talk about Ike, Rose.

(*Silence.*)

ROSE: Zadok's going to be popping in this evening.

BELLE: Zadok, what for?

ROSE: He wants to have a word with Ike.

BELLE: I never understand our brother, Zadok. He's a highly
intelligent man, Oxford-educated, what's he want to talk to
Ike for?

ROSE: Ike's no fool. They were friends long before you married.

BELLE: Don't tell me, it was Zadok introduced us. So what's he
want to talk to Ike about?

ROSE: I'm not going to make a secret of this, Belle. Zadok and I,
we worry about you. And we worry about Ike.

BELLE: I worry about Ike, too.

ROSE: He's a decent man, Belle –

BELLE: Yes, decent –

ROSE: And he's not well, I mean the hand, the leg, his general
health –

BELLE: Rose, I don't want to talk about it, really I don't.

(*Silence.*)

ROSE: Zadok ran into David Figg the other day, you remember
David Figg, the doctor?

BELLE: Remember him? I knew him before he was born.

ROSE: People speak very highly of him. He's thought to be a top
man.

BELLE: So?

ROSE: Well, he and Zadok met, they got to talking, one thing led
to another, and they discussed Ike. David feels that Ike's
problems are psychological –

BELLE: I could have told him that twenty years ago –

ROSE: He feels he should see a psychiatrist –

BELLE: From his mouth into God's ear.

ROSE: Listen, Belle, this is serious –

BELLE: I'm serious. I've always known my husband wasn't

normal. At the age of forty-six his mother dies and he has a nervous breakdown, that's normal? I'll tell you one thing for certain, Rose, when I die he won't have a nervous breakdown.

ROSE: Zadok's going to talk to Ike tonight. He's going to suggest that Ike should see Norman Hurwitz.

BELLE: Who's he when he's at home?

ROSE: Norman Hurwitz? He's Professor of Psychiatry, the top man in the country, Belle.
(*Silence.*)

BELLE: How's the library?

ROSE: Can't complain. People are reading books. You'll encourage Ike to see Norman Hurwitz, won't you, Belle?

BELLE: When's Zadok coming?

ROSE: Any time now.
(*Silence.*)

BELLE: I often wonder, Rose, how Ike and I ever produced someone like Leonard.

ROSE: You're not asking me, a spinster, to tell you about the facts of life, are you?

BELLE: (*Smiling*) Shut up. I mean, when you think about it, Ike's such a peculiar man.

ROSE: Belle, these are the mysteries.
(*Silence.*)

BELLE: When I met Ike I thought he was the handsomest man I'd ever seen.

ROSE: And so he was, he was a wonderful looking man.

BELLE: He was doing so well then. (*Silence.*) I should have had Leonard earlier. (*Silence.*) Where does talent come from? (*Silence.*)

ROSE: It's a shame he's an only child.
(*Silence.*)

BELLE: (*Calling.*) Leonard, come and talk to us, your maths can wait –
(*The front doorbell rings.* LEONARD *puts his head round the door.*)

LEONARD: There's someone at the door –
(*He goes.*)

BELLE: (*Calling*) Leonard, is Uncle Zadok there?

LEONARD: (*Off*) Yes, he's here –

(*A knock on the door.* ZADOK *put his head in.*)

ZADOK: Sisters mine, it's your brudder.

BELLE: Hello, Zadok.

ROSE: Hello, Zadok.

BELLE: Tell Leonard to come and see me.

ZADOK: (*Shutting the door*) Maestro, your mother wants to see you.

LEONARD: (*Off*) Coming, Mom –

ROSE: That's good. Let Leonard be in here while Zadok talks to Ike.

(LEONARD *comes into the room.*)

BELLE: Have you finished your homework?

LEONARD: Nowhere near –

(ZADOK *puts his head round the door. He has a chicken leg in his hand.*)

ZADOK: I've stolen a chicken leg.

(*He disappears, closing the door.*)

BELLE: Sweetheart, come and sit, what did you want to tell me?

LEONARD: It can wait, Mom.

BELLE: No, it can't. I want to hear –

ROSE: You can tell her in front of me, Leonard, I'm family, remember?

LEONARD: All right, I'll tell you –

BELLE: Don't do us any favours.

LEONARD: I'll tell you. You asked me to tell you, I'll tell you.

BELLE: Leonard, you're not too old to be put across my knee and given a damn good hiding. Don't get short with me, get short with your father but not with me.

ROSE: All right, choose your weapons, seconds out, now let's behave like civilized human beings.

LEONARD: At my lesson today –

BELLE: Yes?

ROSE: With Professor Kinski?

LEONARD: (*Irritated*) Yes –

BELLE: Leonard, relax, I can see you're tense, relax.

LEONARD: I'm trying to tell the story, you keep interrupting –

ROSE: Gong! Round two. Break clean, keep your punches above the belt, and come out talking.

BELLE: Rose, please. Go on, sweetheart –

LEONARD: He says, Professor Kinski says, he thinks I ought to go overseas to study. To Vienna, he says.

ROSE: Vienna, what's he talking about, Vienna, what's wrong with London?

BELLE: Rose, wait a moment, Tell me exactly what he said.

LEONARD: He said there was nothing more he could teach me.

ROSE: He said that?

LEONARD: Yes. He said – (*Hesitates.*)

ROSE: Tell us, don't be modest.

LEONARD: He said he'd never reached such a point with a pupil before. He said, he was so gentle today, he even wants to take me out to lunch in the holidays, he said he felt helpless. And Mom, I've been feeling for weeks now, he's got nothing more to teach me.

BELLE: You should have said. Those lessons are costing me a fortune –

LEONARD: I know, I know, but what was I to do? Anyway, today he brought it up. He said I really need master classes and the only place I would find them is in Vienna, he said.

ROSE: The man's mad, who goes to Vienna nowadays? Only Graham Greene. And what would you learn in Vienna, the zither? You'll go to London –

BELLE: Rose, wait a moment. Leonard, look, I have to think –

LEONARD: Mom, I know, you don't have to explain –

BELLE: It's a big decision, a big trip, the cost, my God –

LEONARD: Look, I know, I mentioned it to Dad –

BELLE: You mentioned it to Dad, that'll be a great help –

ROSE: Can I ask a question? Everything's taken for granted in this household. I'd like to ask a basic question.

BELLE: Ask.

ROSE: Leonard, do you want to go overseas? (*Silence.*) Do you?

LEONARD: More than anything in the world.

(BELLE *rises and pours herself another cup of tea.*)

ROSE: Do you want to go to Vienna?

LEONARD: I don't know where I want to go, I'd just like to go and study somewhere where I'd learn what I have to learn.

ROSE: That's settled, then.

BELLE: Rose, not so quick, it's not as simple as that.

ROSE: I'm not saying he's going tomorrow, Belle, I'm just establishing the young maestro's wishes in the matter.

LEONARD: I thought I might make some enquiries about New York –

ROSE: New York? What d'you mean, New York? You're another madman –

LEONARD: Aunty Rose, New York's a musical capital –

ROSE: Yes, like my left foot. What's wrong with London?

LEONARD: Nothing's wrong with London –

ROSE: Your Uncle Zadok, your mother and I were all born in London.

LEONARD: Aunty Rose, I know that, but it doesn't make London the musical capital of the world.

ROSE: What have you got against London?

LEONARD: I've got nothing against London –

ROSE: Then what's all the talk about New York? And as for Vienna, I've never heard anything so ridiculous –

BELLE: Rose, Rose, wait a moment. Leonard, I have to think about this –

LEONARD: Of course.

BELLE: At this moment, I'm not so concerned about where you go –

ROSE: Belle how can you say something like that? If he's going to go anywhere he's got to go to London –

BELLE: Rose, for God's sake, I've had a long day and now this to think about.

ROSE: Pardon me for breathing.

BELLE: Rose, look. Money doesn't grow on trees. Not in this house anyway. It's a big decision. I have to be certain I can afford his fare, the fees, his upkeep –

LEONARD: Mom, I know it's probably impossible. I just thought I'd better tell you –

BELLE: What d'you mean, impossible? I haven't said it's impossible, I just want to think about it –

LEONARD: If you say we can't afford it, I won't live the rest of my life eating my heart out.

(*Silence*.)

ROSE: Leonard, I knew this day would come. I've thought about it
often. I want you to develop not only into a great musician but
also into a great artist. I want you to use London, I want you to
– I argue it this way. London's the only place for you. London
is the centre of the world. The most cultured people on earth
gravitate towards London. They have the finest theatres in the
world, the finest libraries. They have art galleries and concert
halls. They have Winston Churchill and that gorgeous
Anthony Eden. They have the finest system of government in
the world. Did you know, Leonard, that in England when a
Cabinet Minister leaves the presence of the King he has to
walk backwards? Please God he should trip. What a system.
And the King. And the Queen. And those two little darlings,
Elizabeth and Margaret Rose. We are talking about a city,
about Mecca, about Jerusalem, about London, about
England. But you know above all what England has? England
has English. Now, this is a language. Imagine, Leonard, if
there'd been no pogroms. You know what you'd be talking
now? Lithuanian. That is not a language. English is a
language. And thank God for the Empire. Without the British
Empire you'd be talking Zulu. How could you go to Vienna?
What sort of language is German? It's a language for shouting
orders. But English. Oh, Leonard, what a language. Take
time to read, I beg you. Music may be your life, Leonard, but,
believe me, without books a person may as well be dead. You
can keep your Russians, your Dostoevsky and Tolstoy, you
can keep your French – Zola and Flaubert are good only for
insomnia. But for life, Leonard, as I always tell anyone who
comes to listen, for life, Leonard, devour William
Shakespeare, drink John Milton, taste Jane Austen, consume
George Eliot, drown in Charles Dickens, glory in John
Donne, whisper Wordsworth when you walk, befriend
Robert Browning and let William Blake invade your dreams
and nightmares. And if you are blue, I know you'll listen to
the music that inspires you, but do me this favour: reach out
for P. G. Wodehouse. Never mind he was a German spy,

genius and decency don't always walk hand in hand – look at
Wagner – but P. G. Wodehouse writes English to make
Thomas Mann illiterate. I thank God that your mother, your
Uncle Zadok and I were born in London. It's given us – it's
given us culture. New York. Please. Americans are about as
cultured as Miss Anna Katz. Have you read this man, Mailer?

LEONARD: No –

ROSE: Don't read him, Leonard, with his fug and fugging. Filth.
But that's America. Norman Mailer. And to what American
did they award a Noble Prize for Literature? Pearl S. Buck,
that's all they could find. Pearl S. Buck, I ask you. Mind
you, she makes even Norman Mailer look as if he can write.
No, no, Leonard. English. England. London. I want you to
promise me you'll read, Leonard, you'll go to theatres and
art galleries – and remember, always wear a tie when you go
into the centre of London. It's the respect you pay a great
city. And one more thing. How would you have managed in
Vienna? At your school they don't teach languages, they
teach Afrikaans. Afrikaans. Pearl S. Buck should have
written in Afrikaans, it may have improved her style.
(*They laugh.* BELLE's *laughter turns to tears, which she tries to
hide.*)

ROSE: Belle, what's the matter – ?

BELLE: What's the matter, what's the matter, what d'you think's
the matter?
(*Silence.*)

LEONARD: Professor Kinski invited me to have lunch with him at
the Waldorf.

ROSE: Well, it's better than having an enema but the results will
be the same.
(BELLE *laughs.*)

LEONARD: He said he was very proud of me. (*Silence.*) I'll go and
finish my homework and then I must practise.

ROSE: Uncle Zadok and your father may be talking privately. Be
discreet.

BELLE: And Leonard – ?

LEONARD: Yes?

BELLE: Give me a day or two –

LEONARD: There's no hurry –

BELLE: I've got a little saved, not much, I may be able to – I've just got to work it out. Just remember, everything happens for the best. I'm a fatalist. What will be, will be.

(LEONARD *opens the door to go*.)

ZADOK: (*Off*) ' – not in our stars but in ourselves,' ourselves, Ike, the fault is in us, in me, in you –

(LEONARD *goes, closing the door. Silence*.)

BELLE: I've been dreading this moment ever since I can remember.

ROSE: I envy you.

BELLE: You need your head examined.

ROSE: To have a child like Leonard. To have a child who's – (*She falls silent*.)

BELLE: I'll find a way, Rose, we won't talk about it, do you mind? I'll find a way, it's my responsibility.

ROSE: We'll all help –

BELLE: Certainly not –

ROSE: You're too proud, Belle, too proud.

BELLE: All right, so I'm too proud.

ROSE: We can all chip in.

BELLE: I won't have it.

ROSE: What do you mean you won't have it? It's only money we're talking about –

BELLE: Yes, only money –

ROSE: Belle, I know you haven't had it easy, but why make money such a big issue? Why let money ruin your life?

BELLE: (*Turning on her*) How dare you, Rose? You don't know what it's like to lie awake night after night wondering where our next meal's coming from. Why let money ruin my life? Because money has ruined my life. All my contemporaries, without exception, have beautiful homes, comfortable lives. I'm nearly fifty, Rose, and I've had to go out to work every day for the last fifteen years. I'm tired, I'm sick of it. You talk to me about Ike. He does nothing. He sits there, day after day, reading those encyclopaedias I bought for Leonard, without two pennies to rub together. He could get a job, he could do something, he does *nothing* to help, nothing. It all falls on me. It's fallen on me ever since the day his mother died and he went to pieces. It's fallen on me, the rent, the electricity, the maid, the food, Leonard's lessons, his pocket-money. When did I last have a new dress? When did I last go to the theatre or a film or a concert? What kind of life are we talking about?

ROSE: You've got Leonard.

BELLE: You didn't listen to a word I say, no one listens –

ROSE: Oh, I listen to you, Belle, I listen to every word you say. You've got Leonard, so stop feeling sorry for yourself. We're born into a world of indifference –

ROSE: Don't lecture me, please, Rose, you and Zadok, you lecture, you philosophize and I have to cope with the everyday, practical misfortunes –

ROSE: Belle, shut up and listen. I won't lecture you, I promise, but I'm going to tell you a story. Once upon a time –

BELLE: Rose, not now –

ROSE: One upon a time, there was a young girl, thought by some to be a very beautiful young girl –

BELLE: Yes, very-beautiful-I-don't-think –

ROSE: Don't interrupt. And this beautiful young girl met a handsome young man. The two of them arrived at that moment in their lives at the end of a strange journey. He from Lithuania, which only the most generous-minded would call a country, and she from London –

BELLE: Yes, but of Polish parents, Rose, I've always thought it's because of my Slav temperament –

ROSE: She from London. By diverse routes, unlikely ever to have met if the world was a friendlier place, the two of them fall in love, yes, she falls in love. I remember, don't worry, I remember you writing 'Belle loves Ike' in the sands at Muizenberg and waiting for the sea to wash the words away. I remember. And this young girl and this young man marry. And very soon, for whatever reasons, no one except you and Ike can ever know, the romance turns sour. Even before Ike's mother died, there were problems. You don't have children –

BELLE: Rose, please –

224

ROSE: You're not going to shut me up, Belle, you're going to listen. All right. So, at last, they have a child, a son. And a year later, Ike's mother dies and he falls apart. His grief is too much for him to bear. Who knows why? A weakness, a sensitivity of which no one was ever aware, and people say it's not natural that a man in his mid-forties should grieve so for the loss of a mother. But it happens, and let me remind you that Hamlet, granted a much younger man than Ike, also grieved for the loss of a parent to the point of madness. So. It falls on the beautiful young girl to keep her family's body and soul together. That was what the Fates decreed. But there was compensation. At the age of five, the little boy, Leonard, goes to the piano in my flat above the library, I remember it as if it was yesterday, and he sits down and, instead of picking out 'Three Blind Mice', he plays a piece he heard on the wireless that morning, a minuet by Mozart. I don't believe in God, but that day was the nearest I came to it in my whole life. So, all right, being what I am, I settle for the Darwin view. By some accident of evolution, by some random disposition of the species, this couple, thrown together at the bottom of the world, produce a child of extraordinary gifts. And believe me, Belle, it's compensation for all the pain and misery and heartache. And something else. It placed on you an obligation which you took seriously and fulfilled to the last letter. You nurtured him, encouraged him, slaved for him. Now, he has to leave. He has to go out into the world so that the world can admire this accident of birth, this comet, this star. Nothing will stop it. Neither the lack of money nor the lack of will. It is inevitable. So, stop worrying. Take pleasure from your good fortune. Believe me, all will be well.

(*Silence.*)

BELLE: I have to let him go, Rose. That's the pain. Not the struggle to send him on his way, but the letting go.

ROSE: I know, I know.

(*Silence.*)

BELLE: Read me the Browning.

ROSE: Promise me you won't worry.

BELLE: I promise you I'll win the Irish Sweep.

(ROSE *takes out a book of poetry*.)

ROSE: Robert Browning. (*Glances at her watch*.) It'll have to be short.

BELLE: But not one of his love poems, Rose, something uplifting –

ROSE: All right, something to cheer you up –

(ZADOK *puts his head round the door*.)

ZADOK: I have to be going –

(ROSE *holds up her hand for him to be silent*.)

ROSE: From 'Pippa Passes' by Robert Browning.

ZADOK: Make it snappy.

ROSE: (*Reading*) 'From without is heard the voice of Pippa singing –

> The year's at the spring
> And day's at the morn;
> Morning's at seven:
> The hillside's dew-pearled;
> The lark's on the wing;
> The snail's on the thorn;
> God's in his heaven –
> All's right with the world!'

ZADOK: Touch wood. I'm off –

ROSE: What time is it?

ZADOK: Quarter past.

ROSE: I'm off, too –

BELLE: Must you?

ROSE: Yes, I must.

(ZADOK *withdraws*. ROSE *gathers her things*.)

Maybe see you at the weekend, Belle –

BELLE: Bring the Browning again –

ROSE: (*Kissing her*) Don't worry too much, Belle, though I know you, if there was nothing to worry about you'd worry there was nothing to worry about –

(*She goes, leaving the door ajar*.)

BELLE: (*Calling*) Len, here a moment –

ROSE: (*From the hall*) Where's Leonard?

ZADOK: (*Off, bellowing*) Leonard!

ROSE: (*Off*) So, Ike, did you have a nice chat with Zadok?

IKE: (*Off*) We had a chat.

ROSE: (*Off*) That's nice.

> (BELLE *takes knitting and a newspaper from her bag and starts to knit while reading.*)

ZADOK: (*Off*) Leonard, your mother wants you. We're just off. (*Pause.*) Where you going? Don't I get a kiss. (*Pause. Then sounds of* ZADOK's *grunts of pleasure.*) (*Off.*) I love this boy.

BELLE: (*Calling*) Leonard, where are you?

ZADOK: (*Off*) Goodnight, I'm off.

ROSE: (*Off*) Goodnight, Len, Ike. See you soon. Goodnight, Belle –

ZADOK: (*Off*) Goodnight, Belle –

BELLE: Goodnight.

> (*After a moment,* LEONARD *enters.*)

Ask your father if he wants cold chicken or eggs for supper.

> (LEONARD *stands in the doorway.*)

LEONARD: Dad, do you want cold chicken or eggs for supper?

IKE: (*Off*) Eggs.

LEONARD: (*To* BELLE *in her room*) Eggs. I'll have eggs, too.

> (*He goes, closing the door. Silence.* BELLE *knits and reads. After a moment a knock on the door.*)

BELLE: Who is it?

IKE: (*Off*) Me.

> (*Silence.* IKE *comes into the room and closes the door.*)

Belle –

BELLE: What?

IKE: Can you – can you lend me half-a-crown?

BELLE: Can I what?

IKE: Half-a-crown, Belle, that's all, I'm broke, I want some cigarettes, I –

BELLE: I'm not a bank.

> (IKE *stands for a moment, trying to control his pain then turns and storms out of the room.*)

IKE: (*Off*) God Almighty, God Almighty – (*Pause, then, a shout:*) Why do you treat me like this? What have I done that's so terrible?

> (*Silence.* BELLE *knits. Lights fade to blackout.*)

SCENE THREE

The hall the moment the last scene ends. IKE *has stormed back into the hall. He sits at the table, trying to calm himself.* LEONARD *is doing his homework.*

BELLE: (*Off, calling*) Leonard. Here a moment.

(LEONARD *rises and goes to the bedroom.*)

(*Off*) Give this to your father.

(LEONARD *comes back into the hall without closing the door. He puts a coin on the table.*)

LEONARD: From Mom.

IKE: Len, do me a favour, pop down to the Greek shop and get me a packet of cigarettes –

BELLE: (*Off*) Leonard, first you have to finish your homework and then practise –

LEONARD: No, no, I'll go now.

BELLE: (*Off*) And close my door –

IKE: I'll do it, you get the cigarettes –

(LEONARD *takes the coin and exits quickly.* BELLE *comes to her door.*)

BELLE: Leonard, close the door, were you born in a barn?

IKE: (*With difficulty*) Belle – Zadok's been talking to David Figg about me. David Figg, the doctor, a top man –

BELLE: I know.

IKE: You know? How do you know?

BELLE: How do I know? Rose told me, that's how I know.

IKE: You know about Hurwitz?

BELLE: About who?

IKE: About Hurwitz, the professor, the psychiatrist –

BELLE: Yes, I know about Hurwitz.

(*Silence.*)

IKE: What you think? (*No response.*) Zadok's going to make an appointment for me. (*No response.*) What you think.

BELLE: (*Intensely irritated*) About what?

IKE: Should I go and see the man?

BELLE: Do what you like.

IKE: I'm asking advice.

BELLE: I'm giving it.

228

IKE: I need some help –

BELLE: You need some help, what about me?

IKE: (*Under his breath*) God Almighty –

BELLE: Yes, God Almighty –
(*Silence.*)

IKE: Figg says my hand's mind over matter. You think it's possible?

BELLE: Yes, I think it's possible.

IKE: I want to use the hand. (*Silence.*) And there's Leonard, this overseas business –

BELLE: You leave Leonard to me –

IKE: Leave him to you, why should I leave him to you? I'm his father –

BELLE: Yes, yes, his father, some father –

IKE: Why should I leave him to you?

BELLE: Because –

IKE: Because what?

BELLE: Because, because –

IKE: Because what, because what?

BELLE: Because what else can you do about it?

IKE: What do you mean, what do you mean, what else can I do about it?

BELLE: You can do nothing about it except leave it to me –

IKE: I can do something about it, I can do something –

BELLE: What, what can you do?

IKE: I'll borrow –

BELLE: You'll borrow –

IKE: Yes, I'll borrow –

BELLE: From whom?

IKE: I'll find someone.

BELLE: Who'll lend you money?

IKE: I'll find someone –

BELLE: You'll find someone –

IKE: I'll borrow some money –

BELLE: Don't talk such nonsense, Ike –

IKE: I'll do it –

BELLE: Do it, do it, yes, do it –

IKE: I'll do it –

BELLE: You talk such nonsense –

IKE: He's my son –

BELLE: Yes, your son, your son –

IKE: I'll borrow some money –

BELLE: Leave me alone –

IKE: When I get the agency for the hangers –

BELLE: When, when, yes, when –

IKE: The plastic hangers, I'll turn the corner, even Zadok thinks so –

BELLE: Zadok, Zadok, what does Zadok know about plastic hangers – ?

IKE: There's a fortune in plastic hangers –

BELLE: There was a fortune in Sir Seymour, there was a fortune in the fish shop –

IKE: I'm talking about plastic hangers –

BELLE: You're talking, you're talking, yes, talking.

>(*Silence.* IKE *shudders, trying to control tears.*)

IKE: What did I do that was so terrible? (*No response.*) It's not a crime to go bankrupt. (*No response.*) It wasn't my fault.

BELLE: No, it was *my* fault.

IKE: I didn't ask to go bankrupt.

BELLE: No, *I* asked for it.

IKE: Shut up, Belle, shut up!

>(*Silence.* IKE *limps back to the table and is about to sit when* LEONARD *returns. He gives* IKE *a packet of ten cigarettes and the change.*)

Give it to your mother, it's your mother's.

>(*While* IKE *lights a cigarette,* LEONARD *goes into the bedroom.*)

BELLE: (*Off*) I don't want it, let him have it –

>(LEONARD *comes back into the hall and puts the money on the table.* IKE *pockets it.*)

>(*Off*) Lennie, were you born in a barn?

LEONARD: What?

BELLE: (*Off*) Close my door.

>(LEONARD *goes to the door.*)

>(*Off*) And, Leonard –

LEONARD: What?

BELLE: (*Off*) Go and practise.

LEONARD: I have to finish my homework first.

(*He closes the door and goes back to the desk.*)

IKE: Len –

LEONARD: (*Weary*) What, Dad?

IKE: (*Lowering his voice*) I owe you a couple of cigarettes.

LEONARD: Dad, don't worry about it.

IKE: I do worry about it, I always pay my debts.

LEONARD: When I need, I'll ask.

IKE: That's a deal.

(BELLE *comes into the hall.*)

BELLE: Leonard, don't you want supper?

LEONARD: I'll make myself a sandwich later.

IKE: I'll have a sandwich, too, Len can make me a sandwich, all right, Len?

LEONARD: Mom, Dad and I have been talking about my going overseas.

BELLE: That's nice for you.

LEONARD: I'm not absolutely certain about Vienna. As I said, I'm keen on New York, but Aunty Rose says London –

BELLE: Aunty Rose always says London.

IKE: We should take advice.

(LEONARD *sits at the table.*)

LEONARD: Yes, yes, I agree, that's right, we should take advice.

IKE: It's not what you know, it's who you know.

BELLE: And who do we know?

LEONARD: Well, I was thinking, there's Miss Katz –

IKE: Anna Katz?

BELLE: Anna Katz, Leonard, please –

LEONARD: Mom, she's a patron of the arts in Cape Town –

BELLE: With her money she can afford to be –

LEONARD: Everyone says she's very cultured –

BELLE: Cultured, Leonard, please, like my left foot she's cultured.

LEONARD: She came to my recital. She was very impressed.

BELLE: I didn't see her there –

(BELLE *sits at the table.*)

LEONARD: She told me I looked like Rachmaninoff.

IKE: Rachmaninoff? Rachmaninoff? What's she talking about, Rachmaninoff? He was bald.

LEONARD: She meant when he was young, Dad.

IKE: Rachmaninoff, you're nothing like Rachmaninoff. I've got pictures of him in Sir John Hammerton, Rachmaninoff looked like a pickled cucumber.

LEONARD: Not when he was young, Dad –

IKE: When he was young he looked like a young pickled cucumber. Rachmaninoff, the woman's mad. You're more like Ronald Colman.

BELLE: Don't be a bloody fool, Ike –

IKE: I'm telling you, he's more in the Ronald Colman style –

LEONARD: Ronald Colman's got a moustache.

IKE: Well, if he had one at your age he must have been very precocious, that's all I can say –

BELLE: Anyway, Ronald Colamn's an actor.

IKE: Leonard can look like an actor –

BELLE: What's he want to look like an actor for?

IKE: It's not who he *wants* to look like, it's who he *does* look like. I'd like to look like King George VI, but I don't, so what can I do about it?

BELLE: (*Laughing*) You talk such rubbish, Ike.

IKE: All I'm saying is, he can't help who he looks like. He could look like Winston Churchill, it's the luck of the draw.

BELLE: Winston Churchill –

IKE: People say I look like Walter Pidgeon –

BELLE: That I can see –

IKE: There you are, I look like an actor, why shouldn't my son look like an actor? And you, Belle, you look like the late Queen Alexandra, Edward VII's wife.

BELLE: I wish I had her money.

IKE: She was a beautiful woman, Belle. All I'm saying is, you can't help who you look like.

BELLE: I wish I did look like Queen Alexandra.

IKE: She was as deaf as a post.

LEONARD: Who was?

IKE: Queen Alexandra.

LEONARD: Was she, Dad?

IKE: Certainly.

BELLE: Was she, Ike?

IKE: The poor woman couldn't hear a fanfare from a full orchestra.

BELLE: Perhaps she didn't want to.

IKE: What are you saying, deafness can be mind over matter?

BELLE: Why not?

(*Silence.*)

IKE: I've been meaning to say, Belle, you've got terrible rings under your eyes.

BELLE: I've got what?

IKE: Rings under your eyes, dark circles.

BELLE: Ike, are you feeling all right?

IKE: I'm fine, why?

BELLE: Because I've had these rings under my eyes for twenty-five years and it's the first time you've noticed them.

IKE: I've had other things to think about.

(*A sort of laugh between them.*)

Look, we're going to find a way, Leonard. God is good. He'll find a way. We're not in Pompeii –

BELLE: What are you talking about? What d'you mean we're not in Pompeii?

IKE: I'm talking about Pompeii and Herculaneum. We can't sit here worrying about volcanic eruptions. We just have to believe that things get better not worse. Perhaps Zadok's right. Perhaps it's up to us. I don't know. Sometimes I'm full of hope, other times I'm in Pompeii and Herculaneum. Anyway, get rid of those shadows, Belle, sleep easy, we'll find a way.

(*Silence.*)

LEONARD: I could work for a year.

BELLE: What?

LEONARD: After I've done my matric, I could work for a year, save as much as possible, that'd help, wouldn't it?

BELLE: How much d'you think you'd earn?

LEONARD: I don't know, twenty, thirty pounds a month, I could save half, that'd help –

IKE: Nonsense, nonsense, I'll work –

BELLE: Ike, please –

IKE: I'll work –

233

BELLE: Ike, you haven't worked for two, three, four years –

IKE: I'll find a job –

BELLE: You say that –

IKE: I mean it –

BELLE: What kind of job – ?

IKE: I don't know –

BELLE: What's there for you to do?

IKE: I'll work, I'll work –

BELLE: Yes, yes, you'll work –

IKE: Give me another week, I'll know about the plastic hangers –

BELLE: Plastic hangers –

IKE: Give me a week –

BELLE: Give you a week, I've given you twenty-five years –

IKE: I'm asking for a little time, a week, that's all, maybe ten days, I'm waiting to hear, it's not my fault.

BELLE: Not your fault, not your fault, whose fault is it, mine? If it's not your fault I'd like to know whose fault it is –

LEONARD: Please, please –

BELLE: Leonard, don't interfere –

IKE: I've had bad luck, that's all, I've had some bad luck –

BELLE: Other people have bad luck, it seems to change, your bad luck lasts a lifetime –

(LEONARD *goes into the sitting room.*)

IKE: (*Without pause*) It's only been difficult since the war –

BELLE: It was difficult before the war, that's when you had the nervous breakdown, before the war –

IKE: My mother died, Belle –

BELLE: You won't have a nervous breakdown when I die.

IKE: I've had my troubles –

BELLE: You're telling me –

(*In the living room* LEONARD *starts to play the piano loudly and furiously: Rachmaninoff's Prelude. Opus 3, No. 2. In the hall,* IKE *and* BELLE *instinctively raise their voices.*)

IKE: It wasn't my fault I went bankrupt –

BELLE: You've been bankrupt all your life –

IKE: You've got no pity –

BELLE: No one's got any pity –

IKE: What did I do that's so terrible? I keep asking the question

234

but I don't get the answer. What did I do?

BELLE: It's what you didn't do –

IKE: Where's your pity, then, where's your pity?

BELLE: Pity for what, pity for who?

IKE: For me, for me, I'm a sick man, yes, pity for me –

BELLE: For you? For you? Pity for you?

IKE: Yes, for me, for me, pity for me –

BELLE: Me, me, me, me, me, me, me –

(*There is a banging on the ceiling, which they ignore.*)

IKE: Belle, the world hasn't treated me well –

BELLE: Oh, shut up, shut up, for God's sake, shut up, the world, me, but never you, Ike, never you –

IKE: I was given a hand with fours high –

BELLE: Given what, a hand with what, given what?

IKE: Fours high, fours high –

BELLE: Fours high, fours high, you're mad, what are you talking about, fours high, your mind's disturbed –

IKE: My mind, my mind –

BELLE: Zadok's right, you should see a psychiatrist, go and see a psychiatrist –

IKE: Why don't you go and see a psychiatrist? You're also in need of treatment –

BELLE: You can always divorce me –

IKE: Divorce you, yes, divorce you –

(*More banging on the ceiling.*)

– and what about Leonard? How can I divorce you when we've got a child like Leonard?

(BELLE *storms into her room.* LEONARD *continues to play the piano in the living room.* IKE *sits at the table and then suddenly starts to have difficulty breathing. He tries to calm down but gasps noisily, like awful moans. He tries to stand but can't. The music continues. At last* IKE *manages to stand. He staggers to Belle's bedroom door.*)

Belle –

(*He collapses.* BELLE *opens her door.*)

BELLE: (*Almost a scream*) Ike!

(*She goes to him.*)

Ike, what is it – ?

IKE: I can't – I can't – catch my – my breath –

BELLE: (*A scream*) Leonard!

(*The music continues.*)

(*Louder*) Leonard!

(*The music continues.*)

(*Shouting*) Leonard, come quickly –

(LEONARD *comes into the hall.*)

Get a doctor, run to the corner, get Dr Simons –

LEONARD: What's happened, what's the matter with Dad?

BELLE: Just go –

(LEONARD *runs from the house.* IKE *hyperventilates.*)

The doctor's coming, Ike, the doctor's coming –

IKE: I can't – I can't – I can't –

BELLE: Don't try to speak, don't try to speak –

IKE: (*With enormous effort; staccato*) I'm not – I'm not – I'm trying – to catch – my breath –

(BELLE *watches over him. Lights fade to blackout.*)

SCENE FOUR

A week later. Night. BELLE *and* LEONARD *are sitting in Belle's bedroom. The mirrors are covered.*

BELLE: Doctors. What do they know? Meningioma. Sounds like something a poet should die from. Meningioma. Shall I read what David Figg says? A GP. A top man. (*She picks up a letter. Reading:*) 'Meningioma means a tumour growing along the blood vessels on the surface of the brain. It can be either malignant or benign. In your late husband's case, the tumour was benign. We know very little about such growths. The pathologist is of the opinion that the tumour had been present for several years but that its development was erratic. For long periods it would, apparently, lie dormant and then, due perhaps to some emotional or physical disturbance, become active, causing slow progressive damage to the brain. What is puzzling is that Mr Lands did not suffer unduly from the symptoms one would normally expect, such as severe headaches or convulsive seizures. I hope all of this is

236

of some help. I wish you and your son long life. David Figg.'
(*Silence*.) Meningioma. And David Figg was the doctor who
said mind over matter. Doctors. What do they know?
(*Silence*.) You know the worst two words in the English
language, Leonard, in any language? 'If only.' (*Silence*.) It
makes me laugh. Everything these days is psychology.
Everybody's blaming their parents or their nannies,
everybody's suffering from an unhappy childhood or some
shock to their system they can't talk about until Freud
interprets their dreams and life is suddenly bearable again.
Everybody's haunted by their own past. Trust Ike to be
different. With Ike it was never just one thing. With him it
couldn't just be mind over matter, it couldn't just be a
growth on the brain, it had to be both. Such a complex man.
Meningioma. 'If only.' (*Silence*.) Leonard, I wish you'd cry,
I'm stifled with foreboding. (*Silence*.) I should have known
he was seriously ill when he mentioned the shadows under
my eyes. Twenty-five years of marriage and the first time he
says anything about my eyes is on the day he dies. (*Silence*.)
I'm not going to be haunted. I'm not going to ruin the rest of
my life with guilt. I'm not going to apologize. We fought.
We argued. I'm a difficult woman. He was a difficult man.
I'm not going to lie. We only fought about one thing.
Perhaps money was a symbol, who knows? (*Silence*.) I can't
weep either. But that's all right. I've seen those widows at
their husbands' funerals, they throw themselves into the
grave, weep and wail and tear their hair out. They're always
the quickest to remarry. (*Silence*.) I'm never going to lie
about Ike and me. I won't bathe his memory in sunshine.
(*Silence*.) The past is the past. What will be, will be. I'm a
fatalist. We have to make plans, Leonard. We have to think
only of the future, your future. You'll go overseas, Vienna,
London, New York, wherever. Don't worry, somehow
you'll go. If I have to eat one meal a week, you'll go. I'll work
to the end of the chapter. As long as there's a purpose I don't
mind. Because, to tell you the truth, Leonard, there's
nothing else I care about except your future. Not now. I
always thought when I had you that I couldn't be alone ever

237

again. Well, one can always be wrong. I have total confidence in you, I believe in your gifts, I have absolute faith. You're my future, Leonard. The past can go to hell. (*Silence. Lights fade to blackout.*)

ACT TWO

*Thirty-five years later. The studio and control booth of a recording
studio in Maida Vale, London. The studio is dominated by a grand
piano. There are microphones on stands; others are suspended. Music
stands. Chairs. A door to a corridor, which leads to the outside world
and to the control booth, which is separated from the studio by a large
sound-proof window and is fitted with a console and a bank of
sound-mixing equipment, amplifiers, speakers. Chairs at the console.
Behind the main control area is space with chairs.*

SCENE ONE

*Just after 1 p.m. The sound of a Rachmaninoff prelude over the
speakers. A dim light on two* TECHNICIANS *in the control booth. In
the studio,* LEONARD, *now fifty-one, listens and makes notes on a
printed manuscript. Into the control booth comes* JEREMY LANDS *aged
eighteen, smart, contemporary, trendy. He is, however, deeply
unconfident and easily embarrassed by himself and others. He sees*
LEONARD *in the studio. He asks permission of the* TECHNICIANS
then switches a switch on the console.

JEREMY: (*Through the loudspeaker*) Dad – ? Dad – ?
    (LEONARD *jumps with fright then sees* JEREMY.)
LEONARD: (*Into a microphone*) Jeremy! What are you trying to do?
    Give me a heart attack?
JEREMY: They're here, is it all right to bring them in?
LEONARD: Have they had lunch?
JEREMY: Yes.
LEONARD: Where are they?
JEREMY: In the corridor. I thought I'd better check –
TECHNICIAN: Shall we take lunch now, Maestro?

LEONARD: Yes, back in an hour.

(The two TECHNICIANS *leave.* ROSE, *now eighty-six, and* ZADOK *eighty-nine, enter.* ROSE *a little hard of hearing, and* ZADOK *who walks on two sticks, enter the control booth.)*

ROSE: Where is he, I could hear Leonard's voice, where is he?

LEONARD: *(Through the speaker)* I'm in the studio, Aunty Rose –

ZADOK: *(Confused)* Where, where, where – ?

JEREMY: *(Pointing)* He's in there –

ROSE: There he is!

(They stand at the window, waving to him. LEONARD *waves back.)*

LEONARD: Jeremy, bring them round –

*(*JEREMY *ushers* ROSE *and* ZADOK *out of the booth.* LEONARD *goes to the studio door and opens it for them. He kisses* ROSE *and goes to to kiss* ZADOK *but* ZADOK *grabs his cheeks and squeezes them with grunts of pleasure.)*

Where's Mom?

ROSE: She's gone where you can't go for her.

LEONARD: Jeremy, go and wait for Granny. I don't want her to get lost.

*(*JEREMY *goes.)*

ZADOK: Don't worry about her. Belle doesn't get lost that easily. Independent? I've never known a woman like it. I should be so independent. But what can I do with these sticks? I should stick them, that's what I should do, I should stick these sticks where the monkey sticks his nuts.

(He laughs.)

ROSE: Ignore him, he's ga-ga.

ZADOK: I've got to sit down. Can I sit in this chair?

LEONARD: Sit anywhere –

ZADOK: All right, I'll sit on the floor.

(He laughs and sits on a chair.)

ROSE: *(A warning)* Len, you have to tell your mother. You know what I'm talking about.

ZADOK: What's going on, what's going on, what's the big secret?

ROSE: You know the secret, Leonard told me in absolute confidence yesterday, and I told you last night. Now Len's got to tell Belle.

ZADOK: Me, I don't give a damn what you do, Len. But remember this: there's no justice in this world.

LEONARD: As my father used to say.

ZADOK: Ike never said anything like that in all his life. All Ike knew was God is good. And that he got wrong.

LEONARD: So, did you have a good morning?

ROSE: Fish and chips.

ZADOK: You have to shout, she's as deaf as a post.

LEONARD: Did you have a good morning?

ROSE: You know where we went?

LEONARD: Where?

ROSE: To Stepney. To see the house where we were born, the three of us.

ZADOK: Only it wasn't there.

LEONARD: Couldn't you find it?

ZADOK: How can you find a house that's been bombed to bits? The Germans bombed our house. They were totally indiscriminate. I almost wept, me, a dry, dusty, unemotional man. And what they've put up in its place, you can't imagine. Sometimes I think Hitler won the war. What they've done to London, it looks like Albert Speer designed the buildings. You know who Albert Speer was?

LEONARD: Hitler's architect.

ROSE: Of course he knows who Albert Speer was. Leonard reads books. He's cultured. (*Again, the warning.*) You must talk to your mother, Len, otherwise there'll be hell to pay.

LEONARD: Yes, yes, I will.

ROSE: Where is she? She said she was going to the lavatory.

ZADOK: Perhaps she didn't mean in this building, perhaps she meant in Timbuctoo.

ROSE: Ignore him, he's ga-ga.

ZADOK: And when are we going to see you properly, Leonard? We've been here two days, we've hardly talked –

ROSE: He's a busy man, Zadok, a famous man –

ZADOK: So famous men talk to their relations, don't they, how else do you explain nepotism?

LEONARD: Tomorrow, I promise, I've kept the whole morning free. You'll come to the flat and we'll talk. Jeremy will drive you.

ROSE: Thank you, I'd rather take a taxi. That Jeremy of yours drives like he's on the dodgems. But what a beautiful boy, I could eat him. What's he going to do with his life – ?

ZADOK: God forbid he wants to be a chauffeur –

ROSE: Is he still so keen on the theatre? Stella said his heart was set on becoming an actor –

LEONARD: You ask him, Aunty Rose, he doesn't tell me anything. He's extremely bright and extremely obstinate.

ZADOK: Leonard, you still see Stella?

ROSE: Zadok, don't be so tactless –

(BELLE, *aged eighty-four, enters with* JEREMY. *She has aged well, is smartly dressed, well-groomed.* LEONARD *kisses her.*)

LEONARD: All right, Mom?

BELLE: Never better.

ZADOK: We thought you got flushed down the toilet.

BELLE: Ignore him, he's ga-ga.

ZADOK: What about me? Why don't I get a kiss? Have I got impetigo or something?

ROSE: You've had a kiss.

ZADOK: When, when, when did I have a kiss?

ROSE: Leonard, do me this favour, kiss Zadok again or he'll drive us all mad.

(LEONARD *leans over to kiss* ZADOK, *but squeezes his cheeks instead.*)

LEONARD: (*To* BELLE) So, I hear you couldn't find the house.

BELLE: Would you believe it? The Germans bombed it.

ROSE: I was telling Len we couldn't find the house.

BELLE: She's as deaf as a post. She only hears what she shouldn't hear.

ROSE: What time does the recording start? I'm so excited, I've never been in a recording studio before –

LEONARD: At about two. The technicians are having lunch. I've only one more prelude to do.

BELLE: Rachmaninoff?

LEONARD: Yes.

BELLE: (*To* ROSE *proudly*) He's going to record one more Rachmaninoff prelude. I'm sick to death of listening to you on records, Leonard, I want to hear you in the flesh for a change. When you play in Cape Town next year, you must play Rachmaninoff.

ZADOK: (*Disparaging*) British workmen.

ROSE: What are you talking about, Zadok?

ZADOK: The technicians. British workmen. Never finish a job.

ROSE: They've got to eat, Zadok.

ZADOK: Why?

ROSE: (*A loud whisper, to* LEONARD) Please talk to your mother, Leonard. You've got to tell her.

BELLE: What's going on, what's he got to tell me?

LEONARD: And you, Uncle Zadok, I hear you've moved into the Old Aged Home. Are you comfortable there?

ZADOK: Who says?

LEONARD: I'm asking.

ZADOK: I'm comfortable, but have you tried talking to old people? You think Rose is deaf –

ROSE: Who says I'm deaf?

BELLE: You see, what she shouldn't hear she hears.

ZADOK: We've got one fellow there, Abe Bendel, this man couldn't hear a baboon fart two feet away –

BELLE: Zadok –

ZADOK: I'm telling you. He gives us all laryngitis.

LEONARD: But you're happy there.

ZADOK: Happy. Yes, I'm happy. Every morning I wake up, I jump out of bed, I dance the sailor's hornpipe, I sing the Hallelujah Chorus, I open the windows, I shout out, 'I'm so happy here in the Old Aged Home', me, a former Professor of Moral Philosophy, a dry, dusty, unemotional man, I'm so happy I'm singing, I'm dancing, 'Hal-le-lu-jah'.

BELLE: Oh, shut up, Zadok, you get on my nerves, you're about as dry and dusty as a tragedy queen.

LEONARD: And Aunty Rose, you still live above the lending library?

ROSE: If I wasn't near my books I'd die.

ZADOK: So, instead of a shroud they'll wrap you in a dust jacket.

ROSE: (*Her loud whisper*) Leonard, you've got to tell your mother –

BELLE: Rose, if you whisper any louder you may as well shout.

243

What have you to to tell me, Leonard? Is it bad news?
(*Genuinely anxious*.) Aren't you well?

LEONARD: I'm fine, it can keep, so what's all the Sea Point gossip?

ZADOK: Stand by, here comes the obituary column.

ROSE: Poor Miss Anna Katz died.

ZADOK: What did I tell you?

LEONARD: I'm sorry, what was wrong with her?

ZADOK: She was ninety, that's what was wrong with her.

BELLE: (*Mouths the word*) Cancer.

LEONARD: What?

BELLE: (*Again mouthing the word*) Cancer.

ZADOK: Cancer, cancer, say it, you're not going to catch it from
saying it. Cancer. It's a perfectly healthy disease.

ROSE: A healthy disease, he's ga-ga.

BELLE: Leonard, what is it you're supposed to tell me?

LEONARD: Miss Anna Katz, Jeremy, was extremely kind to me
when I was young. She arranged a big farewell benefit concert
for me in Cape Town. They raised a lot of money. Without her
I couldn't have gone overseas.

ROSE: Never mind Miss Katz, without your mother you couldn't
have gone overseas.

BELLE: And she was so looking forward to your welcome back
concert next year. The last time I saw her that's all she talked
about. A week later –

ROSE: Well, that's life, Belle.

ZADOK: No, Rose, that's death.

BELLE: Leonard, I'm filled with foreboding. I've been filled with
foreboding all my life. I always expect something terrible to
happen. I'm always on edge, minute by minute, hour by hour,
day by day, I think the world's going to explode. I can't bear
it. I want to know what's going on.

LEONARD: Tell you what, come through with me into the control
booth, we can talk there. Come on, Mom. Jeremy, you look
after Uncle Zadok and Aunty Rose.
(*He leads* BELLE *out*.)

ROSE: She's going to have a nervous breakdown, I'm telling you.

ZADOK: Listen, Belle doesn't have nervous breakdowns, that was
Ike's department.

ROSE: He should have told her right away.

JEREMY: Yes, but Dad's a coward.

(*An awkward silence.* LEONARD *and* BELLE *appear in the booth and they sit.* ROSE, ZADOK, *and* JEREMY *watch them.*)

ROSE: Life's funny.

ZADOK: I'm not laughing.

ROSE: Look at them, mother and son. Your grandmother, Jeremy, sacrificed everything for your father. Everything. And now he's going to break her heart.

ZADOK: You read too many novels, Rose. Belle sacrificed nothing. She did what she wanted to do. And she's got a heart like a rock. She'll live for ever. And don't get sentimental. I can't bear sentimentality.

ROSE: She seems to be taking it well.

JEREMY: He hasn't told her yet.

ROSE: How do you know?

JEREMY: I know.

(*In the booth,* LEONARD *switches a switch.*)

LEONARD: Mom wants to say something.

ROSE: Oh my God, here it comes –

LEONARD: Speak, Mom, they can hear now –

BELLE: I've got this to say. Stop staring at us. You're making me feel as though I'm in a goldfish bowl. (*To* LEONARD.) They won't take any notice, Rose probably didn't even hear me, in five minutes she'll be looking again, nosy – (LEONARD *switches the switch. He and* BELLE *continue to talk.*)

ROSE: Belle's such a difficult woman.

ZADOK: Talking of difficult women, how's your mother, Jeremy? How's Stella?

JEREMY: Fine.

ROSE: Stella was never difficult, Stella was an angel. I'd love to see her again. You remember when you visited us in Cape Town, Jeremy? What a time we had –

ZADOK: How could he remember? He was three years old –

ROSE: I'd really love to see Stella again.

ZADOK: So would I, what a girl, what a figure.

JEREMY: She said she'd like to see you, but –

ZADOK: And fair hair, I've never seen such fair hair. A suicide
blonde. Dyed by her own hand.
(*He laughs.*)

ROSE: Stella never dyed her hair. She was a natural blonde. How
can you say such a thing?

ZADOK: It's a joke, an old joke, can't a man make an old joke?

ROSE: And the most beautiful complexion I've ever seen. Peaches
and cream, a real English beauty.

ZADOK: No one's got any sense of humour any more.

ROSE: The Honourable Mrs Leonard Lands, what a ring that had
to it –

ZADOK: What's she talking about now?

ROSE: I'm talking about Stella. She's an Honourable. Her father's
a Lord –

ZADOK: I know, I know, my memory's unimpaired, unlike your
hearing –

ROSE: The Mitfords were all Honourable. They had a cupboard.
The Hons cupboard.

ZADOK: What are you talking about. Honourable? One of them
was Hitler's popsy. She had a funny name.

ROSE: Unity.

ZADOK: Unity, what a name. She was a Nazi, she should've
stayed in the cupboard. And one of them married Mosley,
what's so Honourable about them?

ROSE: It's a title, Zadok. (*To* JEREMY.) Please, ignore him.

ZADOK: I don't see why we can't see Stella. Just because they're
divorced, it doesn't mean we can't see her.
(ROSE *looks into the booth.*)

ROSE: You think he's told her yet?

JEREMY: No. He's still looking at her. You'll know when he tells
her. When he turns his back. Dad never looks at you when
he's got something unpleasant to say.
(*An awkward silence.*)

ZADOK: I'll tell you something in confidence, Jeremy. Your
father, he was always a secretive boy.

ROSE: He's an artist. All artists are secretive.

ZADOK: Listen, you want my candid opinion, I always thought
Leonard was a little bit wet.

246

ROSE: What are you talking about? You adored him, you still adore him –

ZADOK: You can adore someone who's wet.

ROSE: Please don't talk like this in front of Jeremy. It's not seemly.

ZADOK: Nonsense. He's family. In a family everything's seemly.

ROSE: Your father came to England when he was seventeen, Jeremy –

JEREMY: I know –

ROSE: – all on his own, his mother let him go, just like that, at seventeen, he was still wet behind the ears, but he coped, he managed and he's had a wonderful career, a wonderful life. Even my hairdresser's heard of Leonard Lands. They buy his records, we're talking about a leading musician, our Leonard, just imagine.

ZADOK: When your father was a boy, Jeremy, you never knew what he was thinking. He never said much. Always very quiet, docile. Cowed. That's the word I want, cowed. And very hard to get at.

JEREMY: That's still true.

ROSE: He's an artist, a musician, a pianist. A pianist doesn't have to think, he doesn't have to speak he doesn't have to be noisy. All a pianist has to do is play the piano and that Leonard does divinely.

ZADOK: (*To* JEREMY) In her eyes your father can do no wrong.

ROSE: He's given me more pleasure than any other human being I've ever known.

ZADOK: What she shouldn't hear she hears –

ROSE: He's also the pride of Belle's life and that's why I'm so concerned that when he tells her – God knows what it'll do to her.

ZADOK: I'll tell you the trouble with your father, Jeremy. He bottles things up inside.

JEREMY: That's what the doctor said after his breakdown. (*Shocked silence.*)

ROSE: Whose breakdown?

JEREMY: Dad's.

ROSE: When? When did he have a breakdown?

247

JEREMY: Five years ago, just after Mummy left him.

ZADOK: Did he have an X-ray?

JEREMY: No, Uncle Zadok, it was a breakdown. You don't have an X-ray for a breakdown.

ZADOK: In this family you do.

ROSE: Zadok, you're not to mention this to Belle. Why weren't we told? Stella should have told us, someone –

ZADOK: How is he now?

JEREMY: I don't know, I don't see very much of him any more. And when we meet all we seem to do is row.

(*Silence. In the booth,* LEONARD *stands and turns his back on* BELLE.)

He's telling her now.

(*They watch.*)

ZADOK: Cramp! I've got cramp. I've got to stand. Jeremy, help me –

(JEREMY *helps* ZADOK *to stand.* ZADOK *stamps his feet.*)

ROSE: Are you all right? We walked too much this morning, are you all right?

ZADOK: It'll go, it'll go –

(ROSE *rushes to the window.*)

ROSE: (*Yelling at* BELLE *and* LEONARD) It's only cramp! It'll go!

JEREMY: Aunty Rose, they can't hear you –

ROSE: (*Yelling*) It's only cramp.

ZADOK: Don't shout at me, I know it's cramp. I'm not deaf, I know it'll go –

(LEONARD *and* BELLE *have noticed the fuss in the studio.* LEONARD *switches a switch.*)

LEONARD: What's the matter?

ROSE: (*Yelling*) Zadok's got cramp!

BELLE: I thought he was having a heart attack.

ZADOK: It's gone. It's all right. Don't make such a fuss. I'm fine.

ROSE: (*To the booth, yelling*) He's fine.

BELLE: I can hear, thank you.

ROSE: He's as fit as a fiddle.

ZADOK: From your mouth into God's ear.

ROSE: (*Whispering*) Everything all right, Belle?

BELLE: (*To* LEONARD) She doesn't realize the microphone's on.

248

(LEONARD *switches the switch but* BELLE *goes on talking to* ROSE *who, of course, can't hear*.)

ROSE: I can't hear! I can't hear!

(BELLE *has a word with* LEONARD, *who switches the switch again*.)

BELLE: – the switch.

LEONARD: It's on.

BELLE: You're sure?

LEONARD: Yes, I'm sure.

BELLE: All right, then. (*To the studio*.) Please leave us in peace, my son and I are having a private conversation.

(LEONARD *switches the switch*. ZADOK *sits*. BELLE *and* LEONARD *continue to talk in the booth*.)

ROSE: You all right, Zadok?

ZADOK: How do I look?

ROSE: You look all right.

ZADOK: Then why ask?

(*Silence*. ROSE *looks into the booth*. BELLE *sees her and waves her away*.)

ROSE: I don't think she's taking it well.

(*Silence*.)

ZADOK: Jeremy, this breakdown your father had, was he very ill?

JEREMY: I think so. He couldn't play for three or four months.

ROSE: Why, was there something wrong with his hands, why, why, why couldn't he play?

JEREMY: I don't know –

ROSE: Stella was right not to tell Belle. (*Silence*.) It's like music.

ZADOK: What's like music?

ROSE: Life. Life's like music.

ZADOK: Rose, I'm the philosopher. You leave life to me. I'll leave art to you.

ROSE: If we left life to philosophers there'd be no art. Life is like music.

ZADOK: She's going to tell us whether we want to hear or not.

ROSE: You have themes, variations, movements, motifs, developments, resolutions –

ZADOK: What are you talking about, resolutions, what resolutions? In life nothing is ever resolved –

ROSE: Take the whole business with Ike. His illness. His tumour and his state of mental health. Think of it as a theme. Now Leonard plays a variation.

ZADOK: And she says I'm ga-ga. And you, Jeremy, what variations are you going to play?

JEREMY: I don't know.

ZADOK: They tell me you're very bright.

ROSE: You still want to be an actor?

ZADOK: How can he be very bright and still want to be an actor?

ROSE: The last time Stella wrote to me she said you wanted to be an actor.

JEREMY: I don't know now. I don't know whether to be an actor or a merchant banker.

ROSE: Are you serious?

JEREMY: Yes. I think nowadays one needs to make money young –
(*He becomes embarrassed.*)

ROSE: That's a choice? An actor or a merchant banker?

ZADOK: Be a merchant banker. It's more precarious.
(*He laughs.*)

ROSE: What does your mother say?

JEREMY: She says I must make up my own mind. I don't think she really cares –

ROSE: Of course she cares. And your father, what's his opinion?

JEREMY: I haven't discussed it with him.

ZADOK: You and Leonard are not close?

JEREMY: No.

ZADOK: So, Rose, what kind of variation is that? You see, Jeremy, Leonard and his father were like that –
(*He crosses his fingers.*)

ROSE: You talk such nonsense, Zadok. Lennie and Ike hardly ever exchanged three words consecutively.

ZADOK: Never mind, I always had the feeling they were thick as thieves. There was something between them. An unspoken understanding. I would say they were close.

ROSE: You would say, you would say, take no notice of him, Jeremy, he's ga-ga.

JEREMY: My father and I have never exchanged more than three

250

words consecutively. He disapproves of me. I disapprove of him.

ROSE: Jeremy, that's a terrible thing to say –

JEREMY: It's true.

ZADOK: What do you disapprove of? Don't you like the way he plays the piano?

JEREMY: My father wants to be loved too much.

ZADOK: Who doesn't? Let me tell you, Jeremy, my wife died after we were married three months, and –

(*He shudders with tears.*)

ROSE: All right, Zadok, all right –

ZADOK: (*Still shuddering*) It's not all right, it's not all right, it's not such a terrible thing to want to be loved.

JEREMY: (*Gaining confidence*) But Dad doesn't want to be loved by me or by Mummy, he wants to be loved by the world. He wants to be thought well of. He wants not only to be on the right side, but also to be seen to be on the right side.

ZADOK: This boy *is* bright.

JEREMY: It's not enough for him to be a wonderful pianist, he has to be a public figure, sign petitions, march, support causes –

ZADOK: And you don't? You don't support causes? I thought all young people these days supported causes.

JEREMY: Only after I've made up my own mind.

ZADOK: That sounds smug, oh God, does that sound smug.

JEREMY: (*Embarrassed*) I'm sorry. That's what I feel. That's why I've decided to visit South Africa –

ZADOK: You're coming to South Africa? When? You hear that, Rose? Jeremy is coming out to South Africa.

ROSE: What? What? I haven't been following, I thought he said he wasn't coming to South Africa –

ZADOK: No, Jeremy, Jeremy's coming to South Africa –

ROSE: Jeremy! When, when are you coming, when?

JEREMY: When I've saved enough –

ROSE: What d'you mean, saved enough? Isn't your father paying? he can afford it –

JEREMY: He's matching me pound for pound –

ZADOK: Another merchant banker –

JEREMY: I'm working at night in a restaurant and saving all I can.

Dad doesn't want me to go. He says I'm doing it for spite. He may be right. But what he actually thinks is that it'll reflect badly on him. I know my father. Anyway, he doesn't really believe I'll save enough. But I've nearly there. I want to see South Africa for myself. I want to make up my own mind.

ROSE: I'm surprised at your father making you work. What a dreadful thing.

ZADOK: Does your Granny know you're coming to see her?

JEREMY: I don't think so.

ROSE: Oh, what a time we'll give you, what a time you'll have, I can't wait to tell Belle – (*She turns to the window. Yelling.*) Belle, Jeremy's coming to South Africa –

ZADOK: She missed her vocation, she should have been a town crier.

ROSE: What's happened in there? (*Yelling*) Is Belle all right? (*To* ZADOK *and* JEREMY.) She looks in a terrible state. (*Yelling*) What's the matter with Belle – ?

(LEONARD *switches the switch.*)

– is she upset, what's the matter with Belle?

(LEONARD *and* BELLE *wince.*)

BELLE: God, I'll go deaf too if you shout like that. (*Wiping her eyes.*) Nothing's the matter. I'm laughing. We had a good laugh. Like the old days. Now, I'm dry as a bone. I'd love a coffee but I'll settle for water.

ROSE: I'd like coffee, too.

ZADOK: Don't leave me out whatever you do.

LEONARD: Jeremy, there's coffee down the passage. It's only a machine, I'm afraid.

ZADOK: These days, everything's a machine –

LEONARD: I'd like one, too. Black for me. Mom?

BELLE: I'll have white.

ROSE: I want a black one, Jeremy.

JEREMY: Uncle Zadok?

ZADOK: Black.

JEREMY: And a black for me. That's four blacks, one white.
(*He goes.*)

ZADOK: Four blacks, one white. It's like being back home.

(*He laughs.*)

ROSE: Has he told you, Belle?

BELLE: Yes, Rose, he's told me.

ROSE: And?

(*Lights fade to blackout.*)

SCENE TWO

The control booth. Approximately the same time as the previous scene. Through the window LEONARD *can be seen leading* BELLE *out of the studio. After a moment they appear in the control room, watched by* ROSE, ZADOK *and* JEREMY, *who are now the ones to be seen but not heard.*

LEONARD: Sit down, Mom, no one can hear us in here.

BELLE: Leonard, before we talk, I have to say something important to you.

LEONARD: What?

BELLE: Your hair's too long.

LEONARD: Mom, I'm fifty-one years old, I've been married and divorced, I'm a father of a grown-up boy, and this is the way I wear my hair.

BELLE: I can't help it, it's still too long. So, what do you have to tell me?

LEONARD: All in good time, it's nothing important.

BELLE: You're not ill, are you?

LEONARD: I'm not ill. Just let's have a nice chat. I've hardly seen you.

BELLE: You haven't changed, Leonard. You were always a bad liar.

(*She notices* ROSE *and the others staring at them.*)

What's she looking at? She's such a nosy woman. I want to tell her something –

(LEONARD *switches the switch.*)

LEONARD: Mom wants to say something.

ROSE: Oh my God, here it comes –

LEONARD: Speak, Mom, they can hear now –

BELLE: I've got this to say. Stop staring at us. You're making me feel as though I'm in a goldfish bowl. (*To* LEONARD.) They won't take any notice, Rose probably didn't even hear me, in five minutes she'll be looking again, nosy –

(LEONARD *switches the switch.*)

– you've never known such a nosy woman.

LEONARD: And how's the new flat. Mom?

BELLE: It's small but I bless you every second for it. And the air-conditioner, you don't know the difference that's made. You'll see it when you come back next year. I can't wait.

LEONARD: So, you're sleeping better now?

BELLE: What are you talking about, please, Leonard, who sleeps? (*An awkward pause.*)

LEONARD: Well, Mom.

BELLE: Sweetheart.

LEONARD: What a long road we've travelled, you and I.

BELLE: Leonard, Leonard.

LEONARD: You look so well.

BELLE: Age is a terrible thing.

LEONARD: You've always looked just the same.

BELLE: From your mouth into God's ear. People say I could pass for seventy-five.

LEONARD: Easily.

BELLE: Yes, yes, you were always such a bad liar. You're sure you're not ill, Leonard?

LEONARD: Mom, I'm not ill.

BELLE: Don't mention your breakdown to Rose and Zadok. It would upset them dreadfully.

LEONARD: You never told them?

BELLE: Are you crazy? They'd have had breakdowns, never mind you. You still have your check-ups?

LEONARD: Mom, I had a CAT scan the other day, I'm absolutely fine.

BELLE: Why didn't you write and tell me?

LEONARD: I've been busy, touring, recording, concerts. You should have told Aunty Rose and Uncle Zadok.

BELLE: Leonard, don't interfere, I know what I'm doing. They've aged terribly. They would never have recovered from the shock. You can see for yourself. With Zadok, I don't know if he's really ga-ga or whether he puts it on. He laughs at his own jokes, always the same jokes, always such old jokes. And Rose. I beg her to get a hearing-aid, but, you know what? She's too vain. What's she got to be vain for? Beats me. Still, they're good for my morale. When I look at them I feel like a young gazelle.

LEONARD: You're sure, when you go back to Cape Town, you don't want to move into a hotel?

BELLE: You mean a home? Don't say hotel when you mean a home, Leonard. I'd die, all those old people, they'd drive me mad. No, I'm better off on my own, independent. Len, tell me honestly, the money you give me every month, can you really afford it? I feel so guilty –

LEONARD: Mom, I can afford it –

BELLE: I don't want to be a burden.

LEONARD: You're not a burden. Do you know what I earn for one concert now? Three, four thousand pounds.

BELLE: For one concert?

LEONARD: Yes, and I give about a hundred concerts a year. Work it out for yourself. And then there are my recordings. That's another three, four hundred thousand pounds a year.
(*Pause.*)

BELLE: You earn more in one night than I earned in my lifetime. Well, well, well. I never thought I'd be able to give up work. Here I am, eighty-four, a lady of leisure. I play cards with my cronies, all the old girls, mind you, they bore me stiff, I'm so easily bored. Sometimes I feel like going out to work again.

LEONARD: And you eat properly, Mom, you look after yourself?

BELLE: Leonard, who eats?
(*Brief silence.* BELLE *is about to speak:*)

LEONARD: Did you get the video I sent? Of the recital in Moscow?

BELLE: Certainly. I think everyone in Cape Town's seen it. They're already queuing up to buy tickets for your concert next year. And Zadok showed it to the Old Aged Home. They've got a video. Seven times he's seen it.

LEONARD: And you?

BELLE: Eight times.

LEONARD: You enjoyed it?

BELLE: Of course.

LEONARD: The Russians were very keen on my Rachmaninoff and that was a big compliment, I can tell you.

BELLE: If I may say so, of course I know nothing, but I have one criticism. I think you show off too much when you play.

LEONARD: What do you mean?

BELLE: People should come and listen to the music, not watch the pianist. You sway and you pull faces and you sweat. They watch you and they forget the music. It pleases the unmusical. A pianist who comes between the audience and the music is no pianist. I love music. I don't love self-assertion. That's my opinion. I know nothing, but it's my opinion. So, next year, when you play in Cape Town, a little restraint won't come amiss. Where will you stay? The Mount Nelson's a lovely hotel. Fancy, Leonard Lands from Sea Point in the Mount Nelson Hotel. (*Silence.*) You're not coming to Cape Town, are you?

(LEONARD *rises and turns his back on her. In the studio the others look into the booth.*)

That's what you had to tell me, isn't it? I can read you like a book, Leonard. I've always read you like a book.

(*In the studio,* JEREMY *helps* ZADOK *to stand.* ZADOK *stamps his feet. Commotion.*)

LEONARD: I'm sorry, Mom, truly I am. It wasn't an easy decision.

BELLE: Politics?

(LEONARD *looks away.*)

Politics, politics, politics.

LEONARD: People, Mom, really, people, people, people –

(ROSE *comes rushing to the window and yells but, of course, they cannot hear her and do not yet see her.*)

BELLE: I hate politics –

LEONARD: (*Noticing the fuss in the studio*) What's wrong with Zadok?

BELLE: Oh my God, he's had a heart attack –

(LEONARD *switches a switch.*)

256

LEONARD: What's the matter?

ROSE: (*Yelling*) Zadok's got cramp!

BELLE: I thought he was having a heart attack.

ZADOK: It's gone. It's all right. Don't make a fuss. I'm fine.

ROSE: (*To the booth, yelling*) He's fine.

BELLE: I can hear, thank you.

ROSE: He's as fit as a fiddle.

ZADOK: From your mouth into God's ear.

ROSE: (*Whispering*) Everything all right, Belle?

BELLE: (*To* LEONARD) She doesn't realize the microphone's on.
    (LEONARD *switches the switch.*)
    (*To* ROSE, *who can't hear*) Rose, the microphone's on, they
    can hear you all over the building, they can probably hear
    you in Piccadilly Circus –
    (ROSE *yells at the window.*)
    Is it on or off, Leonard? For God's sake, I'll have a nervous
    breakdown, stop playing with –
    (LEONARD *switches the switch again.*)
    – the switch.

LEONARD: It's on.

BELLE: You're sure?

LEONARD: Yes, I'm sure.

BELLE: All right, then (*To the studio.*) Please leave us in peace, my
    son and I are having a private conversation.
    (LEONARD *switches the switch. Silence in the booth.*)
    Well. So. There we are. You're not going to give a recital in
    your own home town.

LEONARD: No.

BELLE: Why not?

LEONARD: Because.

BELLE: Leonard, 'because' isn't good enough.

LEONARD: Because everyone has to make their protest in their
    own way. I have only my music. It's a gesture, that's all,
    pathetic, ineffectual, but a gesture. And it has to be made.

BELLE: All these years I waited for this one thing. You, giving a
    recital, being acclaimed in your own home town.

LEONARD: Mom, I have to make a stand.

BELLE: You have to make a stand. Against your own mother?

LEONARD: Oh, Mom, don't be ridiculous –

BELLE: Ridiculous? Ridiculous? Is it ridiculous to ask for a little pleasure out of life? Think of the pleasure you'd give me. Is it such a terrible thing to ask for a little pleasure? When spirits are low, when I'm bored, I think of you, marching on to the stage in Cape Town, the audience rising to greet you, you bowing, and me, sitting there, like a queen, glowing, bursting with pride and pleasure. Is that such a terrible thing to ask?

LEONARD: Mom, believe me, I don't mean to hurt you.

BELLE: Thanks very much, God help me when you do mean it. All right, you won't play in South Africa. That's your decision. That's your right. We won't discuss it again.

LEONARD: Thank you.

BELLE: But why did you tell Rose you weren't coming before you told me?

LEONARD: It just came out.

BELLE: It just came out. Good, that's another reason I'm not speaking to you.

LEONARD: What d'you mean, another reason?

BELLE: That interview you gave.

LEONARD: What interview?

BELLE: In the magazine, with the picture of you in Tokyo –

LEONARD: Mom, I've given a few interviews in my time –

BELLE: Never mind, you know the one I mean –

LEONARD: I don't know what you're talking about.

BELLE: Don't get short with me, Leonard.

LEONARD: What interview?

BELLE: Where you said you came from an unhappy marriage.

LEONARD: Well, I did.

BELLE: I know your father was a very difficult man, but why tell the world?

LEONARD: You want me to lie?

BELLE: Leonard, don't be so clever, your fame doesn't impress me. How can you say such things in public?

LEONARD: Mom, the man asked me –

BELLE: You said being the product of an unhappy marriage had affected you deeply.

258

LEONARD: That's true –

BELLE: How can you say such a thing, Leonard? Can you imagine my embarrassment?

LEONARD: Mom, everyone knows you and Dad weren't happy.

BELLE: But in print, Leonard, in print. No, I think it was very wrong of you –

LEONARD: Mom, it was the making of me –

BELLE: What was?

LEONARD: You and Dad, the unhappiness –

BELLE: Leonard, please, I don't want to talk about it –

LEONARD: Without that pain –

BELLE: What pain? What are you talking about? What pain? You were never in pain. You exaggerate, you strike attitudes, you had a wonderful childhood, everything your heart desired I gave you. What pain, what pain, what do you know about pain?

LEONARD: Mom, pain was the making of me.

(*Silence.*)

BELLE: Well, that's all right, then.

(*Silence.*)

That's why I worry about Jeremy.

LEONARD: What's Jeremy got to do with it?

BELLE: I'm worried about him, that's what he's got to do with it.

LEONARD: Jeremy's all right –

BELLE: I didn't say he wasn't. He's a beautiful boy, I could eat him up, the way he speaks, oh God, what a boy, but I'm worried about him.

LEONARD: Why, for God's sake?

BELLE: Because he's very unhappy. I can tell. He doesn't say much.

LEONARD: Mom, people who don't say much aren't necessarily unhappy.

BELLE: He's withdrawn, he's remote. And he drives that car as if he's trying to kill himself and all his passengers. Thank God Zadok's ga-ga, he would have had a heart attack if he'd noticed the way that boy drives.

LEONARD: Mom, the way Jeremy drives doesn't make him unhappy.

BELLE: I only had to mention your name, he accelerates to a hundred miles an hour and drives at the first car he sees. You think I don't notice these things? (*Pause*) Has he got girlfriends?

LEONARD: I don't know, yes, I think so, I don't know –

BELLE: You want to be careful with him, you know what I mean.

LEONARD: I don't know what you mean –

(BELLE *moistens her third finger and then smoothes her eyebrow.* LEONARD *laughs.*)

Don't be ridiculous, he's perfectly normal.

BELLE: I always used to say to Rose, if I hear Lennie's turned into a 'nice' boy – (*The gesture again*) – I'll take a pair of scissors, I'll go to England and I'll cut it off.

(LEONARD *laughs quietly.*)

You must face it, Leonard. Your son is miserable. And you know why? (*No response.*) Because you should never have divorced Stella.

LEONARD: Mom, I don't want to discuss this –

BELLE: You should have crawled to her on your hands and knees and begged her to come back –

LEONARD: Mom –

BELLE: For Jeremy's sake you should have done that.

LEONARD: It was better for Jeremy we got divorced.

BELLE: Don't say such things to me. You think I endured twenty-five years of hell with your father to be told we should have got divorced? Your father and I didn't get divorced, because of you, for your happiness, for your well-being, for your future –

LEONARD: Mom, please, on't talk such nonsense –

ELLE: Leonard, don't speak to me like that –

LEONARD: I don't want to talk about Stella –

BELLE: You don't want to talk about Stella –

LEONARD: No, I don't want to talk about her –

BELLE: You think I enjoyed the rows –

LEONARD: I don't know –

BELLE: You don't know –

LEONARD: No, I don't know –

BELLE: You think I enjoyed the misery –

260

LEONARD: Mom, I don't care any more –

BELLE: You don't care –

LEONARD: I don't care any more, I don't care, I don't care, I don't care –

BELLE: That's your trouble, Leonard, you've never cared.

LEONARD: Good, fine, terrific, I never cared –

BELLE: You've never cared about another living soul. Only yourself –

LEONARD: That's right, only myself, that's all I've cared about, only myself –

BELLE: Me, me, me, me. You think I don't understand these things?

LEONARD: No, no, I know you understand everything –

BELLE: I understand very well. I don't want you to send me another penny –

LEONARD: What are you talking about now?

BELLE: It's exactly the same as you play the piano. You pose. You strike attitudes. But feeling for people, caring, for your own flesh and blood, never. You give me my allowance and you don't have to think about me for another month. You let Stella walk out on you, and you send Jeremy to boarding-school and he can go to hell for all you care. And when it comes to giving your mother a little pleasure and playing in your own home town, which gave you life, which made you what you are, to play in front of your mother and her family and her friends, what do you do? You strike an attitude. Suddenly you're a political figure –

LEONARD: I'm not talking about you and your pleasure –

BELLE: Don't tell me, I know –

LEONARD: I'm talking about making a stand –

BELLE: You're talking, you're talking, yes, talking –

LEONARD: I didn't ask to be born in South Africa –

BELLE: No, *I* asked for it.

LEONARD: Shut up, Mom, shut up!

(BELLE *is shocked for a moment, then she weeps.*)

I'm sorry.

(ROSE *comes to the window.* BELLE *sees her through her tears.* ROSE *continues to talk.*)

BELLE: What did I tell you? There she is. Give me a moment. I'll pull myself together, switch that switch, Leonard, do as I say for once in your life –

(LEONARD *reaches out and switches the switch*.)

ROSE: (*Her voice booming*) – is she upset, what's the matter with Belle?

(BELLE *and* LEONARD *wince*.)

BELLE: God, I'll go deaf too if you shout like that. (*Wiping her eyes*.) Nothing's the matter. I'm laughing. We had a good laugh. Like the old days. Now, I'm dry as a bone. I'd love a coffee but I'll settle for water.

ROSE: I'd like coffee, too.

ZADOK: Don't leave me out whatever you do.

LEONARD: (*Forcing a smile*) Jeremy, there's coffee down the passage. It's only a machine, I'm afraid.

ZADOK: These days, everything's a machine –

LEONARD: I'd like one, too. Black for me. Mom?

BELLE: I'll have white.

ROSE: I want a black one, Jeremy.

JEREMY: Uncle Zadok?

ZADOK: Black.

JEREMY: And a black for me. that's four blacks, one white. (*He goes*.)

ZADOK: Four blacks, one white. It's like being back home. (*He laughs*.)

ROSE: Has he told you, Belle?

BELLE: Yes, Rose, he's told me.

ROSE: And?

BELLE: (*Sharply*) And.

(*Lights fade to blackout*.)

SCENE THREE

The studio, the moment after the last scene ends. BELLE *enters the studio.*

ROSE: Are you upset, Belle?

BELLE: I'm not easily upset.

ROSE: I've got something to cheer you up.

ZADOK: Jeremy's coming to Cape Town.

ROSE: (*Turning on him*) I was going to tell her –

ZADOK: So, I beat you to it –

BELLE: Jeremy's coming to Cape Town? When?

ROSE: You've become very vindictive in your old age, Zadok.

ZADOK: As I always say, there's no justice in the world.

BELLE: Where is he, where is he? I want to see that boy –

ROSE: He's working to save the money. Leonard's matching him pound for pound –

BELLE: You should only know how much he earns. He's a millionaire and he talks about nothing but money.

ZADOK: I wonder who he takes after.

BELLE: Modern parents, they make you sick –

(JEREMY *returns with the coffee*.)

Jeremy, when you come to Cape Town you'll stay with me. The room's no bigger than a cupboard but at least it will save you paying for a hotel.

(JEREMY *hands out the coffees*.)

(*Continuing*) Someone'll lend you a car, people are very generous. They'll make such a fuss of you, mark my words. You'll meet lots of young people, lots of pretty girls, oh, the girls, Jeremy, you'll love the girls, you'll go to the beach, get a nice tan, what a time you'll have.

JEREMY: Thank you, Gran.

BELLE: (*Confidential*) And listen, I've got a little saved from the money your father gives me each month, you're welcome to it.

JEREMY: Gran, it's not necessary –

BELLE: I'll decide what's necessary. I want you to have the money.

(JEREMY *kisses her on the cheek. She glows*.)

ROSE: And do you read many books, Jeremy?

JEREMY: Not too many. I read music. Dad taught me. He's going to let me turn the pages for him today. Isn't that nice?

ROSE: When you come to Cape Town, you've got the run of my library. Over two thousand volumes and no rubbish.

JEREMY: Thank you.

(ZADOK *stands and crosses to* JEREMY.)

ZADOK: And, Jeremy, will you come and see me in the Old Aged Home?

JEREMY: Of course.

ZADOK: I'll make them put something special on the menu for you. Instead of rice pudding with jam, they'll give you jam with rice pudding.

JEREMY: I like rice pudding.

ZADOK: Hold my sticks.

(JEREMY *does so.* ZADOK *squeezes his cheeks with grunts of pleasure*.)

That boy, I could eat him.

(LEONARD *enters the studio*.)

LEONARD: Perhaps I owe you all an explanation.

BELLE: Leonard, you owe us nothing. There's nothing to explain. What time do you start recording?

ROSE: You know, Leonard, I was thinking, if next year you did come back and play in South Africa, it would have been longer than in *The Winter's Tale*.

ZADOK: What are you talking about now, Rose?

ROSE: The time gap. 'Impute it not a crime/To me or my swift passage, that I slide/O'er sixteen years, and leave the growth/ untried of that wide gap.' In Shakespeare it's sixteen years before we get back to Bohemia. With Leonard it would have been thirty-six before he played the piano again in Cape Town.

ZADOK: So, with Shakespeare you get it wholesale.

(*He loves this*.)

ROSE: Ignore him, Jeremy. It's premature senility.

ZADOK: What d'you mean, premature? I'm eighty-nine, I'm bang on schedule.

BELLE: (*To* LEONARD) What time do you start to record?

LEONARD: The technicians should be back in about twenty minutes.

ZADOK: British workmen.

ROSE: (*To* ZADOK, *a whisper*) Belle's upset, I can see she's upset –

BELLE: Who's upset?

ROSE: Belle, I know you must be upset.

BELLE: About what?

ROSE: About what, she says. About Leonard, of course, about him not coming out. You must be upset.

BELLE: I'm not so easily upset, Rose. And I've got Jeremy to look forward to.

ROSE: Never mind Jeremy, you've talked about nothing else for years. Leonard, at the piano, in Cape Town.

BELLE: What will be, will be.

ROSE: You see? You're upset.

BELLE: Rose, I'm not upset.

ROSE: Not much.

BELLE: Rose, I'll scream in a moment.

ROSE: Scream, it'll do you good.

BELLE: You scream, leave me out of it. (*Long pause*.) God, I hate politics!

ROSE: You see, I told you she's upset.

ZADOK: In the old days, Jeremy, when your father was a boy, we never talked politics. It was strictly *verboten*.

LEONARD: The world's changed, Uncle Zadok.

ZADOK: Don't I know? I'll tell you how much the world's changed, and I've seen it all. In the thirties, for example, no one stopped buying cameras from the Germans. No one stopped inviting Ribbentrop to Cliveden, no one boycotted the Berlin Olympics, that's how much the world's changed. Now the world is full of saints and Mahatma Gandhis.

LEONARD: And about time.

ZADOK: You see, Jeremy, I'm a Pavlovian, a disciple of the Russian psychologist, Pavlov.

ROSE: So, where's your dog?

ZADOK: A very well-read woman, your great-aunt Rose. Listen and learn. Rose, it's never too late. Yes, Pavlov. I believe in the conditioned reflex. I believe everybody in this world is conditioned by where they were born, grew up and lived their formative years. This is not a profound thought. In fact, it's a commonplace. But, there are conclusions to be drawn nevertheless. And the conclusion is, we all think we would behave better in somebody else's country. We all know better when it comes to somebody else. But ourselves?

265

Each man bestows upon his own native heath sanctity.
Remember that, because that's my last word on the subject.

BELLE: Good, fine, now let's talk about something else. Promise
me we won't mention politics again.

ZADOK: I promise. We'll talk about something else. Did I tell you,
Jeremy, we've got a video machine in the Old Aged Home?

JEREMY: No—

ZADOK: Yes. We've got a video machine and they show us films,
two, three times a week. One Sunday afternoon they showed
The Godfather. What a film. Maybe the second-best film I've
ever seen. It's about a fellow born in Sicily who goes to
America and becomes the head of the Mafia, *capo di capi*, the
godfather of all godfathers. And what he does to people and
what people do to him, you wouldn't believe. But the film is a
film with a moral. Ask me what the moral is.

JEREMY: What's the moral, Uncle Zadok?

ZADOK: The moral of the film is, don't get born in Sicily.
(*He loves this.*)

ROSE: This man is totally insane.

BELLE: God, you're devious, Zadok.

ZADOK: Jeremy, you want to know the best film I've ever seen?

BELLE: No, he doesn't—

ZADOK: Yes, he does. It's a newsreel, Jeremy, ask me, what
newsreel?

JEREMY: What newsreel, Uncle Zadok?

ZADOK: The one where Jesse Owens wins a gold medal at the Berlin
Olympics in 1936. He beats the whole Master Race, and
Hitler leaves the stadium as though he's just been told he's got
prostate trouble. I love that film.

JEREMY: Dad's only cancelled his concert because he wants to
impress Mummy.

LEONARD: Jeremy, shut up—

JEREMY: That was one of the very big rows between them—

LEONARD: Jeremy, I'm going to slap you hard—

JEREMY: Mummy said you had double standards, Dad. You see,
he's played in Turkey, in Czechoslovakia, in Russia. Where's
he going to stop? Will he play the piano in Ethiopia? In
Malawi? Libya? Iran?

266

ROSE: What are you, Jeremy, a gazeteer?

JEREMY: I simply want to know where one draws the line.

   (LEONARD *slaps* JEREMY *across the face.* JEREMY *runs out and re-appears in the control booth. Silence.*)

ROSE: And we wanted to come back to London before we died.

ZADOK: Afterwards wouldn't be such fun.

   (*Silence.* LEONARD *marches up to the control booth window.*)

LEONARD: (*Mouthing, a tense whisper*) Come – back – in – here!

   (JEREMY *ignores him.*)

BELLE: Leonard, leave him, please, he'll come back. Control yourself. Where's your self-control? And I beg you, no more, I don't want this aggravation –

   (*She controls her tears.*)

LEONARD: I won't have Jeremy speak to me like that.

BELLE: (*To* ROSE) You see what a broken marriage does to a child?

ROSE: I told you she was upset.

BELLE: Rose, you want me to be upset, I'll be upset, I'm going to kill you in a moment and then I won't be upset.

   (*Silence.*)

LEONARD: Let me just say this –

BELLE: We don't want to hear, we understand what you do is your own business, we don't want to hear –

LEONARD: Look, whatever I am, whatever I've become, the price was paid not by me, not by Mom or Dad, or by any of us here, but by a great mass of people who had no say in the matter. I was able to flourish at their expense. And for that I feel ashamed, deeply, deeply ashamed. I can't help it, that's what I feel.

ZADOK: But where's your pity?

LEONARD: What d'you mean, where's my pity?

ZADOK: What about us? Where's your pity for us? You should feel pity for the oppressors and the oppressed. There are two sides to every story. (*Silence.*) You know your trouble, Leonard? You've never been very bright. And I'll tell you something else. After a lifetime of serious study, in my opinion nothing can be explained.

BELLE: Then why do you explain everything?

LEONARD: (*Angered*) Listen to me, for God's sake, listen to me! The trouble is, you won't listen, you don't want to hear!

BELLE: Leonard, I've decided. I don't want you to come to my funeral.

ZADOK: What's she say?

ROSE: She doesn't want Leonard to come to her funeral.

ZADOK: What's she talking about, she's not dead yet, is she?

ROSE: God forbid, Zadok, that's a terrible thing to say.

ZADOK: She doesn't look dead to me –

BELLE: My mind's made up . Don't waste money on a fruitless journey. I'd rather Jeremy had the money.

LEONARD: Mom, cancelling my concert in Cape Town is my only weapon –

BELLE: I'm not talking about your concert, I'm talking about my funeral.

ROSE: Wait a moment, wait a moment, before we bury you, Belle, I want to ask your son something.

BELLE: I don't want to be buried, I want to be cremated. I've left it in my will.

ROSE: Wait a moment. You said weapon, Leonard, what weapon are you talking about? You're not a soldier, for God's sake, your're a musician, an artist –

LEONARD: Aunty Rose, being an artist is not some divine job description –

ROSE: Not divine? Being an artist is not divine? What a terrible thing to say –

ZADOK: And by the way, there are two things that have never brought a government to its knees. Sanctions and bombing the civilian populaton.

LEONARD: Oh, really, Uncle Zadok? What about Hiroshima?

ZADOK: Hey, that's not bad, Len, I'll try to remember that –

ROSE: Believe it or not, I, too, have something to say. It's no secret I'm a lover of books, a lover of poetry, a lover of art. I believe in art, that's what I believe in. God I leave to the godly, business and politics I leave to crooks. I believe in art. I believe art – I mean literature, poetry, the theatre, music, painting, ballet, the opera – all art is an expression of what's best about each and every one of us. All right, so I'm a deaf,

old spinster who knows nothing, who's never been in love,
who's never been loved —

BELLE: Never been loved? How can you say you've never been
loved, Rose? That's a terrible thing to say —

ROSE: All right, all right, let me finish. I know people laugh at me
behind my back, I know what people say about me, I know,
I know, I know. But no one will take my belief away from
me, and my belief is that art is a solace, art is a benediction.
All right, argue with me, shout me down, call me an old fool
who knows nothing of life, but my world was created,
transformed and blessed by art. My prayers are for more
Shakespeares and George Eliots, my litany is to the glory of
Mozart and Schubert, my worship is of Rembrandt and
Chagall, and the infinite number of artists whose vision has
made me able to bear this life from one day to the next.
Where would we have been, Belle, you and I, without our
poetry, without our Browning, our Wordsworth, our Byron?
There's not a thought in my head, not a feeling in my body
that art hasn't, in one way or another, informed and fired.
And this is what I have against you, Leonard, whom I love
with all my heart, this: that you withhold from your great
mass of people whom you claim paid for your privileges, you
deny them as well as us your ability to bring forth musical
sounds which adds to the glory of being alive. Leonard, are
you listening to me? You want to feel ashamed? Feel
ashamed you've cancelled your concert. You must hold your
talent in very low esteem because it seems you believe deep
down that not one note you play will change a single human
heart. That's where I disagree with you. You see, stupid old
woman that I am, I believe there's a chance that music
might, might, just might, turn the whole world upside
down, all right, not the whole world, I don't believe in
miracles, but one individual world, and that's a chance, in
my opinion, you're meant to take. After all, I speak from
personal experience. That's it, that's what I believe, I'm
finished, now make fun of me.
(*Silence.*)

ZADOK: Sister mine, you make me weep, me, a dry, dusty —

BELLE: All right, Zadok, we know, we know.
(*Silence.*)
LEONARD: You're talking about another time, Aunty Rose, those things belong to another time.
BELLE: More's the pity. Everything seems like a thousand years ago to me. I don't think about the past. I had such hopes – I hate the past.
ROSE: Anyway, you've got Jeremy to look forward to.
ZADOK: Kitchener died and England won the war.
BELLE: His mind's wandering, ignore him.
ROSE: You won't think again, Len?
(*Silence.*)
ZADOK: Where's Jeremy?
(ZADOK *rises. He goes to the control booth window and makes signs to catch* JEREMY's *attention.* JEREMY *switches the switch.*) Are you receiving me loud and clear?
JEREMY: Yes.
ZADOK: Come back here, I've got something to ask you.
JEREMY: I can hear you, Uncle Zadok.
ZADOK: Fine, it's a difficult question. What do you think of your father's peculiar family?
JEREMY: At least you talk about what matters to each other –
ZADOK: Wrong. We skirt the issues, same as everyone else, only we do it more loudly.
(*He laughs.*)
JEREMY: It makes me feel I'm alive.
ZADOK: From your mouth into God's ear. You have only one obligation, and that's to life. That's what kept us all so young. You know what they call me, Jeremy, in Cape Town? Peter Pan. The boy who never grew up.
BELLE: Jeremy, darling, come back in here, please, for my sake –
(JEREMY *switches the switch and leaves the control booth.*) You should apologize to him, Leonard. What you did was uncalled for –
LEONARD: He should apologize to me. And, Mom, don't interfere.
(JEREMY *re-enters the studio.*)
BELLE: Come and sit by me, Jeremy.

(*He does so.*)

Fathers, eh, Jeremy?

ZADOK: And mothers.

LEONARD: I'll tell you something, Mom, I think often of Dad, of my father –

BELLE: You can do what you like, it's not my business.

ZADOK: I was fond of Ike. He had the biggest store of useless information of any man I've ever met. Yet he never knew who he was, what he was, and he had no chance in life, but I liked him. And his father was a wonderful whistler. That's where Leonard gets his talent from.

BELLE: For a clever man, Zadok, you talk more rubbish than anyone else. There was no talent in that family at all. Ike's father. Please. He could hardly read or write let alone whistle.

LEONARD: I wish I'd talked to Dad more –

ROSE: You see, I told you, they never talked.

BELLE: How could anyone talk to Ike? He had nothing to say except the world was against him –

LEONARD: Nevertheless, listen to me. This is interesting –

ZADOK: We'll be the judge of that.

LEONARD: I think now it was as if he and I were, somehow, conspirators.

ROSE: What?

LEONARD: Conspirators!

ROSE: Who?

LEONARD: Me and Dad.

ROSE: You and Ike?

ZADOK: I told you there was something between them.

BELLE: Between whom? Between Ike and Leonard? Please, you're talking about chalk and cheese. And, Leonard, you never cried when he died. I'll never forget that, it upset me for weeks –

ZADOK: I told you, he was always a bottled-up boy.

LEONARD: We were conspirators. We shared a secret. You know what we shared? A sense of failure.

BELLE: Leonard, I've never heard anything so ridiculous in all my life. You a failure? What's success, then? I don't believe I'm hearing these words.

LEONARD: He felt he was washed up in the wrong place at the wrong time.

BELLE: I never heard him say anything like that.

LEONARD: You never talked to him, so how could you hear?

BELLE: Leonard, please, not in front of Jeremy, please –

LEONARD: Well, I remember. And it comes back to me, and it haunts me. When I was a kid, in Cape Town, I used to go down to the beach and spit into the sea.

ROSE: He used to do what?

ZADOK: Spit in the sea. Like old Abe Bendel. He spits, in the sea, on the carpet, in his bed, you've never seen such a spitter. (ROSE *and* BELLE *laugh*.)

LEONARD: All right, you don't want to hear, I won't tell you –

ROSE: We want to hear –

LEONARD: Just so that I can get this off my chest, I'll tell you as quickly as I can. Because I want you to know. I used to spit in the sea and watch my saliva disintegrate into millions of undetectable particles, still me, but also part of the ocean being carried who knows where, reaching out to other islands, seas, continents, other people, all people, eternity, the whole universe. I was at one with the world. I felt I embraced the world.

ZADOK: All this from spitting in the sea?

LEONARD: All right, all right, very funny, but the point is this. I've never felt that again. Even here, where I've lived most of my life, I'm not at home.

BELLE: You've lived in this country thirty-five years and you don't feel at home here?

ROSE: How can you say you're not at home in London? It's not possible.

ZADOK: Perhaps he should spit in the sea more often.

LEONARD: The truth is, I'm an alien wherever I am.

ROSE: I don't understand this. What more does he want? What more is there? You play your music all over the world –

JEREMY: Except in South Africa –

LEONARD: Jeremy, when I need another comment from you I'll ask for it.

BELLE: Jeremy, darling, enough now.

LEONARD: Aunty Rose, I wanted, I wanted – what did I want? I think all I wanted was to be somebody.

ROSE: So?

LEONARD: (*Smiling*) I still want to be somebody. That's why – I don't know – perhaps that's why I do what I do. Perhaps that's why I'm making this stand. Stella said I had no backbone. Perhaps this is my backbone.

BELLE: Why you're not coming to Cape Town to play? To be somebody? To have a backbone?

LEONARD: Perhaps. I don't know. I tell you these things because I don't want you to think that the decision was easily arrived at.

ZADOK: I'll tell you something, Leonard. It's not where you are, it's who you are.

LEONARD: Who am I, that's the point, who am I?

ZADOK: 'The fault, dear Brutus, lies not in our stars but in ourselves –'

LEONARD: Yes, yes, yes, yes –

BELLE: Zadok, no more philosophy, please, it drives me mad –

ZADOK: Fine. Not another aphorism do I utter. Except this. There's no justice in this world.

LEONARD: As my father used to say.

ZADOK: I said it –

LEONARD: No, Uncle Zadok, my Dad said it –

BELLE: Leonard, forgive me, now you're talking nonsense. How could your father say such a thing? Leonard's father, Jeremy, your grandfather, was a very simple man. Difficult, but very simple. Mind you, he never raised a finger to Leonard. But all he knew was what a bad hand he was dealt.

LEONARD: All right, all right, whosoever said it.

ZADOK: I said it.

LEONARD: All right, all right! You've all believed in me so much for so long, perhaps it's now time I should believe in myself.

JEREMY: Cue music.

LEONARD: Shut up, Jeremy.

JEREMY: No, I won't shut up, because I can't talk to you when we're alone. You take the easy way out, that's what I can't stand, you take the easy way out –

BELLE: Jeremy –

JEREMY: Not going to South Africa is easier, because if you wanted to make a real stand, you'd go. But no, no, you do what's expected of you because it's easier. And all the talk about the great suffering masses. I always like that bit, Dad, when you become so impassioned about the great suffering masses while you sip your champagne in the back of a chauffeur-driven car doing the social whirl –

ZADOK: Now, that's unfair, Jeremy. You mustn't blame your father for enjoying what the world pays him. And you don't have to be good to do good, remember that –

BELLE: Zadok, don't interfere –

JEREMY: And the music he plays, he plays what comes easiest to him. Rachmaninoff. All the critics say he plays too much Rachmaninoff –

BELLE: I read those critics, Jeremy. They were Germans. Enough said.

LEONARD: Jeremy, please don't talk of things you know absolutely nothing about. When I first played the piano –

ROSE: In my flat, above the library, a Mozart minuet, I remember it as if it were yesterday, he was five years old –

LEONARD: Yes, I was five years old. I just went to the piano and played. Gran didn't arrange for me to have lessons in the hope that I'd have talent. The talent came first, and she arranged for lessons as a result. Talent has always been the taskmaster, and yes, I don't deny, in certain respects, it came easily to me. At nine years old I sight-read the Beethoven C minor piano concerto. But it wasn't just a sight-reading, it was a *performance*, as though I'd worked on the piece for months. And everyone marvelled, and I couldn't understand why because it was as natural to me as drawing breath. And it still comes naturally to me, yet why is it I have to practise and that sometimes I play sublimely and others like a blacksmith? On the good days I don't suddenly develop extra fingers or muscles, I don't have bionic arms or a computerized nervous system. So why is it that sometimes I have to struggle and fight and, yes, Mom, hammer the keys until the sweat pours down my face and back? Why? What's the problem, what's the secret? The problem is that the world impinges. When you're nine years old, or on the good days, you and the world are one, or there is no world, or there's just your world. The truth is, I can only play really well when the chasm between who I am and what I do disappears. That's why I practise. I practise to make the piece I play easy so that my physical actions are secondary to everything else. That's how it is. What I am is how I play. Yes, and I enjoy cigars and champagne and parties and restaurants because I need to be with people, and because most of my life I spend alone at a piano, or in foreign hotel rooms, after a concert, watching television programmes in languages I don't understand. And I play Rachmaninoff, Jeremy, because his soulfulness puts me directly in touch with my own emotions, aspirations, doubts, insecurities, innermost feelings. And I require that, like a drug. Because what I am is how I play.

BELLE: Is that what you meant when you said pain was the making of you? (*Silence.*) I must have done something wrong. I don't want to think about it, I can't bear to think about these things, and I was so looking forward to – (*Breaks off.*) Everything's poisoned. Where's the pleasure in life? Where's the pleasure?

LEONARD: (*To* BELLE) Dad used to talk about being in the wrong place at the wrong time. I feel that. I curse the fact I was born where I was born. It's crippled me.

BELLE: Leonard, you're driving daggers through my heart –

LEONARD: And I am obsessed by the impermanence of things and I remember Dad talking about being swept away – he used to talk to you, Uncle Zadok, about these things – about sudden disaster, volcanic eruptions, you remember, Uncle Zadok?

ZADOK: I never heard Ike mention a volcanic eruption in his life. He had trouble with his bowels, that I remember –
(ROSE *and* BELLE *laugh and so does* JEREMY, *and eventually* LEONARD, *too.* ZADOK *chuckles and wheezes. They all become a little hysterical.* LEONARD'S *laughter turns to tears. He sobs. The others stop laughing.* LEONARD *holds out a hand.* BELLE *hesitates, then takes it.* LEONARD *cries. Two* TECHNICIANS

enter the control room. One of them switches the switch.

TECHNICIAN: We're back, Maestro. Ready to record?

(*All, except* LEONARD, *swing round to look at the booth.*
LEONARD *continues to cry. Lights fade to blackout.*)

SCENE FOUR

The control room, an hour later. In the studio LEONARD *records a
Rachmaninoff prelude: 'Elégie, Opus 3, No. 1'. He plays with great
stillness.* JEREMY *turns the pages for him. The music is relayed into
the control room where* BELLE *sits between* ROSE *and* BELLE, *behind
the two* TECHNICIANS, *who wear headphones.* ZADOK *sleeps.* ROSE
*listens with a sweet, unwavering smile. It is uncertain whether or not
she hears what is being said.*

BELLE: He never looked like Ronald Colman.

(*They listen.*)

No, no, no, Rose, I'm not going to think about the past. (*She
takes out a handkerchief and wipes her eyes, blows her nose.*)
You see, he's been my life for so long. Sometimes I ask
myself why we have children.

(*They listen.*)

No, no, all's right with the world.

(*They listen.*)

Videos, broadcasts, recordings, that's all I ever hear of him
these days. Where's the life, Rose, where's the life?

(*They listen.*)

Rose, in confidence, I gave him such a piece of my mind
when we were alone. Did I let him have it. Mind you, I think
he's playing better as a result. He's not pulling faces, he's not
swaying, he's not sweating, altogether less self.

(*They listen.*)

My honest opinion is that Jeremy won't come to Cape Town
either. Is Leonard going to have trouble with that boy! Well,
what can you expect from a broken home? Oh, Rose,
children, children.

(*They listen.*)

Never mind children, this child, this particular child, this

Leonard of mine, light of my life. He's been a perpetual excitement to me. I remember him setting off, carrying all my dreams and hopes and longings. What a blessing promise is. I still pray every night. But never for myself, never. You should pray, Rose, although if God heard from you after all these years he'd probably die of shock.

(*They listen.*)

You know what Miss Katz said to me the last time I saw her alive? She said she envied me. I told her she needed her head examined. With all that money and she envied me.

(*They listen.*)

I'm going to tell you something in absolute confidence, Rose. I'm pleased he's not coming back to Cape Town. I'm pleased he's cancelled his concert whatever his reasons, politics, people, who knows? Perhaps one can never go back. No, no, I'd never tell him to his face but I think he made the right decision. For his own sake. And for mine. Because I learned a lesson from him today and for that I thank him. I used to think people couldn't change. Maybe I'm an exception. Rose, you know what I've learned? To let go. He's been my life for too long. We can't cling for ever. I think everybody has to learn to let go.

(*They listen.*)

I've never minded anything so long as there's a purpose.

(*They listen.*)

Let's just hope things get better, not worse.

(*They listen.*)

This is odd. I used to have a feeling of terrible foreboding. It's gone now. It was like a premonition, I'd go to sleep with it, I'd wake with it, I just knew that something terrible was going to happen, a catastrophe, a disaster, something awful. But it's gone now. And you know why I think it's gone? Because perhaps it's happened.

(*They listen.*)

Who knows? Who knows?

(*They listen.*)

Where does he get it from? Where, where, where does he get it from?

277

(*They listen.*)
Leonard, oh my Leonard.

ROSE: Your Leonard, Belle, and Ike's.

BELLE: What she shouldn't hear she hears.

ROSE: And Ike, Belle. Yes, Belle, and Ike.

BELLE: Yes, yes, all right. (*Pause; irritably, sharp.*) And Ike.
(LEONARD *finishes the piece triumphantly.* ROSE *rises and applauds wildly.* ZADOK *wakes and struggles to his feet.*)

ZADOK: Bravo! Bravo!
(ROSE *and* ZADOK *applaud. the* TECHNICIANS *look back at them.* BELLE *glows.*)
(*Lights fade to blackout.*)